The title tells you exactly what's inside. This is a very handy manual on how to bring Jesus and your neighborhood together. Fusing ideas from missional literature and the practice of asset-based community development, Austin Maxheimer shifts your church's thinking from traditional "outreach ministry" toward the fuller, more kingdom-focused work of neighborhood revitalization. Passionate and practical.

MICHAEL FROST, Morling College, Sydney

If one of the chief questions close to the heart of Jesus is, "Who is my neighbor?", then as followers of Jesus, we must contend with this question on a daily basis as well. Maxheimer's contribution through connecting this key question to the power of asset-based community development provides Christian leaders with a practical way to be a neighbor and to invite and include our neighbors as a chief part of the kingdom of God.

REV. DR. EUN K. STRAWSER, lead pastor, Ma Ke Alo o, Honolulu, HI; cofounder, 'Iwa Collaborative; author, *Centering Discipleship: A Pathway to Multiply Spectators into Mature Disciples* and *You Were Never Meant to Lead Alone: The Power of Sharing Leadership*

This book calls us back to the heart of Jesus. It invites us to see our neighbors not as problems but as partners in restoring communities. If you want a practical faith that gets its hands dirty and walks where Jesus would walk, this book is for you.

CRAIG GREENFIELD, author, *Subversive Jesus*; founder, Alongsiders International

Neighborhoods and Jesus is a timely, Spirit-infused call for the church to rediscover its role in the restoration of marginalized communities. Austin Maxheimer beautifully weaves Scripture, personal story, and practical frameworks to show how churches can move from outreach as charity to empowerment through partnership. Grounded in the asset-based community development model and animated by the ministry of Jesus, this book challenges believers to reimagine mission as incarnational neighboring.

ALAN HIRSCH, author of numerous books on missional spirituality and practice; cofounder, Forge Missional Training Network and Movement Leaders Collective

Neighborhoods and Jesus is a timely, powerful call to live out faith where it matters most—in our own neighborhoods. Austin Maxheimer beautifully weaves theology with practical steps, showing how everyday connections can reflect the love of Christ. Inspiring, accessible, and deeply convicting, this book is a must-read for anyone wanting to make a real impact right outside their front door.

ERIC TILLMAN, resident engagement specialist, Evansville, Indiana; founder, E2 AGBTG Music Entertainment & Apparel

Neighborhoods and Jesus is a game changer for anyone thinking about loving their neighbors like Jesus did. Austin's deep theology, coupled with example after example, flips the script on traditional outreach by showing how marginalized communities are full of wisdom, strength, and hope. The "Love Your Neighborhood" framework isn't just a theory—it's a proven, practical, compelling roadmap for long-term, resident-led transformation. If you want to do ministry *with* people instead of *for* them, this book will inspire, equip, and challenge you in the best way.

ERIC SWANSON, cofounder, City Leaders Collective; coauthor of five books including *To Transform a City*

Austin Maxheimer shares a personal and relatable perspective of the church and its impact on his neighborhood and neighbors. This book truly captures what it's like to be a Christ-follower doing the work in your neighborhood, as well as what it's like when that engagement is absent. *Neighborhoods and Jesus* is insightful, heartfelt, and, for those who love Jesus, inspirational to read. It leaves the reader with no choice but to think, *How can I be a part of benefiting my community/neighborhood in a Christlike way?* For any ministry or organization questioning the "Why" of community outreach, this book is a must-read. It is the answer!

ROXANNE CALHOUN, chef; community leader, Tepe Park, Evansville, Indiana

This book is for every person following the way of Jesus, but it is a must-read for church and nonprofit leaders who are mobilizing ministry efforts to the marginalized. This is an opportunity to learn from a fellow practitioner who has committed his life to living out the mission. Austin lives in the neighborhood he felt compelled to serve, has the biblical and theological depth needed to write this book, and gives us a prophetic imagination for seeing our city look more like the city God would build. He is real and honest, with a hopeful vision and tone. He demands we rethink or even stop many of our approaches while recognizing and celebrating the small things, done over time, that lead to real change. I know very few people who live lives worth imitating, and even fewer who take the time or have the skill to call the church to embody God's love to their neighbors through a book like this. Austin is both. His courage is contagious, and this book will encourage you to love your neighbor, wherever and to whomever you are called.

ROSS CHAPMAN, DMin, CEO, Denver Institute for
Faith & Work; founder, For Evansville; author, *Faithful Work:*
In the Daily Grind with God and for Others

Neighborhoods and Jesus offers a complete and compelling picture of the integration of our faith and place. Austin Maxheimer delivers a wealth of wisdom from lived experience on the clear call of Jesus to love God and love our neighbor. It is an invaluable guide to helping re-place our faith.

JARED MACKEY, executive director, Sacred Place

NEIGHBORHOODS & JESUS

NEIGHBORHOODS & JESUS

PARTNERING
with COMMUNITIES
for INSIDE-OUT
TRANSFORMATION

100 MOVEMENTS
PUBLISHING

AUSTIN MAXHEIMER

Published by 100 Movements Publishing
www.100Mpublishing.com
Copyright © 2025 by Austin Maxheimer

The author has no responsibility for the persistence or accuracy of URLs for external or third-party internet websites referred to in this book and does not guarantee that any content on such websites is, or will remain, accurate or appropriate.

Library of Congress Control Number: 2025909147

ISBN 978-1-955142-68-7 (print)
ISBN 978-1-955142-69-4 (eBook)

First edition published in 2023 © by Austin Maxheimer

Cover design and interior design by Jeremy Secrest

100 Movements Publishing
An imprint of Movement Leaders Collective
Cody, Wyoming
www.movementleaderscollective.com

For the eager expectation of creation is in the hopeful awaiting of the revealing of the sons and daughters of God.
ROMANS 8:19 (AUTHOR'S TRANSLATION)

This book is dedicated to all of those children of God who step out every day to offer up their lives as sacrifices to love their neighbor, and in so doing, invite them to know Jesus.

CONTENTS

PREFACE TO THE REVISED EDITION

This book carries within it years of my life—over a decade of ministry experience interwoven with the insights gained from my doctoral research. This revised edition centers on the same core intention as the first edition: to inspire and equip everyday followers of Jesus to actively participate in neighborhood revitalization as a powerful expression of ministry to those on the margins.

The people I hope to reach remain the same: individuals committed to following Jesus who are looking for practical ways to engage in holistic ministry.

The heart of the message also remains: exploring the biblical foundations for why neighborhood revitalization is such a fitting ministry for local churches and Christians, sharing personal stories from practicing the work, and integrating sociological research from my dissertation.

What you'll find different in this edition is the result of a dedicated process of refinement. Through professional editing, the message has been carefully shaped and polished to enhance its clarity and flow. The structure has been improved, and the content streamlined, all with the primary goal of creating a more engaging and impactful experience for you, the reader.

In the three sections of the book, you will see my intention to work from strong biblical foundations, to develop these into principles that can be applied in many different contexts, and to share the practices and stories of how this work has taken hold in the neighborhoods I have had the privilege of being part of. This new flow in this revised edition will hopefully enable you to navigate these building blocks for neighborhood revitalization in the way of Jesus.

My deepest hope is that this revised form will more effectively activate the people of God into the mission of God. I believe the church is a vital source of hope for the world, embodying God's vision for the kingdom of heaven to be experienced, even in part, today. Your involvement in this work is a meaningful contribution that God can use to bring about transformation in your own life, the lives of your neighbors, your community, and ultimately, the wider world. It is my sincere hope that this revised work encourages you toward that very purpose.

INTRODUCTION

One random Saturday morning, in the Spring of 2012, I answered a volunteer call to go door knocking and listening to neighbors in the east end of Henderson, Kentucky. I did not know it at the time, but the church our house-church network had recently merged with was kicking off a neighborhood revitalization effort in the area. I knew nothing about neighborhood work, asset-based community development, or community mobilization for sustainable change. At that point in my life, it just sounded like something Jesus would do, so I went and did it.

That Saturday, as I interviewed seven neighbors in the east end, asking them what they thought the strengths, weaknesses, opportunities, and threats of their neighborhood were, I began a journey that radically transformed how I viewed "outreach ministry." While it has been a slow process of moving from ignorance to understanding, one immediate realization I had that day was that neighbors are not people to be pitied but experts to learn from. Every neighbor I talked to was full of insight, passion, dreams, hopes, skills, and capacity.

What I uncovered moved me closer toward how God sees his creation: people of inherent dignity and infinite worth.

Over the next ten years I went from being a learning volunteer to a community mobilizer to an overseer of small-group church ministry to a civic leader in multiple neighborhood initiatives and finally culminating in a vocational shift in 2017 to take the position of neighborhood revitalization director for a local Christian nonprofit.

Throughout this journey, God was revealing and deepening my understanding and conviction that neighborhood revitalization is a means through which God desires for his people to join with him in holistic ministry to our marginalized neighbors. Holistic restoration of marginalized neighbors is a calling, dare I say a command, for the people of God to actively participate in as a testimony and witness to the reconciling work of Jesus Christ.

Yet the church seems to be largely missing from this ministry and mission field. While there are a smattering of Christians serving in neighborhood revitalization efforts, there certainly isn't a flood, and the presence of organizational churches is almost nonexistent. Instead, churches are mainly focused on serving the needs of their congregations—they might participate in some outreach ministries but, although well-intentioned, these often ignore the worth and abilities of the people they are trying to help.

My concern about this gaping hole of church presence in neighborhood revitalization led me to do research for my dissertation on this topic. The title for the thesis was, "What are the biblical understandings and experiential catalysts and sustaining forces that lead toward Christian engagement in neighborhood revitalization as a ministry to marginalized neighbors?" A bit of a mouthful, I know! Basically, I wanted to find out why followers of Jesus participated in neighborhood work and how we could help others do the same.

My research involved asking church leaders, congregants, and participants in neighborhood revitalization efforts about the intersection of their beliefs, their view of the role of the church, and how they put their faith into action. I wanted to understand how we could move disciples into participating in neighborhood revitalization, and what experience would catalyze and sustain this engagement.

The results of these surveys offered an explanation as to why the church and most congregants were missing from the neighborhood work I was participating in, and pointed toward positive actions that could be taken to encourage engagement. I found that the Christian community has actually done a pretty good job of transferring concepts that inform our collective faith. You could say that the vast majority of Christians are "thinking right." But right thinking has not led to right acting. What's more, it seems the church as a whole has lost, or is losing, our sense of calling to our marginalized neighbors. What we see clearly communicated in the Old Testament as a primary concern of God for his people, lived out by Jesus in his ministry, and the bedrock of the early church's revolutionary power and spirit, was indicated as the lowest concern for the pastors and congregants I surveyed in relation to the role of the church; and it was the lowest in frequency of congregants' faith in action.

We need to rediscover our mandate for ministry to marginalized neighbors and help the church participate.

Who Is My Neighbor?

Our neighborhoods are desperately in need of transformation. Eleven million (of seventy-four million) children in the US are living in poverty. Black, Hispanic, and American Indian/Alaska Native families have on average half the annual income of white families.[1] Of those living in poverty, many are in concentrated "poverty areas," with an average 21.1 percent of those in poverty living in these neighborhoods, ranging from 5.2 percent in New Hampshire to 42.4 percent in Mississippi.[2]

These statistics only touch on the physical poverty experienced by these people. There are much further-reaching implications for their emotional, relational, and spiritual well-being that are impacted by the financial deprivation they experience. Life expectancy, health, income and career opportunity, likelihood of being involved in criminal activity—all of these areas are negatively impacted for these neighbors and the neighborhoods they reside in.

If we are to make the case that followers of Jesus collectively are called to neighboring those marginalized among us, we must be careful in our definition of "marginalized neighbors." As I will explain, the approach I am putting forward in this book is "asset-based." Therefore, we see those who are marginalized neighbors not simply as "those in need" but as neighbors who are the key to bringing about change in their neighborhoods. This means our meaning of the term

---

[1] "2003 State of America's Children Report: Child Poverty," *Children's Defense Fund*, accessed March, 4, 2025, https://www.childrensdefense.org/tools-and-resources/the-state-of-americas-children/soac-child-poverty/.

[2] "Share of People Living in Poverty Areas Fell by 6.6 Percentage Points Since First Half of the Decade," *United States Census Bureau*, February 8, 2021, https://www.census.gov/library/stories/2021/02/fewer-people-living-in-poverty-areas-2015-2019.html.

"marginalized" has to be handled carefully. The broadest definition I would give is this: those pushed out from the center of society.

Every human society has a set of foundational beliefs, values, mores, etc., that bind it together. It has an "operating system," if you will—often referred to as "culture." Culture is a complex web of underlying philosophical views, religious/spiritual beliefs, politics, media, art, and good-old-fashioned mob mentality. We are often blind to the cultural realities we move in and are shaped by because it is simply the water in which we swim. The larger and more diverse a society becomes, the more the center moves and shifts and has layered sub-cultures with their own centers. At any given moment there is in fact a center, and those closest to it have the greatest opportunity to experience a flourishing life.

A marginalized neighbor, then, is one who has been pushed out from the center of a culture and is living on its edge. Out on the edge there is less of everything—power, influence, resources, peace, etc. These neighbors are unable to access the flourishing life that others have as they are derailed or barred from the intended or directed purpose of the cultural center. They can even be cut off or at least hindered from participation in the larger community.

If we are to follow Jesus' command to love our neighbors (Matt. 22:39), we need to think about how this extends to the marginalized neighbors who often live in neighborhoods that have been pushed from the center of our culture.

At my workplace we talk about neighboring (loving neighbors) in two distinct categories:

- Neighboring *where we are*—where we live, work, play, and worship
- Neighboring *where we're called*—to marginalized neighbors

The first—neighboring where we are—is applied in the broadest terms and is inclusive of the Hebrew-Greek understanding of "neighbor"— literally "the one next to you," a fellow human being you are proximate to, who you encounter in the course of your everyday life. Neighboring in this context is extremely important, and would include actions like sharing our faith at work, investing in church unity (love of other Christians), loving strangers, living missionally, gospel-based city movements, and of course loving your next-door neighbor. These are all important, crucial even, to the Christian way of life. However, what we are primarily concerned with in this book is neighboring where we are called.[3] God's missionary people are collectively called to love marginalized neighbors. This means we need to readdress the issue of where we spend our time and efforts so that we can be God's people, involved in his mission.

We must reorient and shift our ministry activities to align with this calling—not run a program or deliver a service but bring restoration and activation to neighbors created in the image of God.

This book aims to bridge the gap between what is and what could be. In every neighborhood that faces barriers to flourishing, there are churches and Christians waiting to be sent for kingdom transformation. We dream of a city that has no poverty, no kids killing kids, no hungry bellies, no person without a home or community to belong to. Followers of Jesus give hundreds of millions of hours of service and money every year. What if a small portion of that was redirected to developing the communities we live in or live next to?

What Is Asset-Based Community Development?

In the mid-1980s, after witnessing the failure of twenty-five years of government programs designed to address poverty, two faculty

---

[3] I'm intentionally using the plural "we." While we all take on the identity of Christ's mission as individual disciples and should each individually love marginalized neighbors in our own way, the restorative practices referenced throughout this book are what I believe is the imperative for the collective body of Christ, the assembly, the church as a whole. It is what *we* are to be doing. I would also note that the word "called" is a very biblically loaded term; one difficult to deploy without full acceptance and understanding of the metanarrative of Scripture. For now, let "calling" stand in for a summary of the command, invitation, promise, and identity of the collective people of God that we see throughout the biblical narrative.

colleagues, John McKnight and John Kretzmann, decided to figure out a way to end generational poverty.

For two years they traveled around the nation and visited hundreds of disinvested neighborhoods, collecting thousands of qualitative data points by asking one question: "Tell me a time or story when people came together to create positive change in your community."

Their radical thought was this: Every community already has everything it needs to create positive change and build the neighborhood they desire to see. Need proof? Well, you just told me a story about it actually happening!

This idea was built on the premise that the very structures, institutions, organizations, and programs we create to alleviate poverty are actually contributing to cycles of dependency which perpetuate the problem.

Using the data from the collected stories, Kretzmann and McKnight proposed that an asset-based approach to community development, as opposed to a deficit-based approach, would enable a community to build itself from the inside out.[4] Instead of focusing on what was wrong with a community and what they do not have, the focus would be toward what is right and good, what is already present, and build from there. In this way, neighbors are empowered and resourced to design what they want to see in a flourishing community instead of having expectations placed on them from the outside.

DEFICIT-BASED	ASSET-BASED
• Focus on deficiencies	• Focus on effectiveness
• People are consumers of services	• People are producers
• Community members observe as issues are being addressed	• Community members participate and are empowered

---

4 John P. Kretzmann and John L. McKnight, *Building Communities from the Inside Out: A Path Toward Finding and Mobilizing a Community's Assets* (Evanston, IL: The Asset-Based Community Development Institute, Northwestern University, 1993).

Of course, the greatest asset in any neighborhood, the residents themselves, become the center of the work. Their voices design, their skills build, and their talents activate; they make the change. Residents become the focal point of investment.

As I discovered the asset-based community development (ABCD) approach, I immediately saw its compatibility with the ministry of Jesus.

This book makes a case for the biblical mandate God has given to his people, throughout the story of Scripture, to be those who bring restoration and activation to marginalized people. This includes understanding how God embedded this mandate in the Law for the people of Israel, how Jesus fulfilled this Law, and how he shows us the way to live this out. I also share my experience from the last fifteen years in this work and how my team engage in ABCD through our Love Your Neighborhood initiative. Love Your Neighborhood is Community One's unique approach to neighborhood revitalization, grounded in asset-based community development principles, and shaped by Jesus' ministry. Community One is a Christian nonprofit that partners with neighbors of the Tepe Park neighborhood in Evansville, Indiana, to implement Love Your Neighborhood. In addition, four other neighborhood-based organizations are utilizing the Love Your Neighborhood framework in their own neighborhoods. I have been leading, building, coaching, and practicing this work since 2017.

Here is an overview to help you navigate the book:

Section one: God's design for all to flourish. These chapters unpack our biblical understanding of caring for marginalized neighbors and explore the systemic problems that are pushing people to the edges of our society.

Section two: Mindsets for working **with** *marginalized neighbors*. This section looks at some of the ways churches currently do outreach and ministry in a "needs-based" way and how we can align ourselves with an "asset-based" approach that will value and empower our neighbors.

Section three: The power of asset-based community development. Here I share the processes we use for neighborhood revitalization through our Love Your Neighborhood initiative. The final chapter looks more closely at the issue of churches engaging in this work.

Peppered throughout the chapters, you will find stories from our neighborhood that will hopefully bring to life some of the learnings I share. The transformation we have seen in our neighborhood is only because of our wonderful neighbors, and so these stories are central to communicating what this work is all about.

Note that, throughout the book, I use the language of "neighborhood revitalization" and "asset-based community development" largely interchangeably, though they have slight differences. Neighborhood revitalization is the overarching process of actively improving the quality of life of an under-resourced or disinvested neighborhood by addressing neighbors' lived experience, e.g., housing, education, infrastructure, safety. Asset-based community development (ABCD) is one approach to neighborhood revitalization. ABCD recognizes that a deficit-based approach has not been successful in eliminating generational poverty and instead aims to build on the latent and existing assets within a community in order to bring about sustainable change from within. Love Your Neighborhood is the specific approach we take in neighborhood revitalization, built on the foundational approach of ABCD, with an emphasis on resident engagement and incorporating practices from the ministry of Jesus for the restoration and activation of marginalized neighbors.

The last fifteen years in this work have shown me just how committed God is to bringing restoration to marginalized neighbors but also just how central those neighbors are in this work. It is through their activation that true transformation can be brought about.

I have found my involvement in neighborhood revitalization as an expression of Jesus' ministry to be life-giving, and I want to help others experience this as well. In addition to stories and anecdotes, we will look at research to discover biblical themes and real-life experiences that can help mobilize local churches to do holistic ministry to marginalized neighbors in under-resourced neighborhoods and to identify potential barriers that keep churches and disciples from engaging. Collectively, these findings can help inform the practice of ministry through creating experiential learning opportunities among marginalized neighbors, leveraging the local church for transformative missional impact, and helping local congregations rediscover the calling of the church to restore "the least of these"[5] living in urban centers. I believe that neighborhood revitalization is not merely a vehicle for missional engagement but is also a participatory ministry of Jesus that can help shape disciples into the likeness of Christ.

This is the call I believe Jesus has given to all who follow him—to love our neighbors and to see them restored and activated into the work of kingdom transformation he has invited us to. What's more, as Christians and churches engage in this work, we ourselves are transformed more into the likeness of Christ. These are surely worthy reasons to address our worn-out methods of serving the poor and consider a different way—one aligned with the way of Jesus.

---

[5] See Matt. 25: 39–40.

PART ONE

GOD'S DESIGN FOR ALL TO FLOURISH

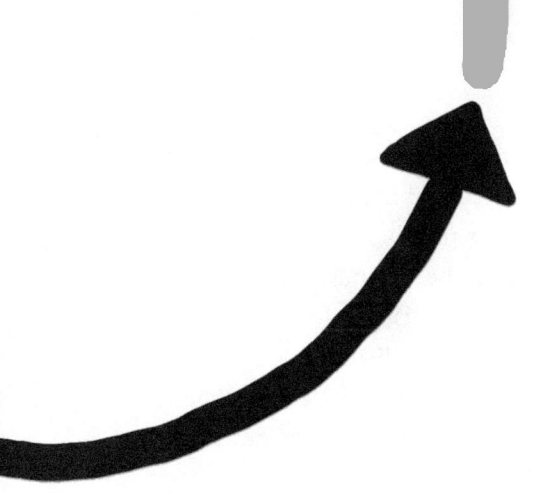

1
JESUS'
PURPOSE
STATEMENT

Jesus gave a life purpose statement: "I came so that they may have life, and have *it* abundantly" (John 10:10). The original language he used would have conveyed a sense of a "full" life. A good visual would be an overflowing vessel.[1] Jesus came so that humanity could experience an overabundant, flourishing life.

What does Jesus mean by that? What does a flourishing life look like?

Let me offer a few clarifiers of what I can confidently say Jesus was *not* putting forth as a descriptor of a flourishing life:

- A life full of "stuff": square footage, vehicles, toys, money, closets full of clothes.
- Positional authority or career achievement: plaques on walls, names on degrees and certificates, letters before and after names on business cards, occupying a spot high on the org chart.
- Heavenly guarantee and earthly complaint: *only* a future orientation of hope—going to heaven when we die or when Jesus comes back, while ignoring, complaining, or being apathetic to life now.
- Religious piety: being so holy that we are removed from others, closeting ourselves against the stain of the world to take the moral high ground but, in doing so, not interacting or loving others.

---

[1] *Dictionary of Biblical Imagery*, Lelan Ryken, James C. Wilhoit, Tremper Longman III, eds, s.v. "fill, fullness" (IVP Academic, 1998), 284–285.

To be clear, none of these things are inherently bad, or wrong to possess in and of themselves. They may even contribute to a flourishing life. But they are not the end destination, or fulfilled image, of what Jesus was talking about. If we read through the Gospels, follow Jesus on his way to the cross, see what he does, and listen to what he says, we struggle to make a case for any of those things listed above.

What did Jesus mean by a flourishing life then? This is a definition that I believe encapsulates the whole canon of Scripture and therefore bears witness to a Christian view of a flourishing life:

- Wholeness of being—thriving in all of your heart, mind, soul and strength.
- Having a directed purpose—finding mission, meaning, and significance.
- In community—life lived with one another.

Wholeness of Being

For a Jewish person living in the Ancient Near East (ANE), the *Shema* set their worldview: "Hear, Israel! The LORD is our God, the LORD is one! And you shall love the LORD your God with all your heart and with all your soul and with all your strength" (Deut. 6:4–5). The *Shema*—which means "to hear" in Hebrew—was something that was spoken aloud every time the people of God gathered together and was also repeated individually when addressing God in personal prayer.[2]

Jesus famously affirmed this outlook on life when he was asked what was the greatest commandment, or "way of life," in Luke 10:27. The various parts he listed (heart, soul, mind, and strength) are what make up the whole of our being, so it could just as easily be stated, "Love God with your whole self."

People living in the Western world today do not have such a unifying statement. We struggle to agree on what *being* is, let alone how to pursue

---

2   Gary H. Hall, *Deuteronomy: The College Press NIV Commentary* (Joplin, MO: College Press Publishing Company, 2000), 138.

wholeness. However, without going down that rabbit trail, I believe we can draw the following parallels to the ANE *Shema* worldview:

- Heart = Emotional Life
- Mind = Intellectual Life
- Soul = Spiritual Life
- Strength = Physical Life

Again, these are all parts of the whole. Each element affects the others. Separating them out is not an attempt to compartmentalize but rather a way to differentiate the disparate parts that make up the whole. You can be constantly filled with joy emotionally while being out of shape physically. You can be stimulated mentally while dead spiritually. Gauging your relative health in these areas is how you can go about shoring up deficiencies in your being. If the above statements are true about my life, I may want to start walking thirty minutes and meditating for ten minutes a day! Current science is showing just how integrated the parts are. A classic example is how exercise releases endorphins that stabilize your emotional state.[3]

I believe it is good and right to begin talking about human flourishing in terms of being whole in all the various parts. A flourishing life looks like a healthy and integrated wholeness of being.

Directed Purpose

Wholeness of being, however, is not the finish line. This is perhaps one of the differences between Jesus' teaching on fullness of life and the narrative about wellness that has boomed in the West in recent years.[4]

---

[3] See Center for Family Medicine, "Mental Health Benefits Of Exercise: What Are Endorphins & Serotonin?" accessed April 29, 2025, https://centerforfamilymedicine.com/general-health/mental-health-benefits-of-exercise-what-are-endorphins-serotonin/.

[4] "In the United States alone, we estimate that the wellness market has reached $480 billion, growing at 5 to 10 percent per year." See McKinsey and Company, "The trends defining the $1.8 trillion global wellness market in 2024," January 16, 2024, https://www.mckinsey.com/industries/consumer-packaged-goods/our-insights/the-trends-defining-the-1-point-8-trillion-dollar-global-wellness-market-in-2024.

An entire industry has popped up around wholeness and has been marketed to us as the answer to life: Health is wealth, invest wisely! Choose health, choose happiness! Your body deserves the best! Stay fit, stay fabulous! Eat right, live bright! Be active, be awesome!

But it begs the question: What happens when you are whole? In fact, without a directed purpose, you will not be able to achieve fullness of being. An integral part of building up the emotional, intellectual, spiritual, and physical is exercising all the parts *while pursuing a purpose.*

There's an interesting statement in the Gospel of Luke about Jesus—it's almost a throwaway line: "When the days drew near for him to be taken up, he set his face to go to Jerusalem" (Luke 9:51 ESV). We know what happened in Jerusalem and the theological ramifications (crucifixion, resurrection, and ascension). The end of that journey saw the accomplishment of what Jesus came to do: fulfill and complete God's mission to reconcile heaven and the cosmos.

Jesus knew about directed purpose. And it was this purpose that drove him to love God with all of his heart, mind, soul, and strength, even when he was facing rejection, persecution, and horrific death. He knew the purpose God the Father had called him to.

We have to question whether the erosion of Christianity's central role in Western thought has coincided with an unmooring of purpose in the everyday lives of people. Or whether, as Christians, we have lost our sense of purpose in what God has called us to, which, in turn, has meant we've lost our wholeness of being. How much of the apathy we see in the pews of our churches is down to a lack of purpose?

Yet modern science again gives us a glimpse into the importance of letting God recapture our imaginations. It turns out that people reporting a sense of purpose have a higher sense of wholeness and well-being.[5] If you know where you are going, why you are going there, and how to get there, it turns out life is better.

---

[5] E. S. Kim, J. S. Nakamura, Y. Chen, C. D. Ryff, and T. J. VanderWeele, "Sense of purpose in life and subsequent health and well-being in older adults: an outcome-wide analysis," *American Journal of Health Promotion*, 36 (2002), 137–147.

I don't think it's a big mystery to say we all long to have genuine meaning in our lives. A flourishing life looks like a whole being going somewhere purposefully.

Community

Community is about all of the above, plus doing it with others! Jesus famously chose twelve disciples who were with him nearly all the time during his three-year public ministry. Scholars think it could have been anywhere from 80–120 hours a week.[6] They were his ministry team.

What doesn't get as much publicity is that Jesus was seemingly always with people of all sorts. He is frequently imaged "reclining at the table," not only with his disciples and friends but also with the untouchables and social outcasts, as well as people of authority and social dignitaries. He was among the crowds constantly. He had other friends, such as Mary, Martha, and Lazarus, that we do not know much about. Jesus was always helping, teaching, healing, and loving others. It's fair to say that Jesus' life was others-centered.

Given that Jesus is God Incarnate, and the Christian faith posits a Triune God—one being in three persons existing in a perfect, perpetual relationship of self-giving and receiving love—you could say that Jesus was merely living out his very nature.

Study after study shows the benefit of community, of belonging to and with others. Here are just a few of the benefits:

- Having a support network has a strong correlation to overall well-being. It seems the more connections you have, and the deeper they run, the happier you are.
- A secure sense of belonging leads to a deeper sense of purpose, and purpose leads to a sense of fulfillment. A strong sense of purpose can even help you live longer!

---

[6] This approximation is based on several different sources including, but not limited to, Robert E. Coleman, *The Master Plan of Evangelism* (Ada, MI: Baker, 2006); *Dictionary of New Testament Theology*, s.v. "disciple"; and The BEMA Podcast series, https://www.bemadiscipleship.com/episodes.

- The feelings associated with belonging to a community have health benefits such as lowering stress and anxiety, while replacing them with positive benefits such as a sense of joy and overall reporting of happiness.
- People reporting that they belong to a community show higher levels of resilience.
- Those reporting that they are part of a defined community have more ideas, display better communication skills, and have better executive decision-making capabilities.[7]

Besides all that, we intuitively know that life is simply better when it is done with others! It is why we invite people to our kids' birthday parties, witness weddings, look back fondly on our school days, and have people over for the Super Bowl. Shoulder to shoulder, face to face, a group of friends can make the most mundane situation a dynamic experience. What's more, when directed purpose is added to a community, there is exponential power added to fulfillment of being. If you have ever been part of a healthy sports team, military corps, dance studio, theater troupe, orchestra, hacker crew, etc., then you have tasted the sweetness of a community of purpose.

Bringing it all together: A flourishing life looks like a whole being, going somewhere purposefully, with others.

We see these strands throughout Scripture: We see this flourishing life in Creation where humanity was made to thrive, to rule and subdue the earth, and to do so with others. We see it in God's rule of life given to the Israelites through the Law which set out how they should pursue godly living, directed them to the Promised Land, and gave boundaries for how to live as a community, set apart for him. With Jesus' coming, this Law is ultimately fulfilled and, once again, we see his life demonstrate the flourishing that he calls us all to live out—loving God with

7   A. H. Howard, G. Dadirai Gwenzi, L. Newsom, B. T. Gebru, and N. Gilbertson Wilke, "The Relationship between Sense of Belonging and Well-Being Outcomes in Emerging Adults with Care Experience," *International Journal of Environmental Research and Public Health*, 20 (13), July 7, 2023, https://pmc.ncbi.nlm.nih.gov/articles/PMC10341974/.

our whole being, seeking first his kingdom as our purpose, and being in community with others. And finally, we see this flourishing life pointed to in Revelation, which highlights how these three elements will come to ultimate completion.

The Kingdom of Heaven

A flourishing life is what God has made us for, what Jesus offers, and the future hope we look toward. The glorious image of heaven in the book of Revelation has captured the imagination of every generation of Jesus-followers: a multitude of ethnicities; no hunger-or-thirst-tears; constant singing and music; cities and streets of gold; streams and greenery of life; wedding banquets ... all communicating a vision of peace, health, abundance, and joy.[8] In other words, *flourishing*. We long, yearn, desire, and look forward to the experience, to taste and see that the Lord is good (Ps. 38:8).

Yet we do a disservice to Jesus' life and ministry—and therefore a disservice to our lives and ministries as his living and active body in the world—when we push off heaven to an exclusively future event. Even the teachings of Revelation have been relegated to a future-only orientation for many Christian faith traditions, far from the encouragement and buoy for the present life it would have been for the original recipients of the ancient text.

Revelation literally means "apocalypse," which means uncovering or unveiling.[9] What is being unveiled and uncovered is the kingdom of heaven, which incidentally, from a proper theological understanding, is happening now.[10] Jesus said the kingdom of heaven is near (Matt. 4:17 NLT). By incarnating into creation, Jesus began the reconciliation of heaven and the cosmos, transcendence and immanence, the kingdom of God and the kingdom of humanity. The completed works

---

[8] See Rev. 7:9; 21:4; 4:9–10; 21:9–14; 22:1–5; and 19:6–8.

[9] See *Bible Hub*, s.v. "revelation," https://biblehub.com/revelation/1-1.htm#lexicon.

[10] N. T. Wright, *Surprised by Hope: Rethinking Heaven, the Resurrection, and the Mission of the Church* (New York, NY: HarperCollins Publishers, 2009).

of Christ—crucifixion, resurrection, and ascension—moved us into a new epoch in which we exist in an "already but not yet" state of heaven. In Christ we are citizens of heaven. This is a descriptor of our real-life lived experience now—today, tomorrow, and into eternity.

So, when we consider Jesus' purpose statement—"I came so that they may have life, and have *it* abundantly" (John 10:10)—we have to see it as a statement for you and for all *and* for now. We are to know the abundant life today precisely because of Jesus' completed works and our citizenship in heaven. And we are active participants in the process! Whenever we move something from darkness to light, we are participating in the reconciliation of heaven and earth. Whenever we experience peace, patience, gentleness, self-control, or love, as opposed to tumult, anxiety, divisiveness, or hate, we are living into the kingdom of heaven. When we create order out of chaos, we allow others to see the image of God and his kingdom. This is the era Christ ushered in when the Father of heaven raised his one and only son, Jesus, from the dead, seated him on the throne of heaven, and then poured out his Spirit from heaven to flood the cosmos with his presence.

Jesus' purpose—promising flourishing of life—is not meant to be a static idea on a page, nor a down payment on a future-only reality; rather it is a very real, lived experience. And if it's available to all, then it should be something we are ushering in for every person—including our marginalized neighbors.

The Counterpull

At this juncture it is important to note that much of our culture acts as a counterweight, if not outright hostile opposition, to the above-offered description of flourishing for all:

- Phones drive us into ourselves and take us away from the moment at hand.
- Streaming services keep us entertained and away from boredom.
- Cars, suburbs, and privacy fences isolate us from neighbors.
- Invitation overload creates decision and engagement paralysis.

- Social media "likes" replace hugs, and buttons and notifications replace more natural dopamine hits.
- Internet connection splits our personas into many disparate pieces.
- We are made to believe that differing ideologies represent people, and to position those people as enemies.
- Success is defined by material possessions and/or status.
- There is no common bedrock of being—no agreed purpose, and no knowable truth.

I could go on ...

The point is, evil or injustice may very well be caused by the intentional acts of some sinister characters, but much more damaging is the cultural water we swim in. We are not even aware of all the insidious ways we are constantly being driven away from the Christian definition or understanding of flourishing.

This is what I will refer to as "systemic" sin—the embedded systems, structures, institutions, policies, environment, etc., in which we collectively participate. In fact, it is the interplay between individual action and systemic realities that is so damaging—the countervoice in your head in collaboration with the marketing strategies that tell you to have one more drink, watch another episode, swallow your pain, stay on the couch ... etc.

There will be a constant and consistent counterpull, both personal and systemic, away from experiencing flourishing. Recognizing it is half the battle.

Every one of us experiences this. But when we begin to look at the systemic sin that pulls us away from the flourishing Jesus intended, we see a range of inequitable experiences that restrict access to flourishing for some more than others.

This leads us to consider what it is to be "marginalized" or a "marginalized neighbor." Before moving on to the definition, let me state this unequivocally: Scripture and the Christian faith are very clear that we are *all* marginalized. Through sin, we are all separated from Jesus Christ (Rom. 3:23–26), and apart from Jesus we can do absolutely nothing to earn our status in the kingdom of heaven (John 15:4–5). Similarly, being a "marginalized neighbor" is simply positional and situational language that describes a person's relationship to a society's prevailing norms. Being a "marginalized neighbor" is not commentary on a person's worth and value.[11] If anything, the early, consistent, and sustained concern God shows for marginalized neighbors throughout Scripture is proof of their inherent dignity and infinite worth. The recognition of our own marginalization before God allows us to adopt the posture and approach of humility in all areas of life, including our interactions with our marginalized neighbors.

That said, the simplest understanding of a marginalized neighbor is someone who has been pushed to the edges (or margins) of a society or community. They encounter barriers or difficulties staying in or entering into the center of the community where the majority resides.

This marginalization can occur through two basic processes:

- Systemic injustices pressed upon an individual through contextual cultural realities. (I will detail some of these in chapter three.)
- Personal choices pressed upon by the individual themselves.

These two processes are completely and totally interrelated and cannot be extracted from one another. For example, living in the reality of systemic injustice may lead someone to make personal choices they may not have made had they not faced such experiences. In addition, it is often the personal choices of individuals in the "center" of a society or community (often those with the most power) that lead to the existence of systemic injustices that others have to live with. The relationship between these two are horribly and helplessly intertwined.

Here is the tricky balance we must find when using the term "marginalized": On the one hand, we must recognize our universal

---

[11] For a helpful exploration of this issue, see Seth D. Kaplan, *Fragile Neighborhoods: Repairing American Society, One Zip Code at a Time* (New York, NY: Little, Brown and Company, 2023). The second chapter of his book, "The Rich are not Alright," addresses the problems of categorizing people and the implications that certain groups are represented as having lesser status or value, when the reality is that we all have problems.

commonality as those "marginalized" from the fulness God has for us; but on the other hand, we need to utilize terms and definitions that create alignment across different groups, which can help us to recognize the systemic sin that God would have us work against. Seeing the value and agency of those who are marginalized is a key focus of the work I do and the main premise of this book. I would never want to create unhelpful categories that cause harm to our neighbors—I believe Jesus calls us to work against the systemic marginalization that happens in our communities, and that his way was to be among the marginalized, empowering and equipping them to have the flourishing life he came to offer, and for them to be instrumental in taking that good news to others.

We participate in ministry to marginalized neighbors as Jesus did—seeing that all people hold inherent dignity (created in the image of God) and are of infinite value (Jesus died for all), to bring about restoration of whole people (heart, mind, soul, and strength) and whole communities (lived experience of flourishing), helping to activate them in the mission of God by loving God, self, others, and the world.

So, to be absolutely clear: Non-marginalized neighbors are not any better than marginalized neighbors. But if we avoid the term "marginalized," we might be in danger of failing to recognize marginalization, or ignoring the harm done to those we would refer to as marginalized.

When we talk about marginalized neighbors, we are using the term as an unfortunate necessary reference point in order to address the loving ministry that God has called his people to participate in—the ministry of reconciliation and holistic restoration. We do this ministry in recognition that we are called to help bring our marginalized neighbors to the center, and part of that process is removing the barriers and obstacles in their way.

Jesus and the Marginalized

The answer to so much of this is to look to the life and example of Jesus. When we become followers of Jesus who understand and imitate his ways, we are able to become partners with God in ushering in his kingdom on earth. Jesus' life was marked by ministry to the marginalized. The narratives of the Gospels are absolutely littered with stories highlighting his ministry priority. A few examples:

- He picked his twelve disciples, his ministry team, out of the leftovers from the Jewish religious system—unpromising students who had already begun other vocations (Luke 5:1–11).
- He touched the unclean and healed the helpless (Luke 8:43–48).
- He reclined at the table with tax collectors and sinners (Mark 2:15–17).
- He traveled through regions his countrymen traveled around (John 4:4).
- He allowed women to sit at his feet and learn in a time where that was not allowed (Luke 10:38–42).

While these may seem like mundane "so what" actions to us today, they were rather heroic and controversial in Jesus' cultural context. This way of life busted every established tradition, custom, and value held close by the Jewish society he was part of. Jesus did not do these things for rebellion's sake, or to give someone the finger, or to put forward a persona on social media; rather, Jesus lived this way because it was the fulfillment of God's intended way of life for his people. Jesus took these scandalous actions simply because marginalized neighbors are real people, created in the image of God, and therefore those who hold inherent dignity and infinite value.

We know that Jesus' ultimate mission was cosmic redemption, but his ministry was marked by holistic restoration and activation of marginalized neighbors. This was the kingdom he came to bring.

We also know that Jesus came as a fulfillment of the Law that God had given to his people, the Israelites, through Moses (Matt. 5:17).[12] This means that we can learn a lot about God's attitude toward

---

[12] For a more detailed analysis on Jesus' role as the fulfilment of the Law and the Prophets, see "How Does Jesus Fulfil the Law?" *Bible Project*, March 7, 2024, https://bibleproject.com/articles/how-does-jesus-fulfill-law/.

marginalized people, and how he wants us to care for them, by looking at the relevant passages in the Law books of the Old Testament.

What follows in the coming chapters is a proposal about a recurring group we meet throughout the Old Testament—the Orphans, Widows and Sojourners (OWS). In the time of the Israelites in the Old Testament, this group represent those facing the greatest barriers to living a flourishing life: hindered from loving God with all of their being—heart, mind, soul and strength. The OWS were marginalized in their society and therefore faced restrictions on their most fundamental human rights. God called his people to adopt an identity and a set of practices that restored the OWS, removing those barriers, and giving them the opportunity to join or rejoin the larger faith community, Israelite society.

I believe the closest approximation to the OWS in our current American culture are our neighbors stuck in generational poverty, and the vast majority of those neighbors are usually concentrated in a few urban neighborhoods of each town or city that have experienced decades of disinvestment. This makes understanding the OWS and God's direction to the Israelites for how to care for them vital as we consider how we might include and empower our marginalized neighbors today. As the people of God, our call to love our marginalized neighbors remains the same: to help remove those barriers through a common identification and adopted set of practices that foster holistic restoration and open pathways to loving God with the whole of their being.

By learning from the approach to OWS in the Old Testament and by observing how Jesus brought this to completion in justice for the marginalized, we can allow our personal and collective ministries to be shaped and formed into a missional expression that aligns with God's revealed heart. We can subvert the ways of the world and bring about the flourishing life Jesus wants for all people.

2
A
BIBLICAL
MANDATE

The Ancient Near East (ANE) is the cultural context in which the Bible was written. The timeframe of authorship from the start of the Old Testament to the close of the New Testament spans almost three thousand years, so generalizations—like the one I'm about to make—can be dangerous, because cultural shifts and nuance vary greatly over such a span of time. But for the most part, scholarship allows us to say with a fair amount of certainty that in the ANE, society operated under an agricultural-patriarchy.[1] As a point of contrast, America could be categorized as a culture of consumeristic-individualism.[2] This is in no way a value statement on either culture; it is simply a statement of observable cultural characteristics.

So, what does an agricultural-patriarchy entail?

Agricultural: There can be a certain amount of romanticizing of rural America where people used to own their own land and grow their own food. Or maybe that's just because I grew up in the farm fields of Illinois! But even those of us who have lived in agricultural settings in the US are removed from the ANE farming culture. This is largely due to the influence of the industrial revolution, which shaped the John Deere tractor and cornfields scenes more familiar to us from the last seventy years. A society that revolves around agriculture, like that of

---

[1] R. K. Harrison, *Introduction to the Old Testament* (Grand Rapids, MI: Eerdmans, 1969), 396.

[2] Bryant L. Myers, *Walking with the Poor: Principles and Practices of Transformational Development* (Maryknoll, NY: Orbis Books, 2011), 55–58.

the ANE, is vastly different from what we experience today, because so much of day-to-day life was determined by land. You received your sustenance from what grew and was raised on your land. Your status in the community was determined by the amount of land and its prosperity. Your home, which really was more like a mini-village with extended family, was in the center of your land. Religion revolved around agriculture too, as fertility gods, offerings, and local cults were dedicated to crops or weather that determined your livelihood. Even for the Israelites, who counter-culturally rejected agricultural idolatry, the religious system required sacrifices from your livestock or harvest as an offering (see Lev. 1–5). The social calendar was in sync with the harvest, as the festivals largely followed the cycles of planting, growing, and reaping crops. The few city-dwellers either had land outside the city gates that they farmed, or a trade that they used to barter for food.[3] Every aspect of life was informed and affected by agriculture, beyond the simple fact of needing food to survive. It was the basis for all interactions in a community—social, religious, economic, and even entertainment.

Patriarchy: A patriarchal culture is one in which everyone's identity, economy, status, and profession, stems from the family line which begins with the patriarch, or eldest father.[4] Prosperity passed through the generations through the male line. Typically, multiple generations would live together in a large household or multiple households on the same land, and the head of the family would ultimately be responsible for everyone's care, business dealings, the settling of disputes, etc.[5] To make a modern-day comparison, it is sort of like the patriarch was the mayor or president of these miniature communities, although this analogy still falls short of conveying the relational side of what the patriarch stood for. While it is true that the patriarch would act as business manager, judge, and even general at times, he was also a husband, father, grandfather, and brother. Patriarchal culture also

---

[3] Ralph Gower, *The New Manners & Customs of Bible Times* (Chicago, IL: Moody Publishers, 2005), 289.

[4] *Merriam Webster*, s.v. "patriarchy," https://www.merriam-webster.com/dictionary/patriarchy.

[5] Gower, *The New Manners & Customs of Bible Times*, 82.

shaped the sense of individual identity in a way that is hard for us in our individualistic culture to fully grasp. Who you were was largely informed by your family lineage. That is not to say there was no sense of personal identity, or individual independence, but it was never separated from the larger family-tribe-nation.[6]

In a culture where all of your sustenance, identity, basic needs, and overall view of what it means to live an abundant life is determined largely by your family line as it comes down through the father, and the land connected to that family line, who faces the most barriers to loving God with all of their being?

The fatherless, the husbandless and the landless.

Orphans, Widows, and Sojourners[7]

When God gave his people the Law, or "way" of following him in everyday life, he revealed his desire for them to be a nation set apart, as a witness to the One Living God (Duet. 7:6). Although the ANE context would mean the Israelites' culture would look similar to many of the neighboring nations, God desired for their relationship with him, with others, and with the world to look distinct in two primary ways:

- How their relationship with God and one another would fit within the ANE context.
- How their relationship with God and one another would transform societal norms found in the ANE context.

---

[6] Walter Brueggemann, *Journey to the Common Good* (Louisville, KY: John Knox Press, 2010), loc 579.

[7] A quick note on "sojourners" because it isn't a word we run across much today: In some translations you may see "alien," "foreigner," or even "immigrants." All of these terms come with baggage in this day and age, which is why I favor the word "sojourner." It also captures the real-life situation of this collective people group. They were, broadly defined, "not Israelites," but could be from any other nation. They were nomadic, often traveling in family units. Sometimes they would pass through and be around only a short time, remaining strangers, but at other times they would settle for an indeterminate amount of time, for a season or possibly years. The one common factor was that they did not, could not in fact, own their own land in Israel. See also, *Dictionary of Biblical Imagery*, s.v. "foreigner," 300–302.

One dramatic but clear example of what we are talking about is the sacrificial system found in the Old Testament. Bringing offerings of livestock and harvest to the local religious temple was a widespread and common practice in the ANE.[8] God chose to reveal himself through this normative practice and laid out the sacrificial system we see in the biblical books of Exodus, Leviticus, Numbers, and Deuteronomy. We know that God was ultimately pointing his people to Christ and would redeem the sacrificial system by reconciling the cosmos through the sacrifice of Jesus; but for these ancient Israelites, the sacrificial system allowed them, in part, to know God in their day and time. In many ways, it looked like the sacrificial systems of the surrounding nations, so it was not some completely foreign concept that held no meaning for the people of God. It was incorporated into the faith community in a way that was accessible to their lived experience, and helped direct their worship to God.

However, while looking very similar, there were also stark contrasts and boundaries in the Israelites' sacrificial system to set them apart from those of their surrounding nations and to keep them pleasing to God. The first, and most obvious, was that instead of bringing sacrifices to the temple of whatever deity they wanted to appease and gain favor from—gods of fertility, war, physical location, or sun—the Israelites worshipped only one God (Deut. 4:35), from whom all of creation had its being, the only one to whom honor and worship was due. Second, the sacrifices were not intended as manipulations of God, to get God to do what they wanted. God had rescued and redeemed his people before accepting their sacrifices, which were meant to be given as recognition of an existing relationship, and love for the God who saves (Ezek. 20:1–32). Obedience and faithfulness to God's promises and commands were expected based on an existing relationship, not as contingencies to a relationship. It is a fine line, admittedly, but one that makes all the difference.

Finally, there were some sacrificial practices that were so abhorrent to the holiness of God that God wanted to protect his people from

---

[8]   Gower, *The New Manners & Customs of Bible Times*, 289.

them—namely sexual sacrifice and most especially child sacrifice (Lev. 18:21–23).

In this example, you can see how God used a normative ANE practice—the sacrificial system—and revealed himself through it, but also, he redeemed and transformed it in particular areas so that his people could be a light to the surrounding nations. The testimony of Scripture is that God uses the familiar aspects of a culture to reveal the transcendent. He enters into the mundane parts of human existence and works it for his glory and our good.

This directly influences our inspection of the OWS and the marginalized of society. God accepted a cultural reality—agricultural-patriarchy—and then called his people to live counterculturally in a way that not only cared for the marginalized of the ANE context but also was intended to restore them holistically back into the people of God. Here was a group that the "system" had forgotten—their ability to care and provide for themselves had been taken from them, their identities lost and cut off, with their physical lives threatened constantly. They were stripped of their dignity and self-worth. This is the very definition of marginalization. And these are the very people God repeatedly calls his people to remember and restore.

A closer examination of the Scriptures that highlight God's care for the OWS can inform our understanding of how to care for the marginalized in our cultural context. Here are some of the key passages.

Exodus

> You shall not oppress a stranger nor torment him, for you were strangers in the land of Egypt. You shall not oppress any widow or orphan. If you oppress him at all, *and* if he does cry out to Me, I will assuredly hear his cry; and My anger will be kindled, and I will kill you with the sword, and your wives shall become widows and your children fatherless.
>
> EXODUS 22:21–24

This is the first instance where the OWS are placed together, and it sets the precedent for all the following occurrences. The first thing to note is that the OWS are there. Thank you, Captain Obvious! It may seem a silly, unneeded point to make, but the unfortunate truth is that we would rather sweep the marginalized under the rug and go about life as if they do not exist. The OWS in Israelite society could have easily been the invisible minority forgotten by the masses and leveraged for personal satisfaction by people operating out of evil motives and positions of power. Instead, God worked the OWS directly into the Law. This inclusion was designed to keep them from becoming unnoticed or forgotten.

The second seemingly obvious statement is that the OWS were at risk in the whole of their being. If they were not at risk, you wouldn't see a command from the Lord to make sure they were treated appropriately. If there were no threats to their person, there would be no warning.

This passage is smack in the middle of the laws God is giving the Israelites as they move their identity from slaves in Egypt to the people of God living in the Promised Land. The passage is used as a warning of what not to do—wrong, oppress, or mistreat—and is especially remarkable as it carries a connotation of leveraging power and/or position to steal the dignity of another human being. We are not talking about an accident or mistake, nor even acting inappropriately out of ignorance, arrogance, or hubris. The verbiage used here is one of intentional oppression and injustice. God simply says, "Don't do that!" But the Law makes two important moves in doing this. First, it asks the Israelites to identify with the OWS by remembering their own past—they were once slaves in Egypt and were rescued through no action of their own, but by a free gift of God. Second, it communicates that God himself will act on behalf of the OWS to restore justice. To our eyes, this seems incredibly harsh and possibly even ungodly— but set aside for a moment if you can the anachronistic reading of the text and understand that God was revealing himself to ANE people through ANE culture—an eye-for-eye type of justice system. God was communicating that he would act on behalf of the marginalized to restore justice. This was certainly good news for the powerless!

The key points we can draw from this passage are:

- Marginalized neighbors were present in the community.
- Marginalized neighbors were at risk in the whole of their being.

Deuteronomy

The book of Deuteronomy fashions itself as Moses' farewell speech to the Israelites and is the most formative book for the practices of the people of God before Jesus came. It just so happens to be chock-full of references to the OWS. There are more clues in these verses to help us know these neighbors. Deuteronomy 10:18–19 once again states that God intervenes by giving the OWS food and clothing: "He executes justice for the orphan and the widow, and shows His love for the stranger by giving him food and clothing. So show your love for the stranger, for you were strangers in the land of Egypt." This is repeated in 24:17–21, reminding the Israelites of their experience in Egypt. Chapter 14, verse 29, says that the OWS are in the towns—which suggests they would have gathered in concentrated geographical areas and is synonymous with their lack of land. This is also reinforced in 16:11–14 where their presence in towns is mentioned two more times. In 26:11–13, we see that the OWS are at least partially dependent on other people's decisions to provide for them; and 27:19 shows that they were at risk legally, showing that they could easily suffer injustice.

We continue to build our profile of the OWS:

- Marginalized neighbors lacked basic daily needs of survival.
- Marginalized neighbors were concentrated in populated areas.
- Marginalized neighbors were forced to be dependent on others.
- Marginalized neighbors regularly suffered injustice.

Jeremiah, Ezekiel, Zechariah, and Malachi

The books of the Prophets contain reminders to the people of God about the importance placed upon their care of the OWS. It is telling of the Israelites' neglect of the OWS that the Prophets needed to remind them over and over again of God's instruction in the Law.

Jeremiah speaks to the Israelites of their place in the Promised Land that is predicated on their treatment of the OWS: "*If* you do not oppress the stranger, the orphan, or the widow, and do not shed innocent blood in this place, nor follow other gods to your own ruin, then I will let you live in this place, in the land that I gave to your fathers forever and ever (Jer. 7:6–7). The book also speaks of the importance of subverting power: "Do justice and righteousness, and save one who has been robbed from the power of *his* oppressor. And do not mistreat *or* do violence to the stranger, the orphan, or the widow; and do not shed innocent blood in this place" (Jer. 22:3).

Ezekiel and Zechariah specifically address "extortion"—which highlights how the OWS are economically at risk: "They have oppressed the stranger in your midst; they have oppressed the orphan and the widow among you" (Ezek. 22:7; see also Zech. 7:10 and Mal. 3:5).

Further Scriptures from the Old Testament echo the call to protect the OWS. The psalmist decrees they must be protected from the wicked: "Vindicate the weak and fatherless; Do justice to the afflicted and destitute. Rescue the weak and needy; Save *them* from the hand of the wicked" (Ps. 82:3–4). The OWS seem easy prey for the purposefully malicious. There are those from the outside who attack and exploit their position of weakness for their own gain.

So, our final three profile builders for the OWS are:

- Marginalized neighbors were economically challenged.
- Marginalized neighbors were preyed on by the malicious.
- Marginalized neighbors were easily forgotten by the very people who were supposed to protect them.

Now that we have built a picture of the agricultural-patriarchy of the ANE and the experience of the OWS as a marginalized subset of the population, we can return to God's key purpose statement for his people, the *Shema*, to consider what implications this had for the Israelites' treatment of the OWS.

The *Shema*

Here's the scene: Moses had gathered up all the Israelites to give one parting reminder of who they were as God's people. It was a strange parting because, while the Israelites had a faint sense of themselves as being the people of promise and their ancestry through Father Abraham, their identity had been ruthlessly and systematically erased through four hundred years of slavery in Egypt. They had become the people of bondage, crying out to return to slavery even after being freed. But free they now were.

Here they stood, on the precipice of stepping over the line into a completely new identity, one already declared over them by God and established freely through God's actions, and Moses gives them the statement that became the bedrock for the Israelite nation, uniting them as a people and affirmed by Jesus as the greatest commandment.

The *Shema* is the name of the prayer, but also the first word, "hear" (Deut. 6:4).[9] The ancient Hebrews would not have interpreted that word as "listen," as a cognitive exercise, like we do today; but instead, they would have understood it as intricately tied to action. It would not have been considered "hearing" unless there was associated action in response.

A fuller rendering of the *Shema* could be, "understand and obey." This has echoes of Jesus' introduction to his well-known parable in Matthew 7: "Therefore, everyone who hears these words of Mine, and acts on them, will be like a wise man who built his house on the rock" (v. 24). Hear and obey.

> Hear, Israel! The LORD is our God, the LORD is one! And you shall love the LORD your God with all your heart and with all your soul and with all your strength.
>
> DEUTERONOMY 6:4–5

---

9 Gary H. Hall, *Deuteronomy: The College Press NIV Commentary* (Joplin, MO: College Press Publishing, 2000), 138.

The full *Shema* statement declared the truth that God is the foundation of reality (the I AM), both personally and corporately. It set the meaning for everyday life and the life of the community. The second part of the declaration was about relationship: "The LORD *our* God." This transcendent God who is the grounding of all existence had revealed himself, first to promise, then to rescue, and finally to establish an eternal relationship.

All of that, and more, is located in the *Shema*. The key here is that this declarative statement requires a response, and at the heart of the response is love—understand and obey, Israel, because the LORD your God is One ... "and you shall love the LORD your God with all your heart and with all your soul and with all your strength."

The centerpiece of the Christian faith has always been love. In everything, Christianity should reflect the overflow of God's great love for his people, and it should be the first thing others see. The reflection of that love should be overwhelming in its capacity to blind people with its power, which incidentally, is why Jesus says that the second part of the greatest commandment is to love your neighbor as yourself. Your "self" has been infinitely loved by the transcendent God who became immanent and exchanged his identity for your own in order to dwell in the presence of raw, unaltered existence. What love indeed! How can we not love our neighbors in response.

The call of the *Shema* is to recognize God's existence, his great love for us, and in response to his very being and actions, to love him in return with all of our being—heart, mind, soul, and strength and then to love others in return.

As mentioned in the previous chapter, the heart, mind, soul, and strength are idiomatic of the totality of your being—and in our modern terminology we might equate this with all our emotions, intellect, spirituality, and physicality. Yes, we can separate them out and work on each one, but first and foremost we should understand ourselves as whole beings. And that is how we are to love God—with all that we are. This is the response called for in the *Shema*—to place primacy of relationship within the totality of our being, all aspects of our self, and all moments of our life; to give over ourselves with reckless abandon, to radically reorient a life of love toward God who is the giver and sustainer of all being.

So how does this fit with the importance of God consistently and repeatedly calling Israel to care for the orphans, widows, and sojourners? Why are they often lumped together as a list of three? And what does this have to do with being the people of God?

Put simply, in their cultural context, the OWS were the ones who had significant barriers to loving God with all their heart, mind, soul, and strength. And the barriers they faced could be removed by a community of people living out their faith.

By virtue of being landless and fatherless in a society that was ordered around land and fathers, the OWS were at risk in every aspect of their being. The cultural norms and societal expectations were against them at every turn:

Physical (strength): This was the most practical. If a person didn't have access to land, they couldn't grow food or raise livestock. Proper nutrition would have been a real problem. Their physical bodies would become at risk as they were never sure where the next meal would come from. What is more, if they had no land, they had no home. There would have been a constant threat of exposure to the elements and therefore a heightened susceptibility to sickness, disease, and natural wear on the body.

Intellectual (mind): If the physical body was in a state of constant stress, the mental state would soon follow. Never knowing where their next meal was coming from—or whether it would come at all— and exposure to the elements would eventually destroy their mental processes. The societal structures were conveying the understanding that they didn't belong. Physical marginalization led to the belief that they were in fact disenfranchised. Being one of the "least of these" became a mental state, instead of a mere set of circumstances.

Emotional (heart): Once the raw physicality became identity, they would begin to make decisions based on that identity. Not knowing where sustenance was coming from meant decision-making became pragmatic. Hopes and dreams for life or community took a back seat to finding a way to fill the belly. Emotionally, they would become defeated, as they got stuck in the state of always being in crisis. Their will and decision-making would seem to no longer be their own.

Spiritual (soul): The soul was the reality of the self and the direct link to a reality beyond. It was the connection to the deities or deity. In most ANE cultures, the sacrificial system seemed to be the method through which you could make yourself right before your god. It was an appeasement of the god so that it might go well with your soul. Even for Israelites worshipping God, the sacrificial system represented communion with—or entering into the presence of—God; the grounding of your being in the source of all being. Those without land had no produce or livestock to bring as an offering. This effectively cut them off from both communion with God and the people of God.

An Israelite would have connected their being to their soul and heart when hearing the pronouncement of the *Shema*. All of their might (strength) would have been connected to the responsive actions taken, e.g., loving their neighbor. The soul represented their being, their living self, who they were as a person. It was a commentary on their internal reality. The heart, on the other hand, was the counter-side, speaking to the external reality. The heart represented the will, or decision-making, and was therefore concerned with doing. An Israelite would have understood the command to love the Lord their God, to do so with all of their being and doing, with all that they are, and with all of their actions. Therefore, belonging in the community of the people of God meant the giving over of the whole of yourself in communion with God; precisely what the cultural systemic structures obstructed the OWS from.

Israel's Ministry to the OWS

The question looming for the people of God was what to do with their marginalized neighbors. There were people living among them who were essentially cut off from communion with both God and the larger community due to the reality of living inside a patriarchal-agricultural society. Without the protection of inherited land, the OWS often found themselves among the beggars, prostitutes, indentured servants, or dead. The Lord intervened through the Law, calling for care of the OWS and continuously calling for the Israelites to remember their commitment articulated in the words of the Prophets.

Sadly, it was the failure of Israel to act on behalf of the OWS that violated their covenant relationship with God. This failure reflected a lack of intimacy with God, who cares for the marginalized and executes justice on their behalf, to incorporate them into the people of God. If the Israelites would not align their actions with God's own, then they would not know him and could not be known by him (see Jer. 7:5–7).

The Exile (see Jer. 52, 2 Kings 25, 2 Chron. 36) became the judgment for violating this relationship. The Israelites were at war with one another—Israel and Judah, a divided nation—and failed to act on behalf of the OWS. God brought judgment, in this case via the nation of Babylon, as a consequence of their separation.

As exiles in Babylon, they were once again sojourners. They had no land to call their own. They were fatherless and landless, cut off from their inheritance, left at the margins of the Babylonian culture. They had been brought low and reminded of where they came from; what they were called to remember in the Law. In this way, God was shaping his people for when he would bring them home in order that they could become a people who would indeed act on behalf of the marginalized.

The thematic flow of Judgment—Exile—Return—New Relationship, is completed in Jeremiah 31, a passage that shows the fulfillment of the Law in Deuteronomy and the exhortation of the Prophets in Jeremiah 7:5–7. God's Law would no longer exist outside of the individual or community but would one day be written on their hearts (through the coming of Jesus and the impartation of the Holy Spirit). The promise is that when God returns his people from Exile, they will operate under a renewed relationship, one where the Spirit of God himself is imprinted on the hearts of his people. The covenant community will act toward others in full alignment with the character and will of God, which has been shown to be uniquely oriented to the marginalized of society.

And it does not simply end with a reorientation of the heart and mind but continues through the restorative practices given by God for his people to enact, bringing tangible transformation in the lives of real people, in a real time and place, in real ways.

Practices for the People of God

Over the years, I have laid out the case for the people of God today to step into the Israelites' original calling—to care for and include the OWS of our times. Whenever I share this, the typical response is affirmation and head nodding. The issue(s) arise when we move out from the why, to the what, and especially begin to discuss the how. How do you achieve restoration and activation? What exactly does that mean?

To begin to talk about the how, we will return once again to the Israelites' neighbors, the OWS. We can learn from God's instructions to Israel, see how they were to minister to their marginalized neighbors, and then draw on these principles in our context. As I've studied these passages, I've observed how God repeatedly charged individuals representing the collective people of God to reorient their minds and simultaneously adopt normative practices—tangible actions—aimed at holistic restoration of heart, mind, soul, and strength of marginalized neighbors. Here are a few examples:

Gleaning (Deut. 24:17–21): The practice of leaving a part of the harvest in the field for the OWS to harvest themselves. This allowed them to bring in their own sustenance and have their strength restored.

Listening (Ex. 22:21–24): If the OWS were mistreated they were to cry out, and God would hear their cry. By giving them a voice in the community, their heart (will or decision-making) could be restored.

Executing justice (Deut. 10:18–19; 27:19; Ps. 146:9): Biblical justice can be understood as aligning reality with the character of God. When the people of God executed justice on behalf of the OWS, they were restoring their heart and soul.

Incorporating into the tithe (Deut. 14:29; 26:11–13): A landless, fatherless, husbandless individual would have no offering to bring to allow them entrance into the presence of and communion with God.

Incorporating the OWS into the tithe of the people gave them access to worshipping God and would ensure their soul was restored.

Including in celebration (Deut. 16:11–14): Incorporating the OWS into the tithe was not merely entrance into a religious ceremony. In ancient Israel, the various offerings were also to be enjoyed through festivals. They were to feast and commune together, and therefore be restored in mind and strength.

Protecting (Deut. 24:17–21; Jer. 7:6; 22:3, Ezek. 22:7): The Law and Prophets built in protection to cover those most exposed. This included physical and economic protection. Knowing that protection was present allowed for freedom in decisions, and freedom to make decisions was a restoration of the heart and mind.

Mourn with (Ps. 94:6): Orphans and widows had, by definition, experienced loss. Similarly, sojourners had experienced loss of family, culture, and identity. The exhortation for the people of God was to mourn with the OWS. When a community empathized with the hurting, they were restored in their heart, soul, and mind.

Care for (Zech. 7:10; Mal. 3:5): This seems the most basic, but the prophets Zechariah and Malachi lamented that the people of God simply did not care for the OWS and therefore were not after God's own heart. Caring for others and showing the marginalized compassion restored the wholeness of a person.

We can begin to see the connection between the things God commanded the Israelites to do and the holistic restoration of people. These were synchronistically formative practices for Israel as a whole. When Israel did not perpetuate predatory lending practices against the OWS, marginalized neighbors won, but so too did Israel itself. The nation had become holy as God is holy. And to top it all off, other nations—those needing to come to know God—perked up with interest when Israel lived a collective countercultural way of life, reflecting the glory of God, and serving as a witness to how things could possibly be different. In this way, Israel was a blessing to the nations.

From these Old Testament practices above, I believe we can draw three principles that inform our interaction with marginalized people in our culture today.

Common identification: It can be easy for us to view those on the margins of society as less-than. Where the ANE culture of agricultural-patriarchy meant that individual status was formed around land ownership and family, in our culture of consumeristic-individualism we have other metrics of status that can cause us to judge individual worth. These can be metrics such as job status, home ownership, education, and financial security.[10] Therefore, in our culture, when we observe those who have fewer possessions, a perceived "lower" job status, or lack educational attainment, we assign them less power and influence. Even when one's orientation toward the marginalized is to help and not to leverage, it is easy to create the "other"—the one who needs help, the one who can benefit from charity, the one who is lesser. The exhortation for the people of God to remember that they themselves were once sojourners in Egypt was to serve as a refrain that played in their minds as they interacted with the marginalized. It rooted them in a common identity. The call was not only to remember but also to put this into empathetic practice as Israel was to listen and mourn with the marginalized. The inclusion in celebration was an invitation to the table. The common identification moved the OWS from "they/them" to "us/we." We need to consider today how we can find a common identification with our marginalized neighbors, to work from a place of humility as we look to raise up and restore.

Compelled by love: As already established, the Law and Prophet's repeated injunction to care for the marginalized flows out of God's character and is evidenced by his will—his willingness to act on behalf of the OWS. Jesus himself summed up all the Law and Prophets with the command to love God with all that we are and to love our neighbor as ourselves. The people of God are to love others because God first loved those whom he elected to live with in a covenant relationship. Taken together, this presents a people compelled by love—not obligation—to act in love toward the marginalized. The definition of this love, from a

---

10 Donna M. Beegle, "Overcoming the Silence of Generational Poverty," *Invisible Literacies*, The National Council of Teachers of English, October/November 2003, 12–13.

Christian worldview, is one of self-giving and self-sacrifice. We need to join in the mission of God by joining him in love for the other.

Holistic restoration: Finally, the call to care for the OWS was not one of charity but of the holistic restoration of an individual's mind, strength, heart, and soul, as well as restoration into the community of the people of God. Whether it was by restoring their strength through allowing them dignity by harvesting their own food, through including them in the tithes and offerings to restore their heart and soul, or through any of the other examples listed above, the aim was not merely to minister to temporal felt needs but to restore and reflect the wholeness of who they are in the presence of God. We need to find ways to bring marginalized neighbors back to the center of our society, empowering them to experience flourishing life for themselves and to be part of a community that is experiencing flourishing life. This is what we would describe as reintegration into community, where those in need are no longer left on the margins as they experience restoration but are returned to the center. This sense of belonging is part of sustaining that restored life. Furthermore, this reintegration into the center empowers them to redefine the center, unbounded by the cultural mores they've previously experienced. As those who believe that Jesus offers flourishing of life, this also means our hope is that full flourishing means being rooted in Christ.

Contextualizing this call and command for the people of God today will see us activated into the mission and ministry of Jesus. My argument is that the best correlation to the OWS in Israel and our cultural context are those experiencing generational poverty in certain neighborhoods in our towns and cities. Societal factors in a consumeristic-individualism culture place significant barriers and challenges for our neighbors to loving God with all of their being. Many people experiencing generational poverty are concentrated in disinvested neighborhoods in urban centers where housing stock and overall cost of living match income levels. In order to fulfill the biblical mandate of holistic ministry to marginalized populations, Christians and churches must shift away from short-term personal betterment toward the long view of community development, aiming to raise the overall quality of life for under-resourced neighbors and neighborhoods. The practices we see God command Israel to do for and with the OWS are not exactly the manual for neighborhood revitalization today, but they are close— and can help us shape current principles and practices that will assist them in moving toward a flourishing life.

3
SYSTEMS OF MARGINALIZATION

Everyone knows "that side of town." Yes, in my experience, even the neighbors who live there know that's what it is. You can probably call up the mental image: Neighborhoods where housing is dilapidated, things look run down, crime is high, schools are rough, etc. We have to recognize that these places do indeed exist, and more importantly, very real people live in these neighborhoods. Taken as a collective demographic—rather than focusing on individual experiences—our neighbors living there are economically, educationally, physically, and emotionally disadvantaged in comparison to many in the rest of the city.[1]

Those experiencing poverty in most cities often live within a few specific neighborhoods. For example, in my city, 80 percent of people whose income is below the poverty line live in thirteen core neighborhoods concentrated in our center city.[2] There are many reasons for this, some of which we will explore below; but the most basic reason is that these neighborhoods are where those in poverty can afford to live. Property in these areas becomes affordable to those needing housing. That can mean those with disabilities, or fixed-incomes, or lower-than-living-wage jobs, or who made poor life decisions—or any one of

---

[1]   Beegle, "Overcoming the Silence of Generational Poverty," 12–13; and

[2]   See *For Evansville*, "Are we helping kids succeed," in The State of E Report, 2022, https://www. forevansville.org/stateofe.

many other reasons, often with an interplay of several reasons—end up living in concentrated areas of urban poverty.

These neighborhoods are called "disinvested" areas because investment goes out to the edges of the city as suburban development occurs. From the end of World War II through to the 1970s, a phenomenon occurred called *suburbia*.[3] When cars became more affordable, and it was fashionable to spread out and escape the density of the city, large numbers of people packed up and moved to the outskirts of what is known as the urban core. As you would expect, when the people moved out, business, retail, entertainment, jobs, and education centers soon followed. But, in what turned out to be a very bad city-planning move, it was decided that all of these different sectors would be separated out. So, you'd find houses to live in over here, jobs to work at over there, shopping and entertainment in this center, and some green spaces sprinkled throughout. This is an extremely short explanation of a large issue: suburban sprawl. It did, and is doing, damage to community ecosystems because it fragments peoples' lives. They no longer live, work, play, and worship in the same community, reaping the benefits of those natural interactions and relationships.

But arguably the greatest damage was done to the neighborhoods left in the urban core. All the investment went out to the edges for new development, and much human talent and capital left for the supposed greener pastures. This resulted in a lack of upkeep of infrastructure in urban core areas. Perhaps most concerning was the disinvestment in public schools. Like everything else, schools lost resources as new ones popped up in different areas to accommodate the sprawl. When schools aren't actively invested in, the next generation struggles, and cycles of poverty are perpetuated.

A simple fact: If investment goes to one place, it will not go to another. If investment goes toward a mall in the suburbs, investment won't go into Main Street.

---

[3]   Becky Nicolaides and Andrew Wiese, "Suburbanization in the United States after 1945," *Oxford Research Encyclopedias*, April 26, 2017,   https://oxfordre.com/americanhistory/display/10.1093/acrefore/9780199329175.001.0001/acrefore-9780199329175-e-64.

Where there is no investment, quality of life decreases. This results in an area being less desirable, and core costs, such as that of housing, reduce. In turn, you get concentrated populations of people experiencing poverty because these areas become the only places they can afford. Where you get concentrated populations of people experiencing poverty, you get increased rates of violence, low educational performance, single-parent households, and other factors that tend to put a whole community on a downward spiraling trajectory, one very hard to escape.[4]

The Systemic Nature of Poverty

The data suggests that generational poverty is becoming overwhelmingly difficult to escape.[5]

Advanced longitudinal studies (where they follow people for a very long time), like the Panel Study of Income Dynamics, supports the observation that people who are born into poverty stay in poverty, regardless of race, gender, or religious affiliation. The disparity in education is increasing, not decreasing. In 1970, 16 percent of those in the lowest income quartile were likely to earn a bachelor's degree, but this figure had fallen to just 10 percent by 1996.[6] The American myth of "pulling yourself up by your bootstraps" and the promise of equal opportunity may hold true as a possibility at the individual level, but as a collective demographic dataset, those in poverty overwhelmingly become tied to the lifestyle and pass the same experience down to their children.

In addition, the geographic neighborhood where someone grows up has a direct correlation to their long-term poverty. A 2010 study

---

[4] Kretzmann and McKnight, *Building Communities From the Inside Out*, 2–13.

[5] K. A. McGonagle, R. F. Schoeni, N. Sastry, and V. A. Freedman, "The Panel Study of Income Dynamics: overview, recent innovations, and potential for life course research," *Longitudinal and Life Course Studies*, 3 (2), 2012.

[6] Steve Raphael and Eugene Smolensky, "Immigration and Poverty in the United States," *Focus*, 26 (2), Fall 2009.

by the Organization for Economic Co-Operation and Development showed that appearance—or perception—of peers in a community sets expectations for jobs.[7] What adults do vocationally directly transfers to the next generation. Couple the generational cycle with disinvested areas that create inadequate housing, lack of access to nutritious food and health care, and underperforming education institutions, and it becomes a fight for survival rather than a journey of upward mobility and a high quality of life. These neighborhoods have higher crime and fewer employment opportunities. While they have similar local networks to other areas, this lateral networking is ultimately detrimental due to the persistent poverty. The result is a localized community that reproduces itself.

Unfortunately, this is just a small sample of the data highlighting the pervasive and generational nature of poverty.

Talking About the Things We Don't Like to Talk About

I hesitated to write this section for a couple of reasons: First, the great complexity of each issue—there is so much more that could be said, and yet the limitation of space to explore the issues means that I can't incorporate all of its complexity here. Second, these challenges are not my stories to tell, and I am afraid of misrepresenting the issues as a whole, and the lived experiences of marginalized neighbors specifically. However, ultimately, you cannot tell the stories of cities, neighborhoods, and marginalized neighbors, without mentioning these aspects. So, I'm asking for grace and forgiveness up front in light of the aforementioned points, while we wade into the shallow waters of topics we typically do not like to talk about. These are issues we tend to ignore, pass over, can be opposed to the very idea of, or may be genuinely ignorant to. If you can, try to remember all that has come

---

[7] "Education at a Glance: OECD Indicators," *Organization for Economic Co-Operation and Development,* July 9, 2010, http://www.oecd.org/education/skills-beyond-school/educationataglance2010oecdindicators.htm.

before in our discussion of cities—such as rural to urban migration, suburban sprawl, affordable housing stock, etc.—because they provide key pieces to the complex puzzle.

Redlining[8]

The first piece of the puzzle for us to examine is a practice called redlining. Since the 1930s, those with influence and power designed a way to keep people deemed "undesirable" isolated in certain geographical areas, away from the rest of the population of a city. The idea was simple: Draw a red line around an area, and within it is where lending institutions would approve home loans for these groups of people, and outside of it they would not. Easy peasy.

As unbelievable as this practice may seem today, the reality is it was part and parcel of segregation and post-slavery America while we urbanized as a nation. Thankfully, it was found to be illegal in 1968 with the Fair Housing Act,[9] and then that ruling was supported by several subsequent legislative actions such as the Credit Opportunity Act in 1974,[10] Home Mortgage Disclosure Act in 1975,[11] and Community Reinvestment Act in 1977.[12] The fact that laws, and many to boot, had to be passed, proves without a doubt how widespread and deplorable the redlining practice was.

Surely once these new laws were enacted and a light was shined on such a horrendous, obviously racist practice, it stopped, right? During the 2008 recession and banking crisis, lending institutions were forced to open their books to inspection, and wouldn't you know it, the

---

[8] My insights into the challenges concerning redlining are largely informed by Ta-Nehisi Coates's *We Were Eight Years in Power: An American Tragedy* (London, UK: One World, 2017) and my direct examination of the historical acts and policies of redlining.

[9] The Fair Housing Act of 1968, 42 U.S.C. §§3601–3619.

[10] The Credit Opportunity Act of 1974, 15 U.S.C. §1691.

[11] The Home Mortgage Disclosure Act of 1975, 12 U.S.C. §§2801–2811.

[12] The Community Reinvestment Act of 1977, 42 U.S.C. § 5301.

practice had continued—sometimes through clever new workarounds, but sometimes just flat-out blatantly!

But did it stop in 2008? Well, in 2015, Chicago and Milwaukee got dinged very publicly, and just last year in my home state a public outing of a prominent bank made the newspapers for being found practicing redlining—or at least the spirit of redlining, even if they didn't have a map with a red circle on it.

The actual practice of redlining is so abhorrent to me—it fills me with rage every time I think about it. The ramifications of the practice simply make you want to weep. In addition to the racial wealth gap, redlining has contributed to segregation, educational inequalities, health disparities, and has caused negative psychological and social impact. All of these outcomes are purposefully directed at "undesirables." It is an example of oppression of the marginalized and played a large part in deforming a place and its people.

Learning and understanding about the existence of these practices and their ongoing impact on our marginalized neighbors is of key importance if we are to love them well.

White Flight

This reality was discussed earlier by its more friendly name—suburban sprawl. And no, I do not think the vast majority of white Americans consciously sat around and thought, *Hmm. There seem to be a lot more minorities around here, and I am racist, so I am moving to the suburbs.* However, "white flight" is perfectly descriptive of what actually happened as a historical-sociological phenomenon.[13] As migration into city centers occurred, and the popularity of automobiles brought about a drop in development investment in those areas, those with the opportunity—mainly white people—moved to the outer rings of cities. Again, I think it was much more due to market dynamics than intentional/deliberate racism, but the reality is, for fifty to sixty years,

---

[13] Jeff Speck, *Walkable City: How Downtown Can Save America One Step at a Time* (New York, NY: North Point Press, 2012), 17–34.

investment went into suburban development, where white people happened to be going; and the urban core of cities, where minorities happened to be overrepresented, experienced decades of disinvestment.[14] This is the very definition of systemic racism. If we are part of the majority population, we do not need to get defensive about this. We simply need to recognize it, learn, and try to bring about justice.

Gentrification

Gentrification is a complicated concept to define. Through my research, I discovered a range of conflicting data that doesn't paint a simple "right or wrong" picture. Whatever people believe about it, gentrification is the bogeyman of community development. Even a whisper of the word will shut down any talk of a proposed development. I have seen the word slung at people like a weapon.

Let me unequivocally say that I believe displacement of neighbors through gentrification is wrong in all its forms and should be avoided at all costs, even if that displacement stems from a subjective felt experience rather than overt, physical eviction. Here is what I mean ...

Imagine you have lived in the same neighborhood for thirty years, in part due to redlining legacy practices that you are not even aware of, but here you are. The neighborhood has experienced a long period of disinvestment, longer than you have lived there, meaning it is the environment you grew up in. There were things you would change, sure, but it was home. You had gotten used to the culture—the neighborhood had a certain look, feel, even smell. Then, all of a sudden (relatively speaking), a couple of new stores pop up that don't really look like they fit in the neighborhood. A new barber shop opens that doesn't look like any barber shop you have ever seen. A new housing development opens, and it sticks out like a sore thumb because it is the first new build in over twenty years. There are white people walking poodles! There are advertisements at the bus stops that show people

---

[14] Doug Saunders, *Arrival City: How the Largest Migration in History is Reshaping Our World* (New York, NY: Vintage Books, 2011), 10.

who look, dress, and carry themselves differently than you, your friends, and next-door neighbors.

The neighbor understands, "This place is not for me anymore," and puts their house up for sale.

This type of displacement occurs more often due to gentrification than from other causes, such as the rising cost of living, or forced relocation due to demolition, or acquisition of housing stock—although these things do happen in rare and isolated cases.

Really, gentrification feels like one more injustice to neighbors who have been marginalized through redlining and white flight, who find that urbanization and redevelopment of center cities is now a trendy societal move that forces them out of their neighborhoods. This can feel like violent takeover to those neighbors—*we will come in and retake this area because now we want it*. It is a terrible experience to live through, and the surrounding narratives that accompany such developments are equally atrocious.

Of course, the remedy to the problem is exactly what we have been and will continue to discuss throughout this book. I have never been to a neighborhood discussion where neighbors did not express the desire for a more genteel life. They want grocery stores, new homes, more green spaces, entertainment, and better schools. Gentrify away! Just do not displace us. Let the current residents be the ones to benefit from the development. Include neighbors in the change process.

Migration Further Contributing to Concentrated Marginalized Neighbors

Migration to cities, coupled with exponential population growth, is producing a trend of global urbanization. Every day, 180,000 people move into cities. That's 5.5 million a month, or 66 million a year. In the next five years, more people will move into cities than the United States of America has as its entire population.[15] Globally and nationally, this is occurring as people move from rural areas to urban cores.

---

[15] United Nations, Department of Economic and Social Affairs, Population Division, "World Urbanization Prospects: The 2018 Revision," 2019.

And the shift from rural to urban is growing. In 2011, the world officially shifted away from majority-rural living, and estimates have the percentage of urban dwellers at 68.7 percent by 2050. The urbanization of the globe, referred to as megalopolis, megacity, postcolonial city, or simply the global city, is creating a new reality for billions of people—the migrants, the first-generation urbanites, and the city dwellers themselves dealing with the influx of people in the place they call home.

In America, the population shift from rural to urban happened nearly one hundred years ago. The 1920 census was the first time the American population crossed over to above 50 percent, and the 2010 census topped 80 percent.[16] *Our World in Data* at the University of Oxford estimates that nearly nine out of ten Americans will be living in urban centers by 2050.[17] In other words, pretty soon!

The great migration from rural to urban is due in part to individuals seeking peace and prosperity. There is a perception that the city acts as a shelter against the insulated view of the world prevalent in the rural social structure. In the city you can find like-minded people who do not place the previous generational worldview upon you. Further, economic advancement seems to be either constricting or a dead-end in the rural context, presenting either the risk of relying on an established but uncertain local market or accepting constrained financial growth. In the face of such choices people are voting with their feet. The reality that migrants face is that they enter their new urban context as displaced people even before taking into consideration economic realities.

The rural to urban migration contributes to an increase in marginalized neighbors in urban centers, as the "modern nomads" are themselves displaced. The global trend of urbanization and the profile of those migrating into city centers looks different in America. This is

---

[16] "2010 Census Urban and Rural Classification and Urban Area Criteria," *The United States Census Bureau*, December 02, 2019–March 09, 2020, https://www.census.gov/programs-surveys/geography/guidance/geo-areas/urban-rural/2010-urban-rural.html.

[17] Hannah Ritchie and Max Roser, "Urbanization," *OurWorldInData*, 2020, https://ourworldindata.org/urbanization.

in part due to the fact that, as I said previously, America became an urbanized nation over one hundred years ago, so the move into cities is not primarily the national rural poor, although that population is present. An ongoing source of new city dwellers in America are global immigrants who overwhelmingly prefer cities.[18] Taken together, the national rural migrants and international immigrants make up a collective of urban migration that is pouring into the core of American metropolitan regions.

Also trending is the desire of the Baby Boomer and Millennial generations to become city dwellers. These generations are moving out of the suburbs and back into urban centers. Until 2015, the Baby Boomer generation was the largest ever to date, and they are outliving any preceding generation. As a collective, they are choosing to spend their twilight years in cities, citing affordable housing, consumer-care preferences, and proximity to health care and family as the main impetus. On the polar opposite end of the age spectrum, Millennials—who surpassed Baby Boomers in 2015 as the largest generation in the history of humanity—unequivocally want to live, work, play, and worship in the same neighborhood; necessitating walkable cities and requiring a city center location for living.[19]

While this migration by Boomers and Millennials might seem innocuous—*these are the types of amenities and ease of life I want myself*—it does not occur in a vacuum. Those who have spent generations calling the urban core neighborhoods their home, can become displaced either through objective economic realities or subjective feelings of ownership. Neighbors who are already marginalized are further pushed out of their own communities so that neighbors with higher financial means can benefit from the newly built environments.

This means that certain urban areas become marked by wealth (often linked to gentrification) while other neighborhoods receive an influx of people without the choice of more desirable urban areas or

---

[18] Stephen T. Um and Justin Buzzard, *Why Cities Matter: To God, the Culture, and the Church* (Wheaton, IL: Crossway 2013), 28–42.

[19] Jeff Speck, *Walkable City*, 189.

suburbs. Many of these people, migrating into center city neighbor-hoods, can be characterized by the following verbs:

- Displaced
- Foreigners
- Economically depressed
- Unestablished
- Aged or uncared for
- Detached

This means a growing number of marginalized people—biblically corre-lating to those who experience barriers to loving God with all their heart, mind, soul, and strength—are making their homes in center cities.

Wealth Theft

All of the above-mentioned factors come together to perpetuate wealth theft, leading to "generational poverty," both of which put the onus on the people and groups experiencing poverty. The truth is, as a society upholding these institutions, systems, structures, and practices, we are stealing the potential wealth of our marginalized neighbors. When you force all the undesirables into an area; move all the goods, services, jobs, and markets out of it; and move in predatory practitioners like pay-day loans and liquor stores, you steal generational wealth. When you fail to invest in infrastructure development for decades, you steal generational wealth. When you redevelop that same area without including the people who live there so that they feel alienated and unwanted, you steal their wealth because they do not benefit from the development. When you depreciate home values through predatory lending practices, then buy those homes back for pennies on the dollar before redevelopment comes and appreciates in value, you steal wealth from marginalized neighbors.

Unfortunately, this is merely the tip of the iceberg. At the very least we need to be able to talk about these topics because they directly inform how our cities and neighborhoods got to be how they are today.

Without this knowledge, we cannot truly have the empathy needed to develop the common identification that compels us to love and brings about holistic restoration of marginalized neighbors.

As we discovered in the previous chapter, the biblical example of the orphans, widows, and sojourners in the Ancient Near East are contextualized today as the neighbors in disinvested neighborhoods in urban center cities. Whether through immigration, a shift from rural to urban, or an abutting neighborhood, these neighbors are displaced. Many are not physically connected to their "father's land." They are stuck in negative generational cycles with no collective understanding or perception of how to change these circumstances; or, if they are aware, they feel helpless to do anything about it. They are at risk emotionally, physically, mentally, and spiritually due to such normative factors as economic poverty, high crime rates, lower educational opportunities, and lack of municipal investment in infrastructure.

The following words—displacement, dependence, depression, despair, defeat—all lead toward one anti-biblical sentiment placed upon others in a community: the devaluing of individual human beings. This devaluing of the marginalized is precisely what God tried to guard against in his ongoing concern for the OWS and as he called his people to the holistic restoration and integration of the least of society.

So, what is our response as the people of God today? What are we to do as the church? Well, the answer is the same as it was for Israel—execute justice, show mercy, extend love, restore dignity, incorporate into the community, but the practices have changed … *must* change, in fact. We are no longer agricultural-patriarchal, so gleaning, marriage laws, and festival inclusion don't exactly help our marginalized neighbors.

If you have not guessed by now, yes, I believe the answer is neighborhood revitalization. Specifically, an approach to neighborhood revitalization called asset-based community development (ABCD). I believe this approach not only embodies the characteristics of God's design of holistic restoration and activation of marginalized neighbors but also gives a set of practices that can be adopted to bring about the worth and dignity inherent in image bearers of God. The rest of the book tackles this. But first, we turn back to Jesus.

One Monday night, our neighborhood leadership team was having its monthly meeting. We were finalizing our "Love Your Neighborhood" vision for change plan—our process for neighborhood revitalization. We were wrapping up what had been a three-month process, so we were all excited, and stuck around later than usual to finish the work and chat with one another.

We were meeting in a construction trailer in the neighborhood park, because our normal meeting space was undergoing a renovation. We had received a grant to take an old rundown clubhouse and turn it into a community gathering and learning center. During construction, we met in the trailer, with its one-inch aluminum siding.

As we were wrapping up, a loud POP-POP-POP-POP-POP went off outside. All eight of the neighborhood leaders immediately dropped to the ground. I, on the other hand, was left standing there looking like an idiot. Although I had been working in the neighborhood for a few years, I had only been living there for about four months. I was from the Westside, known more for its rural roots. Whenever I had previously heard sounds like that, it was typically firecrackers, and the only gun shots I had ever heard in person were shotgun shells and one-off hunting rifle reports.

My friends pulled me down, letting me know clearly how much of an idiot I was, and I said, "I thought that was some kids with firecrackers." I was quickly informed, "That ain't no firecracker!"

After the initial shock, one of the leaders—a mom of the neighborhood if there ever was one—stood up and charged outside to see if anyone was hurt. It was incredibly brave and courageous in my opinion. These small types of actions that occur every day in neighborhoods like ours are what gives me eternal hope.

Thankfully, no one was hurt. Yet it was unquestionably a terrifying experience. And based on their collective immediate reactions versus my own, it was clearly an experience my teammates had had enough times to shape their behavior.

Walking out into the empty, silent park, there was a palpable feeling of evil and oppression. It was such a stark contrast to the excited, hopeful, laughing comradery we had just experienced moments before as we solidified a vision for the future of the neighborhood, that ironically included safety! The gun shots ended the discussion, and everyone went home somber and reserved. Evil won that night.

About a month later, we had our annual "Movie Night in the Park." Every year, we rent one of those big inflatable screens, invite the entire neighborhood, a family from my church small group grills some delicious BBQ, and we watch a movie together in the community. As I watched kids run around laughing and playing, conversations turning strangers into neighbors, entertainment and fun being had by all, I saw Scripture come to life before my very eyes; "overcome evil with good."

You see, the movie night took place in the exact spot where the shots were fired. It would have been easy, even sensible, to find a new location, to let darkness overcome. But the easiest way to get rid of darkness is to turn on a light. As followers of Jesus, we are called to be the light of the world. We must be present in dark places, and where we vacate that responsibility, the kingdom of this world reigns. However, where we are, the kingdom of heaven rules.

I wish I could say this was a happy ending and those were the last shots fired in our neighborhood—"Movie Night Ends All Violence Forever!" But just last night, from our bedroom, we could hear shots fired, and there were two murders in the neighborhood last month.

But for one night, neighbors experienced a foretaste of heaven; a glimpse of what could be and is to come; a night where community, safety, full bellies, entertainment, and laughter triumphed over violence, sadness, tears, and oppression.

Our goal is to reduce the latter by multiplying the former. Exponentially.

4

**THE
WAY OF
JESUS**

The Psalms provide a wonderful respite whenever I feel I'm acquiring too much head knowledge and not enough emotive empathy in the work of neighborhood revitalization. It is good and proper to pause occasionally and recenter our faith as a personal connection to a personal Being, while still making sure our discussions are aligning with Scripture and the directed purposes of God.

To that end, I've found Psalm 146 to be a wonderful passage to reflect on and sense God call us into his mission, with his grace:

> Praise the LORD!
> Praise the LORD, O my soul!
> I will praise the LORD as long as I live;
> I will sing praises to my God while I have my being.
> Put not your trust in princes,
> in [human beings], in whom there is no salvation.
> When [their] breath departs, [they] returns to the earth;
> on that very day [their] plans perish.
> Blessed [are those] whose help is the God of Jacob,
> whose hope is in the LORD [their] God,
> who made heaven and earth,
> the sea, and all that is in them,
> who keeps faith forever;
> who executes justice for the oppressed,
> who gives food to the hungry.

The LORD sets the prisoners free;
the LORD opens the eyes of the blind.
The LORD lifts up those who are bowed down;
the LORD loves the righteous.
The LORD watches over the sojourners;
he upholds the widow and the fatherless,
but the way of the wicked he brings to ruin.
The LORD will reign forever, your God, O Zion, to all generations.
Praise the LORD!

PSALM 146 ESV (with amendments for inclusivity)

This psalm begins and ends with a call to praise, for the individual in the opening and then the collective at its close, for the current generation and all generations to come. It is an eternal call of praise for an eternal people serving the Eternal One. This intentional bookending of praise places all that comes in between into the context of praise—meaning what comes between are things the psalmist, and thereby the community of faith when they corporately proclaim and affirm these words, believes God is praiseworthy for. We see a glimpse into the very nature of God by what he does in the world, and those things become activities worthy of doing, and praising, for the people of God.

This psalm gives us a glimpse into God's special concern for the marginalized. We see a God who:

- Executes justice for the oppressed
- Provides food for the hungry
- Sets captives free
- Opens the eyes of the blind
- Lifts up those bowed down

Understand, this is not a sentimental commercial for a nonprofit or charity or church outreach program. This is the very nature of *being itself*. If you are a Christian, you know God more fully by experiencing these actions yourself; and because God's nature is to take these actions himself, we experience abundance of life when we join with God in his nature.

But here's the question we must answer: If Christ is in you and these actions are your inheritance, will you receive that inheritance?

Jesus the Christ fulfilled these concepts and actions. He literally did them as God Incarnate and, as an archetype of eternity, enacted them as normative practices for the church, which is his body living and active in the world, so that all humanity could experience *being itself.*

When Jesus introduced himself as the Messiah, he read aloud these very sentiments as they are expressed in Isaiah 58:6; 61:1–2. Jesus revealed himself as God by taking on God's special concern for the marginalized. His words were a summary of completed actions that are still working themselves out into the future ... but in him are fulfilled now.

In Ephesians 2:22–22, Paul says that we are being built into the very dwelling place of God. This is personal (you) and corporate (you all). However, applying this here and now means that we cannot act in a divergent way from our nature, since the Living God indwells us. We can no longer proclaim the faith without living into these very same actions Jesus fulfilled. Where we fail to do so, we are not living fully into the ways of the kingdom of heaven but are instead living into the ways of the world.

Simply put: Because God *is,* Jesus *did,* now You *are* ... for the world.

When we serve as a witness, what do people see? What is the testimony? Do they see a people executing justice for the oppressed, providing access to healthy and nutritious foods, setting captives free, bringing healing to the hurting, lifting up the lonely, building genuine relationships with marginalized neighbors?

That is the kingdom Jesus came to establish, and has in fact established. It is the kingdom the Lord is reigning over. And it is worthy of praise!

The Missional Frontier

The missional frontier is the place and space where the kingdom of heaven does not reign. It's where the fruits of the Spirit are not readily experienced. Turmoil, divisiveness, defeat, chaos, and violence make up the environment instead of peace, patience, love, gentleness, and self-control. All things are God's, but the missional frontier is where God, out of his great love for us, has allowed us the freedom to reject his ways, which has led to the kingdom territory becoming overgrown, wild, and in active rebellion against God.

Jesus' very nature and purpose placed him on the missional frontier at all times. As God Incarnate, he who knew no sin entered into a world of sin in order that he might reconcile all things to the Father (2 Cor. 5:16–21; Col. 1:20). Jesus left the holiness of heaven to bring the same reality to the created world. Therefore, there was never a moment in the life of Jesus that was not spent on the missional frontier. His life was mission.

Jesus' ultimate mission—why he set his face toward Jerusalem—was the reconciliation of all things to the Father (2 Cor. 5:16–21). His completed works of the incarnation, crucifixion, resurrection, and ascension were and are the fulfillment of his mission. This is cosmically unique—accomplished once and for all in the person of Jesus Christ. When we speak of our mission now, we are talking about joining with God in his mission of reconciliation. Through God's great and abiding love for us, he allows us to participate in his mission.

While we cannot add anything to Christ's completed works, we can step into the characteristics and participate in the transformation of his completed works. I believe this is in part what Scripture is referencing when it calls God's people the body of Christ (1 Cor. 12:27).

The four stages of Jesus' mission provide us with an example of how we can be sent to the world to participate in God's mission:

Incarnation (John 1:14): Jesus enters into creation to be among the people he is ultimately to redeem. He was not only among them but was actually dependent on them for life as a baby and young child. While among them, he lived the perfect life of surrender and submission before the Father, providing the way to follow. The Incarnation compels action-oriented discipleship such as being sent, living among, having presence with, following, and surrendering.

Crucifixion (John 19:28–30): Jesus' obedience took him to death on a cross, whereby the sins of the world are forgiven and all of creation is redeemed and is now being reconciled to the Father. The crucifixion compels action-oriented discipleship such as death to self, forgiveness, and reconciliation.

Resurrection (Luke 24:1–12): Jesus' physical renewal of life after death is the first fruit and foretaste of the coming kingdom of God. It is the announcement that all things will be made new. The old is not gone so much as it is transformed and regenerated. The resurrection compels action-oriented discipleship such as hope, worship, and renewal.

Ascension (Luke 24:50–53): Jesus ascends to the right hand of the Father to reign over the kingdom of God. However, Jesus' lordship is marked by a subversive wielding of power that serves others and brings them into the kingdom of heaven. The ascension compels action-oriented discipleship such as humility, reigning, and love.

Much more could be shared here as these are robust theological terms that have received thousands of years of rich reflection from the historical Christian community. For the moment, these definitions will stand for the foundational mission of God to be identified in the ministry of Jesus.

Jesus' Ministry to the Marginalized

To be sure, Jesus' ministry was not exclusively to or designed specifically for marginalized neighbors. There is a solid case that at least half of his "ministry time," detailed in the Gospels, was spent among religious leaders who occupied the very center of Jewish society. But I do not think it is controversial to say that Jesus' ministry was marked by consistent interaction with the marginalized. I have already provided examples and an in-depth discussion of how Jesus fulfilled God's call for his people to restore and activate the marginalized, so I want to take a different tack here—I believe that this marking of ministry is one of the prevailing reasons Jesus makes a compelling and endearing figure even two thousand years later. It is this upside-down approach to revolution of the status quo that captures the imaginations and hearts of generation after generation, across national and ethnic boundaries and wildly different historical epochs, throughout time.

When Jesus bends down to advocate for the adulterous woman, or speaks words of life into a dead servant boy of no renown, or meets the demon-possessed man in his cave, or touches the untouchable, or dines with the outcasts, or honors the lowly, we not only see a new way of organizing a community, but we can also see ourselves participating in it. We become co-conspirators in the upside-down revolution when we step into his ministry to marginalized neighbors.

This is why some of the data points from my research are so concerning. When presented with six questions about their view of the role of the church, both congregants and pastors scored this statement the lowest:

"The church has a specific calling from God to restore marginalized populations of a community."

Further, when asked about the frequency of participation in seven different expressions of faith in action over the past year, these two were by far the lowest on the list:

"Have served or been present with a marginalized population in my community."

"Have spent time in an under-resourced neighborhood in my community with the purpose of living out my faith."

It should be extremely concerning to the wider Christian community that one of its historically distinctive, attractive, and sustaining aspects is being viewed as optional at best. We seem to be missing a non-negotiable formation opportunity in following Jesus—participating and following him into his ministry.

It's difficult not to hunker down and belabor the point here, but suffice it to say if we differentiate Jesus' mission from his ministry by saying that the former is concerned with the cosmic or existential realities for all of creation, and the latter is how Jesus specifically interacted with real people while he was a walking-talking-feeling human being in a time and place, then I believe we can clearly and definitively state that Jesus' ministry was marked by holistic restoration and activation of marginalized neighbors.

Remembering Community

I do not think it gets nearly enough attention from Christian teachers how significant and remarkable it is that the first thing God Incarnate does when stepping "officially" into his public ministry is to gather a ministry team. Jesus builds a community of mission as a priority of his journey to accomplish what he was sent to do. The Gospels are unified in that after his baptism and temptation in the wilderness, Jesus immediately invites Peter, Andrew, James, and John to follow him (Matt. 4:18–22; Mark 1:16–20; Luke 5:1–11; John 1:35–51). While the Gospel accounts have slight variations as to the specific ordering of events, they are unified in Jesus identifying twelve disciples out of a larger discipleship community to have a specialized relationship with him that included higher ministry responsibilities. Throughout the Gospels, as Jesus pursues his mission and goes about ministry, the disciples are almost always there. They witness everything, participate regularly, and experience Jesus firsthand.

This idea of Christian community being essential to a Christ-centered way of life has gotten distorted by our Sunday-centric church models, relegated to an option by Americanism's idolatry of individualism, and confused by our cultural moment of tribalism and echo chambers. If that sounds too harsh, let me ratchet it up another notch: If you are a Christian and not living in an intentional Christian community of some expression with brothers and sisters in Christ, then you are in disobedience to the way of Jesus (John 17:21), and will not experience the fullness of life God desires for you. In a time where definitive statements are out of fashion, it is difficult for me to write this paragraph, but it is a truth we (myself included) need to remember.

A Framework for Neighborhood Revitalization

From what we have discovered above, Jesus demonstrated three priorities in his time on earth: his mission, ministry to the marginalized, and doing this in community with others. As God Incarnate,

Jesus is the exemplar for how we can be part of this kingdom work. By examining the way he lived his life, what he prioritized, and how he invested all of himself, we can draw principles for how we can engage in kingdom transformation and, in particular, neighborhood revitalization. This is why I regularly say that neighborhood revitalization is discipleship—or at the very least a vehicle or avenue for discipleship. If you are following Jesus, your life will necessarily take on the characteristics, likeness, and formation of these components from his life. So often, churches look at creating programs for discipleship where congregants learn in a classroom environment, whereas the kind of discipleship Jesus modeled was on the road, while in pursuit of God's mission to the world.

By exploring how Jesus lived this way, we can discover a framework for neighborhood revitalization and then look at how churches can adopt these principles.

Neighborhood Revitalization

We see the common threads of mission, ministry to the marginalized, and community in Jesus' life. How can we draw from these in neighborhood revitalization?

Mission. A community needs a shared destination, a *telos*, an intended direction. Especially for a neighborhood that has experienced decade upon decade of disinvestment, there may be a complete lack of vision for what a thriving community and life may look like. Neighbors living in these communities may in fact have never seen such a thing in real life. We call this shared destination a "shared vision for change." A more technical term in neighborhood work is something called a Quality-of-Life Plan, which is precisely what it sounds like—a plan for raising the quality of life for neighbors and the neighborhood they live in.

But it doesn't have to be as formal or large scale. The key is a shared destination a community of people can rally around. It can just as easily be small, purposeful, and concrete: "Let's work together to get fresh fruits and veggies for everyone on our block." But it can be grandiose, systemic, and generational: "Every child born in our neighborhood will be career-, college-, and life-ready. They will succeed, and we will do whatever it takes!"

Ministry to the marginalized. After aligning neighbors behind a compelling vision for change, mutually reinforcing activities must take place in order for the vision to be actualized. In the example of access to healthy foods, some of the strategic steps toward that mission could be a community garden, cooking classes, a nonprofit partnering with neighborhood convenience stores to supply fresh fruits and veggies, or a neighborhood food stand opening up for residents to purchase produce. These activities are ministry—serving the whole of our brothers and sisters of humanity, in order to remove barriers in their being, so that they can experience a flourishing life. When it is centered on the "least of these" or those pushed to the edges of society, it is following in the way of Jesus.

Community. There is a catch phrase in asset-based community development: "building a community from the inside out." It captures the idea that the only sustainable way to bring about transformational change is to empower, equip, and resource the community itself to be the agents of change. You may see this occur in an individual frequently and count it a success (as well you should!), but to affect societal and systemic change, it must move out from the one to the many. Neighborhood revitalization work, in order to be truly successful, must be located in a connected or networked community. This can be done in any number of ways—neighborhood associations, created coalitions, social networks, project working groups, action teams, etc. The important part is that there exists a community of changemakers, aligned to a shared vision, participating together in mutually reinforcing activities that bring the vision to life.

I believe this to be by far the hardest piece of the puzzle when it comes to executing resident-centric neighborhood revitalization. In America, everything is stacked against community—the way we build our homes and cities, the idolatry of busyness that fills up our calendars, our consumption of media that sucks up our free time, and the national ethos of the lone ranger or solitary superwoman accomplishing everything. These are but a few examples. We have no margin for building real relationships.

Plus, relationships in general are hard even in good conditions! Those in a neighborhood are mainly strangers, united only by proximity; and, to top it all off, the complexities of poverty and systemic marginalization make building a community a tall mountain to climb.

I would ask, for the sake of the neighbors you will be working with, that you evaluate beforehand whether you are willing to stick around when the going gets tough. There will be skepticism and mistrust. People will bail. Unjust accusations will likely be hurled your way. You will experience hurt, disenchantment, and low spells. Will you show up again the next day? Will you give it another go? Communicate the same message again? Listen one more time? Connect with one more neighbor? Will you do the hard work of building a community one conversation at a time? My hope and prayer is that you can and will answer "yes."

Church Engagement

Now we'll look at church engagement. All of the points made above apply here, but the application expands to the context of the local church participating in neighborhood revitalization:

Mission. It is very trendy for churches to have a mission statement—or it certainly was ten years ago. Personally, I believe a mission statement to be helpful for a church body if it builds a localized expression for the mission of God (this being clearly set out in Scripture and already discussed in the previous chapters in terms of Jesus' life-purpose statement). Does your church know its intended purpose? Do they have a directional end? Can they see themselves participating and contributing, helping to bring abundant life to the world? If so, well done! If not, that is a likely starting point.

The four theological terms offered earlier can serve as a barometer or measuring tool for any church's "outreach ministry." Here are some thought questions to get you started if you are an organizational leader:

- Incarnation: Are we proximate, present, and listening in the space we're called to?
- Crucifixion: Are we sacrificing for others, giving our time, talents, and resources?
- Resurrection: Are we offering hope, bringing dead things to life, and creating new from old?
- Ascension: Are we giving tangible examples of transformation (previews of heaven)?

Ministry to the marginalized. Evaluating this element for your church is pretty simple—is your ministry marked by holistic restoration and activation of marginalized neighbors? If not, that's okay, but use this as an opportunity to repent and change course. Most church "outreach ministries," especially to those experiencing poverty, while well intentioned, actually contribute to cycles of dependency and perpetuate poverty.[1] There is a time to feed and clothe someone, but a ministry should aim at holistic restoration as the destination.

The insidious, sin-filled, side of outreach ministries that are not built this way lies in the fact that they are not really for marginalized neighbors at all. They are designed for the church. If a church wants to serve itself, they should simply make it explicit and not apologize for it! We are, after all, also called to love the church and build up the body (Eph. 4:12). However, if a church wants to serve marginalized neighbors, then they should do so in the way of Jesus—holistic, relational, restorative, activating. All of that starts with being where people are and listening, instead of telling them to come to you and what they need to do.

Community (of faith). It is *en vogue* to deny the importance of Christian community in an individual's faith formation, especially when it is understood as church attendance. Some of this sentiment can be seen as good and necessary for breaking unhelpful norms.

---

[1] For a much more poignant conversation, see these books: Robert D. Lupton, *Charity Detox: What Charity Would Look Like if We Cared About Results* (New York, NY: Harper One, 2015) and Steve Corbett and Brian Fikkert, *When Helping Hurts: How to Alleviate Poverty Without Hurting the Poor and Yourself* (Chicago, IL: Moody, 2009).

However, your simple evaluative question regarding community is this: Are you living life alongside a group of disciples as you pursue the mission of God and do ministry along the way?

If we are going to follow in the way of Jesus, we have to participate in a community of faith. This goes beyond a group of friends or the team you do work or ministry with. The charge is to enjoy a common union and a common mission that is also forming a radical community of belonging. This is possible when Christ is at the center of the community and its defining characteristics are self-sacrifice, humility, and love.

What's more, the world desperately needs a revelation of God's love through his sons and daughters (John 17:21). When Christians come together, filled with the Holy Spirit, they are capable of producing the fruits of the Spirit in the world. Others can taste and see that peace, patience, gentleness, self-control, and love are possible. Yes, individual Christians may be doing this in their everyday lives, but the collective is a powerful witness because of the beauty of the unity among differing peoples and the weight of numbers. Twelve people deployed on mission together can be more impactful than one, especially when those people should not be together by the world's standards. Other benefits of community are the protection provided and the sustainability of the mission and ministry … and while there are exceptions, it ought to just be more fun!

Alan Hirsch calls this *communitas*—the type of community that develops in the context of danger, an ordeal, or an overwhelming task.[2] When faced with such a challenge, the participants develop relationship with one another in a new and deeper way. The social bonds are strengthened and restructured. Friends become comrades.

In order to transform neighborhoods, we need communitas.

As Jesus pursued his ultimate mission, his ministry was marked by holistic restoration of marginalized neighbors, lived out in a discipling community.

---

[2] Alan Hirsch and Darryn Altclass, *The Forgotten Ways Handbook: A Practical Guide for Developing Missional Churches* (Grand Rapids, MI: Brazos Press, 2009), 170.

Mission. Ministry. Community. The foundations of Christ, and therefore, the foundation for neighborhood revitalization.

Formation Through Service

One of my pet peeves is when people place a dividing line between formation and service, or discipleship and mission, or evangelism and restoration. It is typically presented as a linear pathway: *I just need to be a little more like Jesus, then I can go serve in the community; learn a little more apologetics, then I can share my faith; take this discipleship class, then I will sign up for the mission.*

This is incredibly destructive to the actual formative process God desires to work in us, where service and loving our neighbors is the path to loving ourselves and God—in other words, becoming whole humans that experience abundance in Christ. Jesus clearly showed this in his call to the disciples: Follow me, and I will make you into fishers of people (Matt. 4:19). Becoming more of who God wants us to be occurs through the going, the doing, and the participating. This is real "learning."

This same false sentiment permeates my line of work in neighborhood revitalization:

- If we can get these people out of poverty, they can give back to their community.
- Once we stabilize this household, they can contribute to the neighborhood.
- Once I get a job, I'll start helping with the youth program my neighbor started.
- If only we had more capital, then we could start economic development in our community.
- As soon as I get a job ... get my record cleared ... get that new car ... get that bill paid ...

While this all sounds very reasonable on paper, and I am not against prioritization and planning, it belies the deeper truth that transformation comes through participation. Indeed, I will go so far as to say that transformation cannot occur without participation. This is a basic principle of Christian discipleship in the way of Jesus and of neighborhood revitalization.

It regularly happens that we will meet a neighbor who has no clue that we have a neighborhood initiative underway in the Tepe Park area of Evansville. Despite twelve years on the ground, countless neighborhood meetings, events, projects, quality-of-life improvements, mailers, investment in communication channels, pop-up experiments, etc., I would say that the majority of our neighbors are still unaware of our efforts. Hopefully that majority is down from a super-majority, thanks to our consistency, ongoing presence, and tireless pursuit in meeting and engaging neighbors. But disappointingly, we often get a quizzical look and the question, "Now what are you all doing?" Or an even more defeating, "This is the Tepe Park neighborhood?!" After a quick moment of wanting to hand in my resignation, I smile and launch into, "Yeah, we're a group of neighbors coming together for positive change ..."

But you know who does know? The neighbors participating in the initiative! You may be thinking, *Well, duh*; but sometimes the most obvious learnings are the ones we need to press into more deeply.

Why do the neighbors participating in the neighborhood initiative know that the quality of life in the neighborhood is going up, while their next-door neighbors who don't participate aren't aware? Because that's their respective lived experience. One is experiencing transformation through participation, the other is living into the status quo and therefore not having transformative experiences.

Let me provide a tangible example: At one point, Cathy and Lisa held the same view as the vast majority of their neighbors (77 percent to be exact)—that there were not enough activities for neighborhood youth.[3]

---

[3] The process we follow in neighborhood revitalization, which we will discuss in chapters nine and ten, is Listen-Align-Act-Measure. So, we are always finding ways to measure our impact through resident surveys. This statistic came from one of our surveys at the time. You can see an example of this resident-perspective measurement here: https://www.tepepark.org/about-3-2.

After the catalyst of seeing a kid with a gun spurred them into action (more on this in the "Kid With a Gun" story on pages 98–100), they started gathering youth once a month, which grew into a daily youth program. It was no longer their lived experience that youth didn't have activities to engage in—quite the opposite, in fact. At the same time Cathy and Lisa experienced this very real transformation, I would still hear neighbors voice concerns and complaints about their not being enough activities for youth. Both perspectives were/are "true," but the experience of Cathy and Lisa had been transformed through participation, giving them a more positive and hopeful perspective on change in their neighborhood.

This is why I passionately recruit neighbors to participate in our initiatives. I've seen this experience so many times in all the beautiful micro-transformations of our neighbors' quality-of-life—everything from expressing creativity, to engaging with business development, to gaining a sense of community. I want them to experience the transformation that comes with and through participation. It is what we desire for them.

Incidentally, this is the exact same reason—the only one that makes any sense whatsoever to my finite mind—why Jesus gives us a commission and allows us in on God's cosmic mission of reconciliation: It is in the participation that we experience transformation. It is when we step into the ministry of Jesus that God forms us into the likeness of Jesus. It is not when we get to a certain point in our Jesus-ness that God allows us to serve his mission. Service is formation. Formation is service. This is the way of Jesus.

Stated another way, calling us back to the beginning of our case for neighborhood revitalization as fulfillment of Jesus' ministry to marginalized neighbors: When we "serve," all of our heart, mind, soul, and strength benefit. We become more whole, and therefore are able to love God more fully. This in turns compels us to love others, in a positive cycle of wholeness. This is the very definition of loving yourself—loving God (and others) with your whole self. That cannot happen without participation.

Formation and service are not a linear pathway nor separate vehicles of our faith but rather integrated parts of disciple-making in the way of Jesus.

We often act like serving is something we do wholly for others, when the truth is, God likely wants to do something in you through serving, shaping, and transforming you into the likeness of Jesus the Christ—a flourishing life!

This is what we mean by the theological term "sanctification." By joining with our Father in heaven in his mission of restoration and renewal, stepping into our identities as ministers of reconciliation, God completes our personal transformation. I will take it one bold step further and say that activation is what really begins the process. I believe this is what James is getting at in his epistle when he states, "For just as the body without the spirit is dead, so also faith without works is dead" (James 2:26).

Can you imagine if Jesus had not have gone public with his ministry until the disciples were all trained up? If he had waited until they were all shiny, with seminary credentials, and presentable to the religious system? Of course not! Because it was through the actual doing of ministry that Jesus exemplified the best practices for shaping and forming disciples—not to mention an extreme encouragement to us a few millennia later as we observe these disciples lower the bar for our own participation in the following of Jesus. If we desire to be formed more into the likeness of Jesus, we need to be activated into his ways.

PART TWO

**MINDSETS
FOR WORKING
WITH MARGINALIZED
NEIGHBORS**

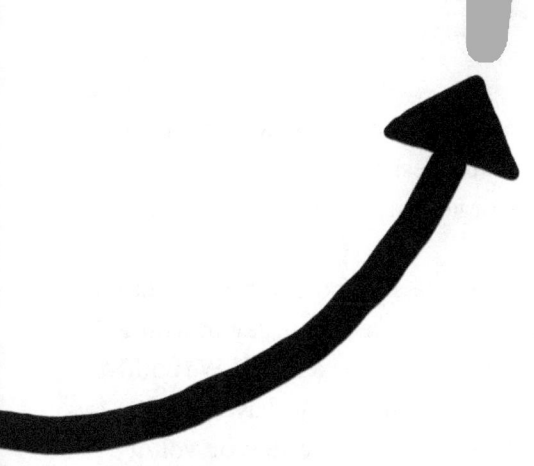

5
BREAKING
CYCLES
OF DEPENDENCY

In the previous chapter I alluded to the reality that most church "outreach ministries," while aimed at helping those experiencing poverty, actually contribute to cycles of dependency and perpetuate poverty. If this is the case, the best thing those ministries can do is to stop. Today.

Despite their good intentions, churches, Christians, and nonprofits can actually produce toxicity through their acts of charity, contributing to cycles of dependency, and therefore often end up hurting the very people they desire to help in the name of Jesus. Though this is well documented globally,[1] the church has failed to respond in our behaviors locally.

Imagine this scenario: Americans see shirtless Africans. Americans give thousands of shirts to Africans. Africans who produce shirts are put out of business, and no new manufacturing businesses are started. Shirts wear out, and Africans need more shirts. Americans send more shirts to Africans. What was motivated by a genuine desire to help a fellow human being actually ends up hurting them in profound ways. There is the obvious problem of creating dependency, which not only robs our African neighbors of dignity, liberty, and freedom, but it also robs them of wealth and community flourishing. Jobs are not created locally, local economies are not infused with capital, and generational wealth never materializes. The ramifications of donating a shirt can be catastrophic.

---

[1]   For a much more poignant conversation, see these books I referenced in chapter four: Lupton's *Charity Detox* and Corbett and Fikkert's, *When Helping Hurts*.

What is more, when we think about our local outreach activities, we might conclude that they are actually designed for the volunteer, the church member, or the church organization itself and not the neighbor in need.

Think about it: We design our volunteer opportunities for the church members. "Come serve for two hours on a Saturday morning when most neighbors are in bed or relaxing on their day off." We build a perfectly curated volunteer experience where all you have to do is show up. We feel good about ourselves after a serve day or volunteering in the soup kitchen line. Many of us share our pictures on social media to show just how socially conscious we are and as a testimony to Jesus' work through us. (It doesn't hurt that we get a couple hundred endorphin boosts from likes and loves!) The serving is largely about us and not those we are serving. Yes, I am saying that most of our local "outreach" ministries are practices in self and corporate idolatry. *Ouch!* This is a hard thing to hear, but we must have ears to hear. It's okay; we are still beloved children of God, and there are indeed many truths to be found, discovered, and retained, even in critique.

It's good to volunteer! It's good and right to help others. It's good to sacrifice time out of your life to love your neighbors. We need more disciples, not fewer, being shaped into the likeness of Christ through serving marginalized neighbors. It is even good and right for churches and Christians to share public witness to the transformational work of the Gospel. The problem is, this type of outreach creates cycles of dependency that don't help our neighbors in the long run. It keeps them in need of our help and fails to recognize their abilities, gifts, and potential to be part of kingdom transformation themselves.

Now that we have ripped that bandage off, we can repent and move forward.

The Development Approach

What I am proposing here isn't that we stop helping people when they're in dire need but that we refuse to quit there. We must put our neighbors on a path to restoration and activation. This approach draws on Lupton's and Fikkert-Corbett's work and the classic illustration: Give a person a fish, and they are fed for a day; teach a person to fish, and they eat for life.[2]

This resonates, but we often pass off the hard work of making it a reality. *Someone should definitely do that. "They" should operate in a more development-centered way! As for me and my organization, well I don't have the time to actually teach someone to fish—we've got five thousand people to feed!*

The development approach is incredibly time-consuming and doesn't look nearly as impressive to funders. We also have to overcome our own feelings of inadequacy and intimidating relational barriers:

- I don't even know how to fish myself! Who am I to teach others?
- I feel much more comfortable showing up to pass out bait and tackle. Can't I just do that?
- Hours, weeks, months spent with a stranger? I don't think I can commit to that!
- We don't even speak the same language. How could I communicate effectively?!

Helping our neighbors experience personal betterment is in no way bad or wrong. It may lead to poor outcomes in isolation, but when personal betterment is a step along a path to holistic restoration, it is part of pursuing the flourishing life Jesus came to give. It's just unfortunate that most ministries stop at personal betterment. Sometimes a person needs to eat a fish! By all means, give them a fish. However, if a year from now, they are still dependent on someone giving them a fish, a new direction is needed.

Here is where Jesus' public ministry can seem like a contradiction on the surface. The Gospel accounts are full of what could be categorized as "personal betterment" (giving a fish). However, we must remember that our American individualistic perspective leads us to focus completely on the specific person in the story and their situation.

---

[2] Lupton, *Charity Detox;* Corbett and Fikkert, *When Helping Hurts.*

Yet, in the cultural context of the ANE, and especially within the story of God and his people, the foundation of a flourishing life assumes community. There is no isolated self-actualization divorced from the larger society in which the characters participate. To be restored is to find restoration into the community of faith and activation into the ministry of reconciliation as an individual and as a blessing to the nations as God's missionary people.

We typically disassociate Jesus' ministry from the development of people and the formation of a community—his activation of whole people into the mission of God. What was Jesus' discipleship of the Twelve if not personal development for the purpose of community development? We just do not use these terms in Christian circles, instead employing the vague and contentious definition of "discipleship."

For three years, very much in the public eye, Jesus' primary ministry was the development of twelve men, shaping them into a community, and empowering and resourcing them to be agents of change in the kingdom of God.

Back to the fish illustration. Lupton takes the classic and intuitive axiom a step further in order to make clear what betterment and development look like at the community level. Community betterment would look like stocking a pond with fish. Now the whole community is better off because they can all go to the pond and feed themselves. But what happens when the pond is fished out? Someone has to stock it again. Just like the personal betterment approach, the community becomes dependent on the source providing the pond with fish, whatever it is and from wherever it comes.

The solution is to move toward community development that could look like any or all of the following:

- Teaching the community sustainable fishing
- Diversifying the economic market—i.e., starting vegetable gardens
- Developing fair trade practices

- Creating a marketplace where entrepreneurs can exchange goods and services
- Identifying trusted representatives to lead the community in crucial decisions

This sort of approach, while a solution (possibly *the* solution), is incredibly difficult to enact, mainly because we have created systems, structures, and institutions that define success inaccurately and reward the wrong things. Here are some countercultural examples that we might imagine occurring if we were to adopt the development approach:

- A pastor of a church only reporting to a board of elders what he is doing to develop twelve disciples—for three straight years!
- A nonprofit talking about the one neighbor in poverty they helped start a business that has no tangible return for their own organization.
- A local government, instead of controlling the development themselves, giving hundreds of thousands of dollars in direct investment to neighbors experiencing poverty so that they can build sustainable change in their own community.

These are seemingly crazy propositions, but they are exactly the types of actions individuals and organizations rooted in the gospel could take when doing ministry in the way of Jesus, moving from personal betterment to development.

Who else has a Lord who willingly gave up his positional authority in order to serve all of humanity?

What other way of life calls us to surrender our lives as we follow our Lord so that we can find life and have it abundantly?

Who else measures success by faith and obedience rather than outcomes?

What else so readily produces a vision for common union and common mission than the Spirit of God who dwells in all who receive?

Where else can the "least of these" hold inherent dignity and infinite value, while pursued relentlessly with radical, revolutionary love?

Who else has a hope beyond death and an eternal timeline?

The church (disciples of Jesus) are perfectly positioned to bring holistic restoration and activation to marginalized neighbors and neighborhoods, moving through personal betterment to community development. But we have to answer the call. We need to stop contributing to cycles of dependency with our well-intentioned yet partially self-serving outreach ministries, and embrace the countercultural approach of Jesus: loving our marginalized neighbors as ourselves.

Roots and Fruits

A number of years ago, I heard a speaker share these words at a conference: "There are thousands hacking at the branches of injustice; be the one hacking at the root."

I was profoundly challenged by this statement, and it caused me to turn to the life of Jesus and ask, "How was Jesus hacking at the root of injustice?"

Of course, Jesus hacked at the ultimate root of injustice through overcoming sin and death, but in keeping with our primary focus, we want to look at the life of Jesus, specifically at his real-life interactions in ministry to marginalized neighbors. Where and how was Jesus striking at the root of injustice in his time and place? What did he do? What did he say? What actions did he take?

Most of Jesus' hacking at the roots of injustice, the way he went about tackling such a complex root system, is the accumulation of all we have discussed so far:

It can be found in his willingness to go to where marginalized neighbors were, entering into their spaces and bringing about holistic restoration, activating them into the mission (John 4:1–42).

It can be found in his relentless pursuit of individuals, bringing real change into the lives of marginalized neighbors so that they could experience transformation, not merely hear about what needed to change (Mark 1:40–45).

It can be found in his presence among the authoritative systems of his day, calling for reformation within these systems, while at the same time creating a new system that was equitable and accessible (Luke 21:37–38).

It can be found in his tireless messaging that turned the status quo upside down, reflecting kingdom values instead of worldly ones, while living out (modeling) those values in his everyday life (Matt. 5–7).

And so much more.

Jesus' way of hacking at the root of injustice was to live an embodied kingdom life that brought justice into the darkness of injustice.

I believe it's also important to note what Jesus did not do. He did not run for a seat in the Sanhedrin, lobby Caesar in Rome, write a treatise or open letter calling for revolution, start an organization and pay staff to rectify policy and run social services, nor develop a program to alleviate some societal ills.

Any or all of these were potential paths Jesus could have taken, but he chose to live his life on earth in closer contact with the people affected by the injustice he'd come to overturn. So, while there is nothing wrong with working in policy, lobbying government, or running a social services program, we cannot do these things without also committing to the close-contact work of seeing individuals' lives transformed.

To use another example: Based on following Jesus through the Gospels, I believe that discipleship or formation in the likeness of Christ does not come through sermons or preaching alone, disconnected from the practices of life. Yet many of my beloved friends and peers give their lives to the preaching of sermons. I affirm (and share with them!) my conviction that, as Christians, we must incorporate embodied practices into our lives—and my belief is that the best way to disciple others is to walk with them and encourage them in this. But at the same time, I in no way want to minimize the faithfulness and sincerity of those who prioritize preaching in their understanding of kingdom work.

There is this strange story in the Gospels where Jesus passes a fig tree, sees it has no fruit, and curses it (Mark 11:12–25). In verse 13, we get a little authorial note that it was not even the season for figs! When the disciples next see the poor fig tree, it is withered. The disciples notice and comment to Jesus, who then uses the opportunity to teach the disciples about prayer and faith—if you have enough faith, praying relentlessly, anything you ask will be done.

A very strange story! In the flow of the narrative, the fig tree scenes are sandwiched between Jesus' triumphal entry into Jerusalem (the King entering his kingdom) and the clearing of the temple of money changers—another image of a broken human system. There are a number of interpretations for this strange bit of narrative, but I believe all of this taken together has much to say about roots of justice and injustice.

If we think of the triumphal entry as representing the root of a system and the money changers in the temple as the fruit, the fig-tree illustration highlights Jesus approach to both these issues.

It's easy to mistake the fruit of a system as the problem—and think that by dealing with the fruit, we've solved it. To be sure, the fruit has to be dealt with, as Jesus showed by overturning the money-changers' tables (Mark 11:15–18). It's commonly believed that the actions of the money changers in the temple were exploiting the poor. But this scene stands out starkly from Jesus' normal ways of operating precisely because it is a relative anomaly—one that sees him enact physical outrage and arguably acts as a catalyst to his ensuing crucifixion, days later.

The root cause of the money-changers' pariah behavior on the vulnerable was a religious system that had corrupted the original intent of the sacrificial system designed by God to restore his peoples' relationship with him. They were taking the means and using it for their own ends, namely for personal gain and profit. Over time, these practices had corrupted their hearts, which produced the behaviors, which in turn produced the fruit of injustice. This scene sees Jesus choosing to deal with the fruit of an unjust system, but we must question whether this would have permanently changed things. Surely, the money-changers would have returned to their usual practices the next day?

On the other side of things, the triumphal entry represents a change at the root of the system as a whole. It was the public announcement that a new way had been enacted by God, and that way is to follow King Jesus into the presence of God. Jesus was on his way to Jerusalem to become the sacrifice, once and for all, so that the entire root system could be changed, allowing us to produce kingdom fruit.

So perhaps this strange incident with the fig tree, sitting between these two events, reminds us of the importance of roots and fruit. Although we must look to remedy the fruit of an unjust system (and can assess whether a system is kingdom-based, depending on the type of fruit being produced), it is only through addressing root causes (and aligning ourselves with those of God's kingdom) that we can see true transformation in the way of Jesus.

This confusion of symptoms and causes, roots and fruit, is often seen in ministry to marginalized neighbors today, and it produces solutions that hack away at the fruit of injustice, rather than the roots. There are too many examples and complexities to cover comprehensively here, but consider a few initiatives that look to address the fruit of injustice, rather than getting to the root of the problem:

- Financial literacy classes for people experiencing poverty
- Feeding programs for the hungry
- Homeless shelters
- After-school youth programs
- Policy advocacy brochures for renters' rights

These are all worthy activities—potentially needed in every marginalized community—but in isolation they do not strike at the root. They are treatments to symptoms. As long as we fail to provide solutions to underlying issues, we merely alleviate some pain in the short-term.

An important note here: Oftentimes a person simply needs relief. As anyone who has ever had a migraine headache knows, just give me the pill so I don't want to die! I can think about holistic healing once this agonizing torture is removed. Remember, Jesus did turn over the tables. This is not a call to stop all symptomatic treatments or to not stand up against the things we see are wrong. But we must question what the long-term impact is of such actions.

After the financial literacy course, the graduate is still in poverty. The hungry come back to the food pantry next month. Youth leave after-school programs and get directly into mischief. Once a policy is adopted, the illegal practitioners find new ways and workarounds to exploit the same systems for their benefit. The root system has not changed. The yard looks nice for a couple of days when you mow over the weeds, but as long as the roots are in the ground, it will look terrible again soon enough.

Getting to root causes and hacking at injustice is horribly difficult work, especially in our cultural moment. Setting aside the complexities of root causes, there are many other societal detractors. We are conditioned for immediate reward gratification. We have lost the sense of faithful presence, opting for short-term wins. Our measurements celebrate volume numbers as opposed to the realism of messy relationships. Stories of change show the great wins or the great need, not the nuance of slow transformation. There is nothing glamorous or glitzy about listening to a neighbor on their porch. If an act of service cannot be posted on social media, did it really happen?

Then there is the overwhelming nature of the issues themselves. I regularly have dark nights of the soul in neighborhood work when generational poverty and its ancillary causes and effects seem too big to bear. How about racism? Hacking at the root of that injustice seems as futile as attempting to carve out the Grand Canyon using only a spoon. Fill in the blank on whatever injustice stings you, and there you will find a seemingly endless root system that your little hatchet is unable to penetrate.

What then to do? Well, I believe there are worthy experiments to try, hypotheses to build questions, and intervention practices to consider. Section three of this book will give more detail on how to utilize an asset-based community development approach, which tries to address root causes, even if it is imperfect and effective implementation is sometimes elusive. For instance, in the conversation around homelessness, permanent supportive housing has garnered significant support as a potential solution Surely there are countless more such approaches out there, and room for many more experiments. Yet the reality is that these broader solutions that focus on systemic change and addressing root causes are often a lot less appealing and satisfying than the personal betterment approaches we see in so many ministries.

After the death of George Floyd in May 2020, I was part of a group that came together, hosted many important conversations, and had a sincere desire to hack at the root of injustice. There was a lot of energy and momentum around minority-owned businesses, Black lending institutions, policy sub-committees, and more—all worthy endeavors. Almost five years later though, none of those ideas have come to fruition. As far as I know, not one person benefitted from all that talk.

But, at the exact same time, a good friend of mine continued with his racial reconciliation ministry, championing a drastically different approach. He brings people from different racial backgrounds together and has them walk a mile together, share a conversation over a cup of coffee, do a service project shoulder to shoulder, and party together.

Now, I cannot claim some grand outcome from my friend's ministry. I can't say I know of a connection that led to some great initiative. However, I do know for sure that at least one person benefitted, because that person is me. Truth is, I know many friendships that have been birthed and real relationships that have begun from participation in his reconciliation ministry—one that followed in the way of Jesus … one relationship, one connection, one real-life experience at a time. That is the only foolproof way to hack at the root that I know of.

Addressing the Whole

In our region, a small group have been championing, advocating, and advancing an approach called "The Promise." It's based on the Harlem Children's Zone (HCZ) model and adapted for our context. If you are not familiar with HCZ and Geoffrey Canada, here is a brief history:

In the early 1990s, after about a decade of running after-school programs in the Harlem neighborhood, Geoffrey Canada and his team decided to pivot their approach due to the lack of transformational change. The programs they were running for youth were doing good things—they could point to success stories—but after twenty years, Harlem was still Harlem, and most of their kids ended up living into the demographics and surrounding narratives. So, they took a courageously bold step, and changed their approach.

They decided they were going to help every child succeed … no matter what. "Whatever it Takes" became their slogan and the name of the book that tells the full story.[3]

In order to do this, they had to shift from a programmatic response to a kid-centric approach. The idea itself is fairly intuitive—place an actual kid, with a real name and story, in the center of whatever you do, and wrap care around that child in order that they have every opportunity for success. Then you walk with that child and their family in an unbroken relationship all the way from cradle to career, so there is no chance for them to slip through the cracks or get lost in the system.

Placing a real kid in the middle of the conversation forces you to build customized pathways and interventions in the context of life experience occurring in real-time. It leaves no room for broad application, assembly-line approaches, and sweeping solutions. One size definitely does not fit all—I think we have run that experiment and found it wanting.

I want to focus for one moment on the idea of "continuity of care." I think this is the magic, or most important aspect, of The Promise's approach, second only to kid-centrism. The concept really came home with clarity for me a few years back when my wife started teaching. She had been a homemaker for fifteen years but moved on to a second career when our kids were older. She loved teaching and is good at it. She fell in love with her first batch of kids, really poured into them, and hoped for positive outcomes for their lives. The sheer volume of kids was a bit overwhelming, but I heard story after story of individual kids she was educating and shaping.

Then the year ended, the kids moved on, and another batch of kids came in and filled the empty seats. Out of sheer self-preservation and

---

[3] Paul Tough, *Whatever It Takes: Geoffrey Canada's Quest to Change Harlem and America* (Boston, MA: Mariner Books, 2009).

practicality, she had to let the previous year's students go, and focus on the next pool of students. She was forced to trust the system—that someone or something would pick up where she left off. Yet in the back of her mind, in all honesty, she did (and does) not trust the system, knowing it is broken. Just the other day she heard about a student from that first year who got a gun charge and is probably facing three to five years in jail and a felony record. Imagine, as a teacher, having to face that situation over and over and over again, not knowing where these students you love and invest your life in are going, who is now loving and supporting them, who is helping them win moving forward. I feel defeated for my wife, and she is only three years in! Imagine how defeated she might be in ten, fifteen, or twenty years!

The Promise seeks to remedy that with continuity of care. Once a family accepts the "promise"—sort of like a covenant between the family and the neighborhood-based organization providing support—there is no pass off to the next grade, the next school, the next program, or the next social service. Technically, that still happens, but the difference is that a wrap-around-care coordinator stays with them, providing that continuity, refusing to allow that student to get lost.[4]

Obviously, there is a lot more to it, but this is the high-level view. While this approach can be used for something as big as the Harlem Children's Zone ($115 million annual budget), the beauty of it is in the potential for innovative churches and neighborhood-based organizations (NBOs) to adopt the approach and transform existing systems and structures. The key is to start small and scale as and when appropriate. Harlem started with ten blocks; Dream Center here in Evansville started with four. You could start with one! Knock on doors, meet families, build relationships, explain the promise, and start ministering for restoration and activation of marginalized youth.

---

[4] Our friends at The Promise report that in the 2023–2024 school year, 31 percent of students demonstrated growth in ELA/reading scores, while 38 percent of students showed improvement in math proficiency. Student attendance also improved, with 47 percent of students attending 94 percent or more of school days, compared to 25 percent of students in the previous year.

At its most simplified, such a ministry requires you to:

- Discover: Build trust, relationships, and equity with families.
- Commit to the promise: Enter into a partnership, helping do whatever it takes to succeed.
- Ensure programs are kid-centric: Place the actual kid in the center, creating a customized pathway.
- Ensure wrap-around services: Fill out that pathway with interventions and solutions.
- Provide continuity of care: Walk with the child and their family from cradle through to career.

At the time of writing, we have three different neighborhood-based organizations in our region that are piloting this approach, "promising" almost three hundred kids. That is three hundred kids who, simply based on where they are born, as a sociological dataset, are on a trajectory to all the negative life outcomes mentioned in chapter three. Now, they have a support system and resourcing to serve as the scaffolding on which they build their lives. They have people and organizations wrapped around them in an unbroken relationship, promising to walk with them through all the trials, successes, and growth opportunities of life. While this is a long-term commitment and full cradle-to-career "proof of concept" is still some time away, the early returns are promising.

These are more than numbers to me. They represent Gina, Tru, and Trey. I first met Gina through the local neighborhood-based organization that is extending the promise to families in our neighborhood. I later found out that she and her family live in our neighborhood. Gina is like so many of the neighbors I have met along the journey of neighborhood revitalization—low income, high capacity. Gina is a quick learner, attentive mother, fantastic event-planner, and recent community gardener. Tru and Trey are her two boys, around seven and four, and they are precocious kids full of hugs, laughter, and joy. Their family has joined our small church plant in the neighborhood, and I have gotten to know them beyond what any one aspect of these connections could entail. They are not just a neighboring family, or just a family that attends my church, or just a family that receives services through a local nonprofit. They are Gina, Tru, and Trey, and it gives me a feeling of faith-filled peace (*shalom*) to know that there is a community surrounding them that will do whatever it takes for them to have a flourishing life.

Start Addressing Roots

The church is perfectly positioned to lead the way in this small-scale, long-term, incremental investment, if indeed it can become the body of Christ living and active in the world. There are potentially more than two billion Christians spread throughout the globe, ready to die to self and worldly expectations in order to create those collisions with the neighbor near them, including those pushed to the edges and margins of society. Whatever sphere we work in (legislative, professional services, grass-roots community work), we must consider how we are attacking root causes, rather than putting Band-Aids on open wounds. Then, in dealing with root causes, we always have to get to the heart of individual lives. Jesus could have spent every day turning over tables in the temple, but on the whole, he chose to invest in the lives of the disciples, seeing the roots of who they were changed, so that they could bring lasting transformation to others. Jesus reminds them with the fig tree that it is their hearts/roots that matter, as that's what will ensure fruit is produced. We need to look for transformational change in people's lives, holistically, rather than addressing symptoms that do not help them to be part of bringing lasting change.

So, start today! Pick up the best root-hacking instrument you have on hand already, the cross, and begin going to work on injustice in your community by following in the way of Jesus. You might not be willing or able to make the commitment of eighteen years. That's okay; just be honest about that. The last thing your neighbors need is a broken promise. Nor is neighborhood revitalization or the Promise approach the only way to fight injustice in the world. What they do need is to have

their agency recognized, for others to be a good neighbor to them—
one who helps remove the barriers to flourishing in their heart, mind,
soul, and strength, and who repairs and expands social networks that
give them access to the same opportunities others enjoy. This is what
neighborhood revitalization work is all about.

Jesus would often start off his parables with the opening line, "The kingdom of heaven is like …" and then proceed to tell a story, provide an illustration, or challenge a popular axiom. At other times, Jesus would start off a public teaching, "You have heard it said … but I say to you …"—completely inverting or shifting the frame of a prevailing cultural norm or truth. Jesus' teachings and parables disrupted the status quo, reimagining for listeners what a holy life looked and felt like. These phrases were dissonance-creators at the highest level. They served two very important purposes: to help people unlearn an established paradigm (way of seeing the world) and to create an opportunity to envision a new paradigm.

Jesus knew that you could not build the truth on top of a faulty foundation. That's why, in our housing rehab work, we always take the house down to the studs regardless of what it may look like cosmetically. Most of the time it's pretty rotten and in obvious need of work, but occasionally we will get a house that looks like it could be salvaged or simply touched up and put back on the market. The temptation is to move on and not do the laborious work needed to tear it all the way down and build it back. But we always do what needs to be done—sometimes with a sigh and groan—because we believe our neighbors deserve quality housing done right.

This was exactly the approach Jesus took with the religious system of his day. He took it down to the studs! And he did this through constantly helping the Jewish people to unlearn–a difficult task for sure. Yet it is absolutely central to receiving the gospel. In fact, you could argue that the gospel is the great unlearning tool, counter to everything we naturally think of in our religious lives. Here are some of the things Jesus came to help us unlearn:

- We earn our own righteousness through good works.
- Our bad actions will be punished.
- The rich and accomplished get the good seats at the table.
- Those with all the good words and prayers are the holy ones.
- What we do with our everyday lives couldn't possibly matter in heaven!
- Our "work for God" happens when we're at church or serving a Christian ministry; what we do the rest of the time isn't at all spiritual.

Obviously, Jesus is talking about and orienting people to the way of life in the kingdom of heaven. Yet, as with most everything we have learned by now, the correlation and application to neighborhood revitalization work is clear: a broken world, a broken neighborhood, a broken neighbor—all are actually places and spaces where the kingdom of heaven can and does reign. We merely have to do the hard work of unlearning and reshaping the narrative so that we can have eyes to see where and how it is breaking through.

Unlearning comes in all shapes and sizes. There are small moments of discovery, like when I learned that 71 percent of my Tepe Park neighbors professed faith in Jesus as the Christ.[1] *Boom!* Unlearning. What I had thought of as a "mission field" or an opportunity for evangelism was actually an opportunity to love my brothers and sisters in Christ. It was a reshaping of my understanding of our work, recognizing it as discipleship, and I had to go to Scripture for a deeper look at God's call to his people to bring about holistic restoration to marginalized neighbors.

---

[1] See "Tepe Park Neighborhood Survey: 2018 Results Report," https://www.tepepark.org/_files/ugd/b91a04_48a03824894e4c99a5e891f03e591884.pdf. Statistics on Tepe Park (and Evansville more widely) in this chapter are taken from this report.

Another example of a small, but powerful, unlearning: For several years, when we would make the case for our work to the wider community, often in the context of either fundraising or recruiting investment into the neighborhood, we would highlight the need, specifically the poverty rate, which was the highest in our city. One day—while talking with a neighborhood leader named Crystal, who shared with us that she could financially afford to live anywhere in the city but chose to live in Tepe Park—I had the epiphany that if the poverty rate is 43 percent, then 57 percent of Tepe Park neighbors are *not* in poverty! The majority. This rather obvious unlearning forced me to quit telling one limited story and start relating a fuller narrative of why we lead a neighborhood revitalization effort in Tepe Park—a narrative more reflective of the lived experience of our real-life neighbors. It is not as simple as, "We need to help these poor people," and communicating the fuller narrative honors neighbors instead of profiling them.

If I go a bit deeper, hit a little harder, and expose some of my own ignorance and latent racism, when I reflected on why Evansville as a whole is 83 percent white and 12 percent Black, yet Tepe Park is 60 percent Black, I had assumed it was due to a mixture of normal human nature to gravitate to communities that reflect ourselves and lasting systemic injustices like segregation and generational economic oppression. Those are indeed factors in a complex situation, but I had to unlearn these simplified narratives, which happened for me through being exposed to information about the practice of redlining.[2]

I had to unlearn before I could see. The issues that have caused continued racial segregation, the Black-white wealth gap, and infrastructure disinvestment that leads to family wealth theft in historically Black communities—all of these go way beyond my "enlightened" narratives.

It is not only the outsiders' narratives that need to be unlearned,

---

[2] See the discussion in chapter three. Redlining was a common practice before 1968 for cities and lending institutions. Officials would draw a red line around areas in the community where black people could and could not live. They controlled housing by not lending mortgages to black people in areas where they did not want them.

but also many of the internal narratives of neighbors within these neighborhoods. Pervasive thoughts like, *You have to get out of the neighborhood to succeed,* and, *These young folks don't care about anything but killing each other anymore* are among the many harmful sentiments that, when vocalized and repeated, become the identity of neighborhoods, and by extension, neighbors living within their boundaries.

We all have to unlearn what it is we are convinced we know, individually and collectively. How much different would our narratives be if we unlearned the worldly perspective and instead took the heavenly view? For example, what if the man-made subtitle in our Bibles rephrased the "Woman at the Well" as the "Samaritan Evangelist"? Or the "Tax Collector" the "Kingdom Economist"? Or the "Leprous Man" the "Bearer of Good News"? Or the "Adulterous Woman" the "Grace Recipient"? The names we give and the narratives we tell go hand in hand.

But the unlearning does not stop there. Christians and churches need to unlearn what it means and looks like to engage with disinvested communities and people experiencing poverty. These are hard things to hear. Just look at the reactions of the religious leaders when Jesus began dismantling their understanding—they wanted to murder him (Matt. 26:3–4). Here are some mindset shifts we might need to make:

- We need to remove the word "outreach" from our ministries.
- We need to cancel one-off serve days disconnected from ongoing ministry.
- We need to stop "mercy ministries" that cannot draw a line toward holistic restoration.
- We need to reconfigure the service-recipient relationship.

We need to stop the above so that …

- We can start building relationships with neighbors.
- We can become rooted in a community and earn trust.
- We can see restoration of heart-mind-soul-strength.
- We can become brothers and sisters in a family.

If you feel a strong reaction upon exposure to these statements, try asking why you feel that way in order to reveal the heart of the conceptual frames that inform your faith and consider how they might be misaligned with the way of Jesus. Like many concepts and practices of our current expression of Christian faith, we have relegated service, or outreach, into an individual-activity space—to be performed as a checklist of what it means to live out Christianity. We have allowed the dualism inherent in enlightenment philosophy to creep into what it means to disciple and evangelize. There is what we do "in here" (church) and what we do "out there" (service). There is the learning of the Christian content of faith (church) and the application of what we have learned in our life (service). There is us (church) and them (service).

What do you need to unlearn? What stories do your narratives tell? Are they ultimately harmful to you and others?

Darell Guder, in his great book *The Continuing Conversion of the Church*, states that across Christian history the challenge has been to form the church's institution to serve its mission, but the problem is the way the institution has taken over and shaped the mission.[3] Jesus' outreach to the poor, disenfranchised, and marginalized demonstrated God's justice, requiring a complete reordering of any and every society.

What a powerful thought: The church could be the catalyst in every community to reorder society, if it would only unlearn its existing systems and structures, die to itself, and be raised to new life (converted to the way of Jesus).

The Importance of Agency

As exciting and hope-filled as this vision is, we have to proceed with caution. We must learn the lesson of previous generations to not overextend our service, stripping neighbors of agency, and contributing to cycles of dependency that produce harm in our communities.

---

[3] Darell Guder, *The Continuing Conversion of the Church* (Grand Rapids, MI: Eerdmans, 2000), loc. 326.

The key to genuine transformation is present in the neighborhood itself, and, as neighbors take action together, they build their own community from the inside out.

Sociologist Rosabeth Moss Kanter once said: "When change is done to you, it is experienced as violence. When you are the agent of change, it is experienced as liberation."[4]

This applies to everyone but has special application to marginalized neighbors. Thinking back to our biblical prototype—the orphans, widows, and sojourners—their being in a cultural context where land and fathers were at the center meant that being landless and fatherless caused them to be at risk. Moreover, just as damaging was the fact that having no way to change their situation sapped an underlying existential value of life—hope.

Agency and hope are interconnected bedfellows. The hope of agency lingers when life circumstances try to beat you down. Real agency allows for the presence of hope. The ability to make choices is part of agency, but agency is more than just making choices. Agency is like choice with purpose. Agency is the ability to make choices that are directional—choices that can determine where you are headed and to what end.

The next level up from choices is decision-making. Closer to agency, decision-making is more meaningful than a choice because it allows for input into the outcome.

It might be said that agency is decision-making plus freedom to select the options. *Merriam Webster* defines agency as "the capacity, condition, or state of acting or of exerting power."[5] So agency is also about power, which is important when we think about shifting the imbalance of power toward neighbors who have been impacted by systems of injustice.

Choice is helpful, decisions are important, and agency is the pathway toward holistic healing. You can make choices and decisions

---

4 Quoted by Cormac Russell in his presentation at the TEDxExeter Conference, "Cormac Russell on Sustainable Community Development: From What's Wrong to What's Strong at TEDxExeter," February 2, 2017; https://singjupost.com/transcript-cormac-russell-on-sustainable-community-development-from-whats-wrong-to-whats-strong-at-tedxexeter/.

5 *Merriam-Webster*, s.v. "agency," accessed February 3, 2025.

and not have agency, but you cannot have agency without choices and decisions. Agency gives you influence over the actual design of choices and decisions, thereby allowing you to be a creator.

I would say agency is the means to have control over your own life and the decisions you make.

Victor Frankl, a holocaust survivor, shares his experiences in his book *Man's Search for Meaning*. As he watched some die in the Nazi concentration camps, while others lived on, he concluded that what differentiated the two was that survivors actively held hope.[6] My own observation in reading through Frankl's account was that he was a master at retaining small snippets of agency in the face of possibly the most agency-stripping experience in human history. The moments when a prisoner gave away their piece of bread to a neighbor who could not get out of bed or spoke an encouraging word to someone who had given up, or decided to write a book of all things—these produced internal wellsprings of hope. There also seemed to be a connection to genuine faith and belief in transcendence—something beyond the current reality—that contributed to survival. Finally, the very last bit of agency was the ability to think and construct worlds in the mind. This is the greatest agency of all, a true gift of life—consciousness—and one that others cannot take away.

Not everyone has the mental fortitude of Victor Frankl to be able to retain agency in such an extreme situation. As with most things, people exist on a spectrum of personal capacity and situational experiences.

If we take another horrific example—American slavery—we find that the vast majority of slaves remained slaves. It is difficult for us in hindsight to understand why there were not more uprisings, rebellions, and revolts. I remember as a kid learning about the few times it did happen—such as Nat Turner's Rebellion and the German Coast uprising—and being confused as to why they did not occur constantly. I now believe it was, in part, to do with agency. Only a small percentage of humans are able to perform extreme actions of agency—like runaways

---

6   Viktor E. Frankl, *Man's Search for Meaning: An Introduction to Logotherapy* (Boston, MA: Beacon Press, 1962).

or rebellions—in a situation like slavery. However, from the few firsthand accounts I have read, it seems that nearly all slaves performed some action of agency along the spectrum, from having a small garden to sabotaging crops. These actions of agency were choices and decisions that created a modicum of hope—which led to a continued existence.

Let's return to a more recent, though still horrific, example—redlining. Redlining, covered more fully back in chapter three, was the act of banks and mortgage-lending agencies to draw lines around where minorities could and could not receive home loans. When you force people into a limited set of options, stripping the fullness of their agency, they can respond in any number of ways. A few remarkable individuals will take extraordinary care of their houses in less-desirable neighborhoods and raise the status of their homes in the face of deteriorating surrounding housing stock and infrastructure disinvestment; but most will look at the long odds, and either consciously or subconsciously decide to spend their agency in other arenas of life rather than investing in a home.

It is crucial to recognize the exceptions to the rule, because some like to hold up the examples on the extremes of the spectrum as "proof"—of what exactly, I am never sure. They say, "See, it can be done; that person there did it!" This is a huge logical fallacy in general, popularly called the "hasty generalization" fallacy,[7] but beyond that it ignores real-life people. Because Frankl survived the concentration camp doesn't negate the fact that six million Jewish people died. The fact that one family on the block kept their house nice and neat through two generations cannot outweigh the fact that the other eight houses on the block are dilapidated and abandoned. The spectrum of agency helps us gain better understanding, and hopefully some empathy for our neighbors.

The point to highlight here is that, while extreme individuals can elevate into a nearly transcendent operation of agency in the face of circumstances outside of their control, the vast majority will take a somewhat different course of action. It is not a marker of their personhood or identity but a truth of existence we all face every day, every moment.

---

7   See Bo Bennett, "Hasty Generalization," at *Logically Fallacious*, https://www.logicallyfallacious. com/logicalfallacies/Hasty-Generalization.

The cryptic passage in Mark 6:5–6 where it states that Jesus could not heal many because of their lack of faith has garnered many different interpretations. As I have reflected deeply on Jesus' ministry to marginalized neighbors, I have come to believe that this passage is about Jesus' transference of agency. Those seeking healing would not have merely been hoping to feel better. In their culture, those who needed healing were suffering in all of their being—pushed to the edges of society, deemed unclean spiritually, unable to participate in social events, fighting a growing sense of isolation and despair that would have contributed to emotional unwellness. Because of these factors, their agency had been reduced and they had been systematically pushed down along the spectrum.

Remember the earlier quote: "When change is done to you, it is experienced as violence. When you are the agent of change, it is experienced as liberation."

To those seeking healing, Jesus offered the possibility of decision-making, so instead of experiencing the violence of change done *to* them, they were able to embrace true liberation and freedom. Indeed, a constant refrain in Jesus' interpersonal healing interactions was, "Go! Your faith has healed you."[8] This flips our understanding because we typically attribute the healing to Jesus. Jesus attributes it to the marginalized neighbors' faith. Interesting. They are the change agents; Jesus is the conduit.[9]

---

[8] See Matt. 9:22; Mark 5:34; Mark 10:52; Luke 8:48; and Luke 18:42.

[9] The topic of healing amidst suffering is difficult to address and requires a longer examination than I am able to give here. However, I want to unequivocally state that I am not suggesting those who are unhealed somehow do not have enough faith. I will join David Bentley Hart in saying, "We are to be guided by the full character of what is revealed of God in Christ. For, after all, if it is from Christ that we are to learn how God relates himself to sin, suffering, evil, and death, it would seem that he provides us little evidence of anything other than a regal, relentless, and miraculous enmity: sin he forgives, suffering he heals, evil he casts out, and death he conquers. And absolutely nowhere does Christ act as if any of these things are part of the eternal work or purposes of God. ... God may permit evil to have a history of its own so as not to despoil creatures of their destiny of free union with him in love, but he is not the sole and irresistible agency shaping that history according to eternal arbitrary decrees." See Hart, *The Doors of the Sea: Where Was God in the Tsunami?* (Grand Rapids, MI: Eerdmans, 2011) 86–87.

This positioning is a major part of neighborhood work done as ministry. The goal is holistic restoration and activation of marginalized neighbors, not to check a box or help people feel alleviation for a day or week. It is not even "getting them out of poverty." If the goal is healing, then even that process must become owned by the one in need of healing. Enacting this will be awkward because we are not used to giving agency. Technically, I don't even really know how to talk about it correctly, because I don't give anyone agency, but we are used to formulating our own verbiage in this patronizing fashion.

Changing this reality will involve growing pains and will be fraught with mistakes. Think about how we normally structure interventions—take "this class we teach where the content is what we decided was best"; "receive this good or service that we have deemed you need"; learn "this skill we offer through our program that trains you for jobs we oversee and write paychecks for." On the well-intentioned side, this is done in the name of efficiency, effectiveness, and best practice. On the sin side of things, it is about control and power dynamics. Both are sprinkled with a fair amount of ignorance and lack of relationships.

I will admit to a seeming contradiction in the Christian view of service and the concept of genuine agency. When we act for others, we inadvertently prevent them from acting for themselves, potentially hindering their own agency. Yet we are clearly called to love our neighbors and to do good works for others. The key to resolving this tension lies in understanding relationships. Unfortunately, we often divorce our actions from relationships, opting for service times and programs, instead of living life alongside those we are trying to help.

This is why our neighborhood revitalization work involves an incarnational approach, whereby we are invested and embed our lives in the neighborhoods we work within. It is also why we believe in the importance of asset-based community development. This means we see the contribution that our neighbors have to offer—the incredible treasure within each of them—and look for ways to work with them to enact change. We bring about change together, rather than acting for them.

You may know of existing programs where agency is seemingly stolen from neighbors, and it might seem too radical to immediately fix the situation, in all of its forms. In the meantime, I would promote the consideration of Robert Lupton's tenants for serving our brothers and sisters in need:

- Never do for the poor what they have the capacity to do for themselves.
- Limit one-way giving to emergency situations.
- Strive to empower the poor through employment, lending, and investing, using grants sparingly to reinforce achievements.
- Subordinate self-interest to the needs of those being served.
- Listen closely to those you seek to help, especially to what is not being said—unspoken feelings may contain essential clues to effective service.
- Do no harm.[10]

Activation Into Mission

Recognizing the agency of those we desire to serve can be a disruptive practice. It makes me think of Anthony, who comes to eat at our neighborhood diner—a free lunch and breakfast once a week. Anthony also comes to serve. Seeing him work alongside the "church-from-the-suburb" volunteers is always a joy. Anthony mostly ignores protocol, roles, and organizational principles, which usually confounds the ones who are trying to follow them. But when the volunteers drive home, he walks a few blocks to where he lives among the neighbors he just served and ate with. He is activated into the mission of loving his neighbors.

In my experience, activating those identified as recipients of service is not something readily discussed in traditional church outreach strategies or civic social services and programs. Incidentally,

---

[10] Robert D. Lupton, *Compassion, Justice and the Christian Life: Rethinking Ministry to the Poor* (Ventura, CA: Regal Books, 2007), 57.

I believe this to be one of the main contributing factors in the "discipleship deficit" in our churches. We talk a lot about "saving people," but not so much about activating them. The end of the journey for you and marginalized neighbors is not restoration but activation. Or maybe it is better stated this way: Activation into the mission of God is the means through which restoration is fulfilled.

In the ANE context, many of the OWS were once sons and daughters, wives, and land owners. They were a part of the people of God, and therefore they had purpose—to glorify God and bless the nations. Once they were pushed to the edges, they either forgot their place or were not viewed by others as living into their ultimate inheritance. By (re)integrating into the faith community, they were immediately activated as missionary people.

Much the same dynamic is present in Jesus' ministry to marginalized neighbors. He fulfilled God's call to Israel and redeemed and restored them in order that the people of God could enact the mission. We see this in the outcomes for those Jesus interacted with: The woman at the well was sent back into her town to bear witness to Jesus, and many believed in Jesus through her testimony; Zacchaeus brought four-fold financial restitution to those he had wronged in Jericho, and gave half of his remaining wealth to the poor, becoming a living testimony of restoration to his community; the leprous man is sent by Jesus right back into the religious community at the temple that would have sent him out into the desert in the first place, to whom he then declared the good news that the healer had come.[11]

Both our current outreach ministries and social services have strayed from this approach. We have moved from people-centric approaches to programmatic-centric and organizational-centric approaches. The focus is on fulfilling the operations of programs and organizations instead of ministering to a person. Some reasons for this are as follows:

---

[11] See John 4:1–42; Luke 19:1–10; and Luke 17:11–19.

- Activation and participation are messy endeavors. As soon as you truly release your power and expected outcomes, you shift agency to others. Not releasing power is a control issue, and for Christians it comes from the sin of self-idolatry. For organizations, the problem is slavery to the logic model.
- Social constructs are applied unilaterally in unhelpful and damaging ways. What is helpful to build cases and make broad sweeping social commentary is rarely pertinent when applied to an individual journeying toward restoration. We have to be able to utilize both the group and individual identity, not pit them against each other.
- Stated very bluntly, it is easier to raise money for things when we deal with "at-risk" people, than when we are raising up "future world changers." The narratives we produce, however, are rarely descriptive of the lived experience of neighbors, and at best they relay only a partial truth of a very complex situation.
- We ultimately are measuring the wrong things, so our activities are inevitably directed away from the very impact we hope to achieve. For example, we might show the success of feeding or housing people, but how do we measure a larger vision of a thriving or nourishing life? We might mobilize one hundred volunteers, but can we measure how they have been formed in the way of Jesus?

What I'm putting forth here is that neighborhood revitalization, rooted in ABCD, is a solution toward activation and participation—which is Jesus' way of serving marginalized neighbors. ABCD aims to build on the assets within a given community, as opposed to focusing on the deficits. The greatest assets of any community are the God-image bearers, the people themselves. The way change happens in ABCD is through the residents themselves and their participation in the change process.

Instead of seeing neighbors living in disinvested neighborhoods first and primarily as people of need, neighborhood revitalization hopes to activate them into the vision for change that they hold for themselves and their community.

This immediately calls to mind some amazing neighbors I have met over the years:

- Melissa, who picked up trash every Saturday to beautify her neighborhood and meet neighbors.
- Lisa and Cathy, who gathered kids once a month to paint rocks and give them a positive activity to do right in their neighborhood.
- Walter, who painted a mural of his own design on the side of his house that we had mistakenly assumed was abandoned.
- Anita, who showed up one day, and then kept showing up to help with every event and activity in the neighborhood.
- Dre, who rolls an old giant tire around to honor his dad's fight against cancer and spread positive messages.
- Crystal, who served on the neighborhood leadership team for years, for no compensation, and quietly bought and rehabbed a few houses in the neighborhood.
- Bernard, who is an incredible entrepreneur, and an even more incredible father.

So many more could be listed. The point is, in a deficit-based system, most of them (not all) would be numbers on a roll of food stamps, nameless/faceless persons to be counted as recipients of social services, or incorrectly lumped into a category based on their address. Instead, they are world changers, activated to love their neighbors using their own unique gifts, and in so doing to love themselves and know their true worth.

It doesn't stop at the neighbors, though. Remember, God's call for Israel to participate in his ministry of holistic restoration was in order to shape them into a people after his own heart, who would in turn stand as a testimony and countercultural witness to the glory of God. Jesus invited his disciples to participate in his ministry to the marginalized for the same purposes. Today, God desires for Christians and churches to do and be the exact same!

Neighborhood revitalization—done correctly—provides an opportunity for the people of God to step into holistic restoration of the marginalized. If there is an initiative going on, neighbors most likely have already given their voice to the issue and have in hand a planned vision for change. They already have a way of gathering and organizing for change that you could join in with. Churches do not have to spend precious kingdom resources starting new programs or initiatives but can instead optimize kingdom resources by placing them into the hopes and dreams of activated neighbors.

Most importantly, this approach changes the definition of success. When a Christian or church participates in neighborhood work, they are participating in ministry to the whole of a person—heart, mind, soul, and strength—and therefore are engaging in transformative work in the world. This is transformative work to the self as well because people are stepping into God's ministry, fulfilled by Jesus, and most likely experiencing more peace, patience, kindness, gentleness, self-control, and love.

Do not become limited by false narratives about what either you or your marginalized neighbors can do. One transformed individual, restored in the whole of their being and activated into mission, can be an incredibly powerful force. Twelve such individuals brought together in a team can bring about cultural revolution if restored and activated. A whole community of restored and activated marginalized neighbors? Well, that is surely what all of creation is groaning for.

Whenever we ask neighbors about their concerns, kids are always a top priority. They are mentioned more than anything else. It preserves my hope for humanity. The next generation is always on the mind of neighbors—they want them to win!

The concerns sometimes come off as complaining: "These kids don't have any role models. There is nothing for them to do. They don't play outside like we used to. They don't have respect for the elders. They cause trouble because they're bored."

I choose to hear those concerns as positive preferred futures: "We want mentoring relationships for neighborhood youth. We'd like to see more youth activities. We need to expand green spaces for recreational opportunities. Let's tap into the creativity and spirit of our youth to build up our community."

But this story begins in the early days of our initiative, when we hadn't begun to reframe the narrative or seen quick wins and early action. There was still a lot of trepidation and hand-wringing about the current state of youth in the neighborhood.

It was compounded one Saturday when a nine-year-old found a gun in the park and was carrying it around. Thankfully, two of our neighborhood leaders, mothers who had connected to the initiative, happened to be there and interceded. But it became what you might call a "Popeye moment" for those mothers—*That's all I can stands, and I can't stands no more!*

Instead of doing an anti-gun campaign, hollering and screaming on social media about how horrible the world is, blaming other parents or the system, or any other fairly reasonable reaction given the terrifying experience, these two women decided to take an asset-based approach toward a solution—one that I believe is a deeply Christian response.

Those two moms decided to start gathering kids every other Saturday to paint rocks. Apparently, this was/is a thing. You paint rocks, place them around your neighborhood, and a virtual community can find and collect them. The specific activity they were doing wasn't really important; it merely provided a focus to allow them to start gathering children to provide positive experiences. They started with what they had—themselves and a public space. That is it, and that is all. They decided to bring a small ray of light into the darkness, to overcome evil with good.

And wouldn't you know it, from those humble beginnings, momentum began to build, their vision expanded, and funding followed. Gathering youth monthly turned into weekly, which then turned into programming, which then turned into a full-blown approach akin to The Promise (detailed in chapter five). This led to more open doors, these moms being invited to lead community conversations, sit on boards of nonprofits, speak at the local TEDx event, and facilitate a breakout at a state-wide community development conference. All of this stemmed from that one catalytic event and decision to take action.

There are about a hundred different leadership lessons in neighborhood revitalization that can be drawn from this short story. Here are a few:

- Start with what you have.
- Never miss an opportunity.
- Take the next faithful step forward.
- Follow your holy discontent.
- Leaders are everywhere if you have eyes to see them.
- Activate your greatest resource: neighbors.
- When in doubt, build relationships.

By gathering kids every other Saturday, those two moms modeled the life of Jesus, and I learned a great deal about him by watching them over the following years. I was formed into the likeness of Christ by their witness.

Lisa and Cathy embodied the principle of being the change they hoped to see. They did not sit around complaining. They did not wait on youth programming or service providers to bring their interventions. Instead, they started with what they had—their agency—and activated their skills, talents, and passions in order to become agents of change.

Now let's take this story one step further in a possibly unforeseen direction—those mothers are not followers of Jesus! In fact, they have a certain amount of hostility toward organized religion of all stripes. Although neither have anything against individual expressions of faith, and would describe themselves as "spiritual," they are not Christians. For me, this perfectly highlights the beautiful mess that is ministry when you move out of the books, theories, and church buildings and into the practicalities of functional ministry ... and, dare I say, the pragmatism of real-life engagement with others. How could a Christian—one with a master of divinity and doctorate of ministry—be discipled by two non-believers? Do we really want children around these ladies if they are not Christians? Shouldn't you be evangelizing them so that they will become Christians?

I no longer feel the need to respond to those questions, doubts, and concerns—that I have myself, for the record. That is one of the interesting aspects of participating in Jesus' ministry; these types of issues do not seem to matter as much when real lives are at stake. The kids in our neighborhood need to experience love, and these mothers are imitating the ways of Jesus, letting the little ones come to them. I have no issues learning about Jesus from them, especially if it drives me to do the same. I have experienced the words of Paul to the church at Philippi, "Some indeed preach Christ from envy and rivalry ... not sincerely ... only that in every way, whether in pretense or in truth, Christ is proclaimed, and in that I rejoice!" (Phil. 1:15–18 ESV). I know the impact of those mothers' decision was deeper and more far reaching than the one kid, but I also know that one kid went from holding a gun in a park to holding a painted rock; from being alone wandering aimlessly to being part of a purposeful community with adult mentors; from being an unknown stranger to a neighbor with a name and story. And in those movements, I find the proclamation of Christ. In that I rejoice!

7

PROXIMITY, PRESENCE, PLACE, POSTURE

Early one morning, Jesus went to the temple, having come from a brief time of retreat at the Mount of Olives (John 8:1–11). This was a regular practice of his, so people looking for him knew where to find him. At this time, many people were seeking Jesus. Once they gathered, he began teaching them the way of the kingdom of heaven. The leaders in the way of the world were none too happy about this, so in order to trap Jesus and discredit him, they brought a woman to him caught in the act of adultery, knowing that Jesus had a soft spot for sinners. They threw her to Jesus' feet, levied the accusations and customary charges, and the test (or more accurately, the trap) was laid. Would Jesus love God by upholding the commands of the Law, or would he love his neighbor by trying to justify her behavior in order to save her life?

Jesus bent down to the level of the woman, said nothing, and began writing with his finger in the ground. The leaders of the way of the world persisted, insisting that Jesus render a judgment on the woman one way or another. With a sigh, Jesus stood and said, "Let him who is without sin among you be the first to throw a stone at her" (v. 7 ESV).

Then Jesus stooped back down and continued writing on the ground. One by one, the accusers left until it was just the woman who was standing before Jesus: Jesus said to her, "Woman, where are they? Did no one condemn you?" She said, "No one, Lord." And Jesus said, "I do not condemn you, either. Go. From now on, do not sin any longer."

In this way, Jesus fulfilled the greatest way of life: loving God *and* loving neighbors.

This insanely beautiful and powerful story is a microcosm of Jesus' ministry. I heard a teaching once offer a little extra-biblical hypothesis that what Jesus was writing on the ground were the sins of the accusers, and, as they were confronted with their personal sin, they left in conviction. It is not in the text, but it certainly fits the story! What is also not in the text is what, if anything, Jesus says to the woman when he stoops or bends down, placing himself in her position, in her space; but I can also imagine him whispering words of comfort, even as his body offered protection from the stones to her body, while saving her soul.

I say this is a microcosm of Jesus' ministry because it illuminates the consistent way Jesus related to marginalized neighbors. Whether it was the woman at the well, Zacchaeus in the tree, the lepers in the desert, or the woman here (plus many others), I believe there are four principles we can confidently draw out that inform the way we go about participating in neighborhood revitalization. These are the four Ps.

Proximity

Jesus bent down to the ground to write in the dust, the very place where the marginalized neighbor was thrown down by her accusers, at the feet of the one who would judge. Jesus tended to find himself in close proximity to the people who needed him most, those desiring holistic restoration. He drew near to them (got proximate) and removed the barriers between him and his neighbor. There was also often a physical element in Jesus' ministry (touching, feeding, even spitting!) that facilitated closeness.

Proximity to our neighbors is vital if we are to know them and work with them.

James is a bi-vocational associate pastor of a church that relocated into our neighborhood. When the church moved in, their lead pastor cast a big vision for all the change that was going to come about in the neighborhood because of their presence. Yet the activities surrounding that vision have looked like every previous tired response: feeding programs, a clothing bank, prayer outreach, and of course Sunday and

Wednesday services in their building. James, on the other hand, has been proximate with his neighbors. He comes faithfully to the monthly neighborhood meetings, is a regular face at events, and has participated in a few neighbor-led projects. He has drawn near to neighbors and entered their space. It has given me great joy to see him in conversations with neighbors as a known person, a friend, as James; and he is now bringing other congregants from his church along to these events as well.

In your following of Jesus, are you proximate to marginalized neighbors?

Presence

First, it is important to say that presence assumes proximity. Each of the four Ps build on each other. Proximity and presence are intentionally related, but a small phrase in the story of the woman accused draws out the difference between the two: "Early in the morning [Jesus] came again to the temple" (John 8:2). Jesus "came again." Now, I want to be careful not to overreach in my interpretation, but Jesus was on an ultimate mission that required constant movement toward his destination, which makes it that much more remarkable that Jesus also created regular rhythms within his ministry. For example, he spent 85 percent of his public ministry in the region of Galilee,[1] regularly taught at the synagogues, frequented the Mount of Olives, and was often found reclining at the table. In this passage he "came again" to the temple. The discipline of regular and consistent presence in the lives of the marginalized offers both an opportunity to become known and trusted by neighbors and to let them know where they can find you when needed.

One of our Love Your Neighborhood[2] partners—an organization executing our neighborhood revitalization approach as lead agency in

---

[1] See John Mark Comer, *Practicing the Way: Be with Jesus. Become Like Him. Do as He Did* (Colorado Springs, CO: WaterBrook, 2024).

[2] Love Your Neighbor is part of Community One, the Christian nonprofit I have worked for since 2017. It's mentioned in the introduction to this book, and our ABCD approach is described more fully in chapters nine through eleven.

their own neighborhood—happens to be a church. To kick off their initiative, they put a giant map of the neighborhood on the wall of their lobby and encouraged members of their congregation to go and be present there, then to share what they did by writing it down on a circular Post-it note and sticking it on the map. It was amazing to watch the faithful presence of God's people fill up the neighborhood: "Ate lunch in the park," "Prayer walked a street," "Had a conversation with a neighbor," etc. The simple act of going to be present with neighbors helped to break down walls, breed familiarity, and provide opportunities for relationships to emerge.

In your following of Jesus, is your presence known by marginalized neighbors?

Place

The opening of the story in John 8 starts with not one but two place-based contextual clues: Jesus went to the Mount of Olives (known by that community to be a place of retreat, resting, and refilling), and he came down from that place to the temple in Jerusalem. In fact, throughout the Gospel accounts, the authors are very careful to include contextual notes on the physical locations of Jesus' ministry and missionary journey. This is because place matters! Place is important in everyone's daily life, but it is especially so because of the intricate link between place and marginalization. Check out these examples from the Gospels:

- "Can anything good come from Nazareth?" (John 1:46). The place of Jesus' birth established his very identity in the eyes of most in his community. This sentiment is alive and well today: "Can anything good come from Southside (this or that neighborhood or area of town)?" We link people's identities, at least in part, to their birthplace.
- When Jesus encountered the ten lepers in Luke 17, they were on the outskirts of the village. This is because, according to Old Testament law, lepers were pushed out into the wilderness or

desert (Lev. 13:45–46). These "unclean" neighbors needed to live somewhere that would not pollute the rest of the community. The undesirable people had to stay in an undesirable place. Whether through low-income housing developments, predatory landlords, or unjust practices like redlining, we are very much still fencing our communities from "the least of these."

- We learn from Jesus' interaction with the woman at the well that Jews and Samaritans did not relate to one another (John 4:9). Samaria was treated as a separate place within a larger community. It was a region where people had a slightly different religious view from that of the Jews, and therefore, the region and its people were isolated and fenced off from the prevailing Jewish worldview. They became their own insular community within the broader geographical context. For many marginalized neighbors, this is very much the case today; whether the driving factor is economic, racial, or ethnic—or a combination of these factors—the sub-community becomes at risk precisely because they are separate, open to attack, and vulnerable on many levels.

Place is a much richer discussion than I can offer here, both in the biblical text and in analyzing our own modern context. Hopefully this sampling at least draws out the importance of place in ministry. Of course, Jesus infamously entered into these to-be-avoided places, drawing near to the neighbors that lived in these forgotten locations, bringing the very presence of God into the lives of those areas the majority deemed God-forsaken.

It was not that long ago that the local parish or neighborhood church pastored in the place it was planted. In fact, that was the entire purpose of its existence. Disassociating ministry from the physical locale has been accelerated by volume metrics. Whether you are tracking number of attendees at Sunday services, small groups, outreach participants, or youth ministry, the more you have, the more successful you are deemed to be. That definition of success has come to replace the importance of a people living in a place. It is counter-cultural, and you will get major pushback, when you declare that, following in the way of Jesus, you are going to focus your ministry on a group of neighbors located in a physical place, in order to bring about restoration and activation. But you will find greater impact for your investment when you stay focused on a place. Try a neighborhood, zone, or even one block.

In your following of Jesus, are you going to the places where marginalized neighbors are?

Posture

The Son of Man came to serve, not be served (Matt. 20:28). Jesus emptied himself even to the point of death, death on the cross (Phil. 2:8). His life was full of stories that showed true humility—not being ashamed or bashful about his position but instead leveraging it for the good of others and the world. Even in the story of the adulterous woman, Jesus bent down, moving from his rightful position of judge standing over the accused, to a squatting position. Jesus humanized the woman, protecting her even as he conferred equal status and shielded her with his own body.

Having the appropriate posture when working with marginalized neighbors is crucially important for restoration. The posture cannot be that of one set apart, better than thou, know-it-all, "we have the answers for how to restore your life." It requires a lowering of your position to create equal footing—not out of superiority but in recognition of commonality—and then leveraging your position and power to raise neighbors to new life based on their unique path forward as an individual and community.

In neighborhood revitalization, the simplest and first move toward correct posture is to listen. This uncomplicated but profound act opens up the possibility to enter into the relationship with neighbors as a learner. You do not have to be the expert, knowing what these "poor people" need, or to have a predetermined solution ready to apply to strangers who may or may not need what you are pushing, let alone actually want it.

In your following of Jesus, are you dying to yourself, conferring value, and empowering others when serving marginalized neighbors?

Incarnation

The four Ps are really just an embodiment of a very important theological term that the Western American Evangelical church lost touch with for a while but has been rediscovering lately: incarnation.

Usually, we only ever really talk about the incarnation at Christmas. It is mainly thought of in relation to Jesus being sent to live among us, to become like us and therefore able to take on our sins to die for us. Incarnation is thought of only in relation to our justification.

But I believe incarnation is important for our sanctification and our missiology as well. What do I mean by that? Well, our sanctification is about becoming more like Jesus and following in his ways. So, if Jesus was incarnate, and therefore fully human, that means we can follow his way of life and grow to be holier, like him. And in terms of missiology (our way of enacting the kingdom of God), God is in the process of reconciling all things to himself, and therefore the incarnation gives us a mandate to follow in Jesus' ways and to join with God in this work. We're invited to embody the life of Jesus (to incarnate him)—to be his hands and feet in God's mission to the world. And we're called to live among those he has sent us to, just as Jesus came to live among us. *The Message* version of John 1:14 literally has it as "The Word became flesh and blood, and moved into the neighborhood" (MSG).

The embodiment of the life of Jesus by his followers has direct influence and application for neighborhood revitalization and ministry to marginalized neighbors. This plays out most strikingly in the ways that we fail to incarnate Jesus as these neighborhoods become places we alienate.

Take the example of the phrase, "that side of town," which conveys a place to be avoided. If you happen to live there, it is a place to escape from. Growing up, I only went to the Southside a couple times. My relationships were not there; it was not the race or class of people that naturally occurred in the flow of my life. What is more, the infrastructure of the city was literally built to go around that area as the city experienced sprawl. As a result, it is easier to drive around the area than drive to it. And because of decades of disinvestment, there is simply no need to go there—no destination, no restaurants, few local shops, no grocery store, and no entertainment, etc. The Southside was like a foreign land in some respects—the people looked different from me, acted different, and the geographical location was a place people I knew talked about, not somewhere they directly experienced.

My lack of proximity and presence ensured I had a lack of relationships there, which ensured a continued lack of proximity and presence. When this kind of segregation is occurring on a wider scale, it also leads to a lack of ministry and holistic restoration of marginalized neighbors. This in turn leads to an improper posture from those who might become involved in ministry to those neighborhoods, as they perceive the people who live there to be either people who need help (best case) or to be avoided altogether (default). This creates a destructive "us/them" mentality, further deteriorating the potential for restorative relationships. Those people on that side of town become the "other"—even to those who truly desire to help.

When this dynamic is present, I have experienced three typical responses to marginalized neighbors: (1) they are ignored, consciously or subconsciously; (2) they are seen as the problem; or (3) they are seen as in need of help.

There is a huge amount we could unpack here—lack of civic education, misunderstanding of the gospel, proper orientation to the other—to name just a few. It is all horribly complex. All I will say here is that none of these mentalities are properly aligned with the Christian faith or with Jesus' way of ministry, which is incarnational—including presence, proximity, place, and posture. (A small, but profound corrective is embodying the "we" mentality of Jesus, which emphasizes shared humanity and interconnectedness.)

These misaligned ways of thinking create ignorance and arrogance, which breed incredibly damaging narratives that are extremely hard to change once they provide the frames through which we see our neighbors. *That side of town has bad schools … it's not safe to go there … they're not educated … they're all poor …* and on and on. Add to that the media's portrayal, which perpetuates the narrative, and then some of the narratives do in fact become self-fulfilling prophecies, which perpetuates the cycle.

The reality is that these narratives are only partially true at best. Remember my earlier example that in my neighborhood we have the highest poverty rate in the city at 43 percent, but that means 57 percent are not in poverty. The majority. Yet the dominant narrative is the poverty one.

The dominant *narratives* are not the dominant *realities* our neighbors face. However, since we are talking about ministry to *marginalized* neighbors, do these dominant narratives even matter?! Followers of Christ are to be harbingers of light (2 Cor. 4:6) and good news (Mark 16:15), literally telling and creating a different story in our communities' darkest places. You would think the darker the place, the more motivated the light would be to become proximate and bring its presence.

But that is not what happens. In a truly insidious turn of the tables, even those who want to help typically do so without living into proximity, presence, place, and posture. In our welfare-state and church-outreach cultures, it often looks and sounds like this:

- Come to our government building, our clothing bank, our food pantry. Stand in line, take your number, get your goods and services as part of a categorized system. Come again next month!
- At our service event, we will stand on this side of the table with our goods, services, and programs. We are here to provide you with what you do not have—that is why you are on that side of the table.
- We host classes or programs at our facility that align with the flow of our work schedule and expect neighbors to come to us, at our most convenient times.

This way of ordering relationships is transactional at best. It perpetuates the narratives and positional authority and communicates, "We are in a good place, you are not; we will help you who need it." Yet, as we have discussed, this does not even really help. Perpetuating self-betterment as an approach to ministry is actually damaging and certainly not reflective of the restorative ministry disciples of Jesus are called to step into.

One of my good friends, who I met through neighborhood work, started getting invited to sit at some influential tables. This was perhaps in part because she was an activated asset for our community and not some "poor person" to be pitied. Her experience of being given opportunities to speak in settings where decisions were being made started out exciting and hopeful and ended with frustration and embarrassment. She told me that she felt like she was nothing more than a box to check—as if the people in those spaces were able to say, "We have a poor person from that side of town at our table! Let's pat ourselves on the back and move forward with our ideas for those people exactly as we had planned."

You can imagine the feeling had it been you in her seat—finally getting a chance to sit at a table where decisions are being made about you, your family, and your community, and then finding your voice at the critical moment of action being overlooked and ignored. You took a risk, stepped into "their world," and were passed over when the ideas, concepts, and solutions were proposed. I can imagine I would have been angry. Others possibly apathetic. No one would leave feeling valued as an image-bearer of God.

Do not perpetuate the narratives with your actions. Refuse to participate in ministry that doesn't recognize the dignity and worth of marginalized neighbors. Follow Jesus into the places, spaces, and lives of marginalized neighbors. Root your presence there, shoulder to shoulder. Above all, do so with the posture of Christ who surrendered his life for you, so you could participate in his ministry to marginalized neighbors.

Being Humble

When we practice the four Ps of incarnation in the context of neighborhood revitalization, we are embodying the presence of Jesus Christ in our neighborhoods. Further, when we approach our kingdom work in this Christlike posture, there is a promise given to us by God. Throughout the Bible, there is a repeated phrase: "The humble will be exalted." This phrase is mentioned by David, Jesus, Peter, and Paul—so it seems something very important is being communicated.

On the surface, this statement seems to be talking about a reward for humility ... which, ironically, might go against any act of genuine humility! But I believe that instead of a promise of future reward, this is a statement of practicality—merely an observation of how Christian service, and dare I say the whole Christian experience of life itself, actually functions.

When we consider Jesus' mission—to reconcile all things to the Father—we often focus on the cross, resurrection, and ascension. What we don't always give much notice to is the time in between his death and resurrection: Holy Saturday.

While the disciples were mourning, scared, and seemed to have forgotten all Jesus had told them about these events, Jesus had descended into hell and was working cosmic restoration for all time (Eph. 4:9). At that moment, Jesus was the epitome of one who is humbled. We could say he was literally "under everyone" as he fulfilled his role as the ultimate suffering servant. But when God exalted him, all who are in him now became exalted by virtue of Jesus' position. Because of Jesus' posture, we are lifted up. This is why Paul says our citizenship is in heaven (Phil. 3:20). *Is* in heaven, not *will be*—because Jesus is now on the throne of heaven, and we have been exalted by virtue of his exaltation, not by any action of our own.

Further, as we take on the posture of Christ, as we humble ourselves, it is God's great joy to exalt his servants, giving us fullness of life with him and the opportunity to bring this foretaste of heaven to those we serve.

This is a beautiful paradox of the Christian way of life—by becoming nothing you will be exalted to knowing God himself.

Posture affects all aspects of ministry to marginalized neighbors. It permeates all the other Ps and the rest of the practices we will cover. Listening takes humility. Entering into alien parts of town takes humility. Repeatedly being present with no public fanfare takes humility. Making a long-term commitment of service with no guarantee of success takes humility. True humility. Because it is not good enough to come and help; you need to die and be exalted by the Living God. We need the power of heaven to bring about transformation.

Transformational change cannot come from the top down, no matter how hard we try, or how good our intentions. The "lowly" will always be crushed down and ultimately pushed out to the margins yet again. It is simply what happens when we wield power. Descending breaks the paradigms, busts the systems, and reaches outside the status quo. It shifts our power to those who have little, just as Jesus gave his power away. Death to self—whether manifesting in positional authority, notoriety, status, salary, or physical safety—is the ultimate equalizer, and therefore holds the greatest opportunity. If you cannot be tempted by wealth, fame, or power, the enemy has nothing to offer. Yet God offers a promise: The humble will be exalted. So, humble yourselves under marginalized neighbors in the greatest act of love, and enjoy the view of God's reconciling work as you experience his exaltation.

STORY
THERE'S AN ARTIST IN THAT ABANDONED HOUSE

After a couple of years of our neighborhood initiative, we created these things called "resident engagement pop-up experiments," or "pop-ups" for short. They are exactly what the name suggests (I'm not too imaginative)—we pop up in the neighborhood, to engage residents, as an experiment. The word "experiment" is tacked on to mitigate against potential failure. Sometimes that failure is that we don't meet any neighbors, but when this happens, we learn something anyway: Neighbors don't want to engage at this time, place, or in this manner. Over the first five years of our neighborhood initiative, we met over four hundred neighbors, many of them through this method.

The idea of pop-ups came from our desire to keep residents at the center of our revitalization efforts. We were a couple of years into the initiative and had a small team of leaders and a fairly strong next ring of neighbors who were engaged, totaling around twenty-five to thirty people. So, we dreamed up a few different interventions, pop-ups being one, in order to meet neighbors and keep us on the ground in the neighborhood, on the streets, and where neighbors actually were.

The motivation was simple: Go to where people are, engage them in their space, do not expect them to come to you, and do your thing. Proximity. Presence. Place. Posture. Embodied in actual activity.

We really didn't want to overthink it, so we bought an E-Z UP canopy, picked a location, day, and time, and came up with an activity of some sort to encourage interaction. Then we "popped up" for a few hours to meet neighbors. Our primary goal was simply to let neighbors know there was a collective group of residents coming together to make positive change in the neighborhood. The secondary goal, if the conversations went well, was to invite them to participate in the initiative and exchange contact information. That was it!

To date, over 1,200 neighbors have connected across five different Love Your Neighborhood initiatives as the work has multiplied.

One day we put a little extra energy into a pop-up, mainly because we had an awesome intern. We bought big pieces of plywood, screwed them together in an accordion style, primed them with white to create a giant blank canvas wall, bought some paint and spray-paint, and invited neighbors to create something. Anything. It was an art pop-up. We found a typical empty lot at an intersection, perfect for pop-ups. We had learned that intersections are the best location because there are four ways of potential traffic.

Next to the empty lot was what looked like an abandoned house. Unfortunately, this is a common sight and narrative in our neighborhood. The vacant lot we were using for the pop-up was empty because the house that used to be on it was torn down. This scenario is the result of a kind of domino effect: A house gets dilapidated, and—after years, sometimes decades—the surrounding home values decrease, so owners don't see the point in investing money in their property when it's next to an eyesore—or they simply don't have the means to keep it up—so they tear it down. Regardless, what you get is an empty lot, and next to it a dilapidated and abandoned house.

The pop-up went great. Neighbors came out, friends joined us, and we had an afternoon of fun and creativity. There is a story and lessons in that for sure. But this story is about Walter, and we didn't even meet him that day!

The neighbors who came out to share their creativity did such a beautiful job on the art that we decided to leave it out on the empty lot for a week or two. Over that time, whenever we would walk or drive by the empty lot, we noticed that the canvases were knocked over, but a day later, they would be back up on display. One day, they were even arranged and placed for better visibility and viewing. We weren't sure what was going on, but we liked it.

A few weeks later, a neighbor named Walter came to a neighborhood association meeting for the first time. He was a very soft-spoken, reserved, and humble guy. Thankfully, our neighborhood champion (staff member on the ground) was an amazing trust- and relationship-builder. Walter slowly opened up to him—although it took a few months. Eventually, we discovered that Walter was the owner of the house next to the empty lot—the one we thought was abandoned! He had been the person picking up and arranging the canvases. What is more, Walter was himself an accomplished artist. He had taught himself how to do airbrush art and had several murals throughout the city—most of them in small churches in our community or on vehicles for his neighbors.

Walter had received the art in the empty lot next to his as a sign from God. He asked if he could use the leftover plywood to shore up his porch. He's resourceful like that. Over time, we found out that Walter had bought his house outright, choosing to pick a rough house over holding a bank note. He knew he had to fix it up and was doing so slowly, but he worked long hours and volunteered at his local church another fifteen to twenty hours a week.

He was always helping others before himself. One time, I saw Walter helping to push a car that had broken down off the nearby highway. He had stopped to help … while I drove right past. *Ouch!*

The meeting that Walter had first shown up to included the announcement of the opening for applications to our neighborhood action projects. This is where neighbors can submit ideas to take immediate action on how they would improve the quality of life in the neighborhood. If their application is agreed upon, they are given a direct investment—meaning we give them cash money to go and turn their idea into reality. The only "string attached" is a photo of the finished project.

Walter had seen the mailer we'd sent out to every neighbor letting them know about the opportunity and had decided to turn the side of his house, the side facing the empty lot, into a mural. He wanted to airbrush a message of encouragement to the neighborhood. The message was "Love Thy Neighbor."

What's more, Walter started rehabbing his house—fixing his porch, siding, and touching up paintwork. He started showing up regularly to neighborhood association meetings. He became an active contributor to the quality of life of his neighbors in small and big ways. It was a joy to bless Walter with a new roof to stabilize his home and encourage him as he continued to improve his property.

Simply being present in the neighborhood led to us meeting Walter—who is now a known neighbor, contributing to a movement of love. Walter is an asset of this community development and uncovering the treasure that he is was a reminder that we must continue to be present in our neighborhood if we are to see all the potential that is there.

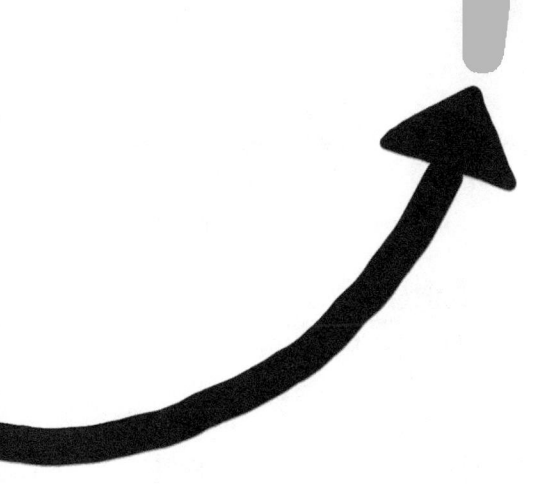

8

NEW WINESKINS

Before we dive into the final section of this book, where I will share how we implement neighborhood revitalization through our Love Your Neighborhood initiative and explore the ways churches can be involved in this type of work, I wanted to take some time to unpack the relationship between individual transformation and the transformation of systems and structures.

Up until now, I have made the case for working incarnationally (rooted in the lives of real people and neighborhoods) and the importance of individual transformation where holistic care doesn't impose "help" onto others or only meets needs. Part of my argument for this is based on seeing the damage that is done when ministries give care at arms-length and when we focus on delivering solutions through structures and systems rather than walking with people and helping them to be equipped for long-term life transformation.

However, the danger with this is that it can create an either-or dynamic. Systems, structures, organizations, and institutions are intertwined with individual lives. So, if inside-out transformation is truly going to happen, they can't be treated as separate entities.

In 2021, I had the opportunity to go to the Christian Community Development Association (CCDA) conference for the first time. John Perkins and CCDA had long been an influence on my life and work, so it was a joy to participate in the learning experience. The conference was impactful on several levels, notably because it was the first time I had been to a conference led, designed, and presented by a minority demographic. It was wonderful to participate in new (to me) cultural worship expressions and to be surrounded by like-minded people who saw neighborhood revitalization as a clear gospel expression of ministry.

It was disruptive and encouraging in all the best ways.

And it was during this conference that I began to see the connection between individual and system transformation.

One of the keynote speakers gave an inspiring and convicting talk about how, in response to white supremacy, white leaders of organizations and institutions should give away or release their influence to raise up minority leaders. This was perhaps one of the first times I had heard people use phrases like "white power" and "white supremacy"—not necessarily in an antagonistic way but merely as the reality of their lived experience.

I was sitting there as a white, forty-year-old male—the very personification of "white privilege"—yet also knowing my own story of growing up relatively poor, working my butt off for a decade straight to get where I was, and overcoming plenty of obstacles along the way. "Austin Maxheimer" certainly did not feel privileged; but, at the same time, I couldn't deny that privilege was something I definitely had!

The revelation I had was that both of these realities can and do exist at the exact same time. I can have an individual experience that seems different from what's happening at a societal level, but that doesn't mean that the societal issue doesn't exist. (This is similar to the analogy I made in chapter six about our tendency to use examples that are exceptions to the rule—like the one kid who gets out of the "bad" neighborhood—to make a case that everyone has the opportunity and thus, ignores the systemic issues.)

This is what I call the individual-societal paradox. Taking the example of white privilege: I can have nary an intended racist action as an individual while still participating in, contributing to, and benefitting from a societal system that oppresses racial minorities. I can even give my life to proactively fighting the injustice of racial inequality as an individual, while simultaneously recognizing that my very fight can muddy the waters of what is good long-term for my marginalized neighbors as a sociological sub-group.[1] The individual and societal are interrelated, complex dynamics.

Through listening to the speakers at the CCDA conference, I gained a greater revelation of how the individual-societal paradox works, and it also made me think about the dynamics that we see in Jesus' relationships with individuals and the institutions of his day.

One morning, during my Bible study time, I came across a line in the Gospel of Luke: "And He came to Nazareth, where He had been brought up; and as was His custom, He entered the synagogue on the Sabbath, and stood up to read" (Luke 4:16). I had read this verse many times before—I'd even taught on it—but (of course) it landed differently that morning as God revealed something to me about Jesus' relationship with systems. From this verse, we can see that teaching at the synagogue was a regular practice during Jesus' ministry. If he did this as part of a regular rhythm, we need to ask ourselves, why?

The synagogue was part of the embedded religious system for the Jewish culture, and just like the insidious drift of human systems, the religious institution of Jesus' day had shifted away from heaven, toward the world. And yet Jesus wanted to spend time within that system.

As I thought about this, I realized that Jesus didn't just do this when he was teaching in the synagogue; there are many other instances where he ministers to the religious institution:

- He reclined at the table with Sadducees, Pharisees, scribes, and teachers of the law.
- He taught in the temple.
- He participated regularly at the synagogue.
- He regularly and consistently interacted patiently with the religious leaders as they asked him questions.
- He turned over the tables at the temple marketplace.

---

[1] This dynamic is discussed in depth throughout Bryant Meyers's book, *Walking with the Poor* but is specifically addressed in chapter seven where he explores the relationship between development principles, practices, and the role of practitioners. See Bryant L. Meyers, *Walking with the Poor: Principles and Practices of Transformational Development*, 2nd ed. (New York. NY: Orbis Books, 2011), 205–238.

- He met with Nicodemus to discuss the revolutionary idea of being born again.

Far from forsaking the dominant religious system of his time, Jesus spent a significant portion of his public ministry speaking into and calling for reform within it. When we consider the way Jesus sought to transform the lives of every person he interacted with, and his kingdom mission to redeem and restore the world, it makes sense that this would extend to the systems, structures, and institutions that impact the way people live.

Yes, And

A popular phrase in recent years, in countering the "either-or" mentality I mentioned above, is "both/and." We could argue that this is what Jesus is demonstrating here—it's *both* transformation for individuals *and* transformation of systems. But I would suggest Jesus had a slightly different approach, which shows the dynamic flow of individual and societal transformation. This is called "Yes, and."

My favorite band of all-time is Phish. They are often categorized as a "jam band," a genre popularized by the Grateful Dead. Phish often play long musical interludes spanning ten, fifteen, or even twenty-plus minutes. During these jams, the band will take the tempo up, drop it down, change leads, and basically wander into uncharted musical territory. A live show is a singular experience because not only is each set different, but also because even if they were to play the same song two nights in a row, the song is substantially changed, as they create new progressions and sounds every time they play. As someone who loves music but is not necessarily musical, this always confounds and leaves me in awe!

I once listened to a podcast, *Long May They Run*,[2] where Phish discussed this approach to their jams. They shared how they had taken

---

[2] Dean Budnick, "Yes, and," October 2, 2019, in *Long May They Run*, podcast, season 1,

an idea from improvisational comedy (think *Whose Line Is It Anyway?*), which is called, "Yes, and." In improv, one actor will deliver a line, and then the next actor's job is to say, "Yes, and ..."—building on what their stage partner had just introduced to the narrative and audience. No matter how seemingly crazy, disconnected, or outlandish, the improviser must connect it to what came before and move it forward ... with humor!

Phish does the same thing in their jams—someone introduces a direction in the music, and the rest of the band has to respond to it, building on where the other is leading, and letting the music go in new directions, ideally with good technical precision! The result is a beautiful, communal experience.

This idea of "Yes, and" has been transformative for me in so many ways because it flies in the face of our typical approach to life, which is "either-or." Admittedly I am a regular perpetrator of this way of thinking. It is so much easier to draw lines and create boxes than to account for the vast complexities and endless nuance that is human existence. It's easy to think that we can only address injustice and see transformation for marginalized neighbors by focusing on one individual or family at a time, forgetting that their experiences are symptomatic of a broken system. On the other hand, it's easy to think that we can only overcome injustice by top-down law and policy changes, assuming that these will have a more significant effect for the masses and that the good we aim to do will be enacted for the individuals.

But "Yes, and" is about seeing individual lives transformed that, in turn, go on to create something new in their social sphere—in community with others, and with the potential to see transformation across the wider society and the systems which uphold those societies.

As I've reflected more on the dynamic of "Yes, and," I've noticed that this is also present in the way Jesus interacted with individuals and systems. Jesus took what was unfolding and built on it, creating a new direction. Time after time, story after story, a person emerges

---

episode 4, https://podcasts.apple.com/us/podcast/s1-phish-ep-4-yes-and/id1479120204?i=1000519270874.

from the crowd, they become seen and known, Jesus ministers to them as an individual, and then he sends them off on a new trajectory, for a transformed life.

Maybe the most paradigmatic example of this can be found in Luke 8. The story of the woman bleeding illustrates how Jesus' ministry combined individual transformation with broader societal impact.

Jesus and his disciples are returning from Gerasene where he healed a man while coming back to Galilee, and the crowd is awaiting his return. A man named Jairus begs Jesus to help his dying daughter and, as they press through the mass of people, Jesus is touched by another person in need of healing. This is a person who would be significantly marginalized in this cultural context: First, she is a woman—a second-class citizen at that time; second, she is an unclean woman—her personal ailment not only would put her at a physical deficit, but her unclean status for twelve years would have also caused untold social-emotional trauma, barring her from community participation; third, she is a poor woman—its seems she has spent whatever money she had trying to be healed, a probable victim of the malpractice of those preying on the vulnerable.

In what can only be categorized as desperation, she touches the "fringes of Jesus' garment" and is instantly healed.[3] It's a wonderful story of Jesus healing, again! This is an example of "Yes."

But then we see Jesus build on this with "and." His act of individual healing has broader implications, challenging the systems that ostracized her in the first place. I believe this is crucial to understanding Jesus' ministry, and therefore our ministry. Jesus certainly could have just moved on, allowed the physical healing to occur—a good work done to a faceless member of the crowd. Incredible, personal transformation. But instead, Jesus stops and asks, "Who touched me?" (v. 45).

What was an anonymous, detached hand among the pressing throng, now becomes a person—a human being with a name and a story. Some question why Jesus stopped and demanded she step

---

[3] See Numbers 15:38–39 for a fascinating insight into the deeper meaning of this small act of touching Jesus' garment.

forward. I've heard some skeptical interpreters even criticize Jesus, questioning whether she wasn't already healed and that she had suffered enough without the spotlight being put on her. Could he not have let the moment pass unheralded?

But I believe something more was happening in Jesus' insistence that the woman come forward from the crowd. Jesus was concerned with holistic restoration and activation. He wasn't content to stop with the alleviation of her physical ailment but desired to see the whole of the woman's being—heart, mind, soul, and strength—restored.

In front of the whole crowd, Jesus addresses the woman publicly as "daughter." To the Jewish audience, this would have been something much larger than a reference to the biological realities of parentage we experience today. It was an inclusive word, one conferring status, placing her in the lineage of the family of God all the way back to Abraham. As such, it was a clear declaration of her standing in the covenant community—a restoration of her social standing. By virtue of this relationship with the heavenly Father, she was afforded God's peculiar care and protection that he always shows his people, especially the marginalized.

Yet even after physical and spiritual restoration, Jesus doesn't stop. He concludes his interaction with the woman with a commission: "Go in peace" (v. 48). Those well versed in Scripture will know that the word for peace is *shalom* and, as usual, our English placeholder doesn't fully capture the dynamic meaning of the Hebrew (or Greek, *eirene*, that's used in the New Testament). *Shalom* means complete or whole— so this final remark from Jesus speaks of the restored life this woman is now able to go and live.

More than this, *shalom* is often used in an active way throughout Scripture. The Bible Project has a helpful study of this word that says, "To bring *shalom* literally means to make complete or restore."[4] So *shalom* is really what much of this book has been about. We see Jesus

---

4 "Shalom/Peace," *The Bible Project*, November 30, 2017, https://bibleproject.com/explore/video/shalom-peace/.

bringing *shalom* to the woman who was bleeding … and commissioning her to go and actively pursue *shalom* in all of her life.

I believe this story speaks of the restoration of this woman, including her participation in the kingdom of heaven, not merely experiencing *shalom* as a passive state of being. *Shalom* includes the idea of rest, but it's the kind of rest where we know that God is at work and therefore that we rest in capable hands. Most importantly, living into that rest is an active way of life. Precisely because we are assured that God's will shall be done, we participate with God in his rest. *Shalom* is the "already" state of the kingdom of heaven—the completed works of Jesus that we can taste and see today. *Shalom* is the indwelling of the Holy Spirit that not only comforts and encourages us but also empowers us to be kingdom citizens everywhere we "go"! There are echoes of the "go" used in the Great Commission that Jesus gives to the Apostles—the sense of being sent as you spread the restorative *shalom* of the kingdom of God.

For the woman who was bleeding, the physical healing to her body was vitally important to her restoration, but the public declaration of her as a "daughter" is also vitally important—bringing healing to her heart and mind—and this in turn brings about reintegration into the covenant community which can bring ultimate healing to her soul.

Furthermore, I believe the words "go in peace" give this woman a mission and purpose. Using her whole being—heart, mind, soul, and strength—she can now step into her inheritance as a kingdom agent, a world changer, and continue to be shaped into the likeness of Christ.

To tie this into this chapter's focus on systems, consider the "Yes, and" nature of what Jesus is doing here: Instead of only targeting individuals for transformation, or only targeting systemic transformation, Jesus understands how intertwined the individual-societal paradox is. He has the ultimate wisdom to adopt the "Yes, and" dynamic and, by bringing transformative restoration to the life of an individual, he knows that she, in turn, will go and be part of the wider transformation happening at a societal level.

We see this time and again in the Gospels where Jesus has an encounter with an individual, brings them healing and restoration but ultimately activates them to go and bring transformation to the society around them. Think of the woman at the well, who became the evangelist to her whole village; or Zaccheus, who brought financial restoration to his community. Jesus takes a "Yes" encounter, adds the "and," and empowers the restored individual to be part of enacting societal transformation.

New Wineskins

One of Jesus' many wise sayings that has worked itself into everyday parlance is, "No one puts new wine into old wineskins" (Mark 2:22). On the surface, this seems to be warning against the blending of the old and new, and has direct application to our current discussion on existing systems, structures and institutions versus new movements. And it certainly does! But digging a little deeper, there is even more profundity in this brief teaching.

First, the wineskins parable is actually couched with another visual in the text—not sewing a new cloth patch into an old garment because it will stretch and ruin the garment (v. 21). This image reinforces the new-wine-and-old-wineskins illustration. The new wine will make the old wineskins burst, resulting in the loss of both the damaged container and the wasted wine.

In all three Gospels where this parable is present, it is told in the context of a question about discipleship—specifically in response to the question of why Jesus did not have his disciples fast like John the Baptist's disciples. Jesus responds, "Can the wedding guests mourn as long as the bridegroom is with them?" (Matt. 9:15). Jesus follows this with the analogy of the new wine and old wineskins and the new cloth and old garment. *Huh?*

The point Jesus is making here is that we are now living in a new reality—one that was ushered in when Jesus established a new covenant with his bride (God's people). Fasting was the old way, the Law, and it cannot be poured into the new without ruining it. Remember though, Jesus came to fulfill the Law not abolish it, so it is not a literalist interpretation. Jesus already accomplished the purpose of fasting—to bring us into a right relationship with the Father—and so now we can freely feast, or fast, in our appropriation of Jesus' life, with full assurance that we do not earn our place before God through the act itself. If earning is our intent, then the new truth will burst the old practice. This is the only way in which we can enjoy spiritual disciplines and practices— they have to be placed into a new vessel.

This principle extends to the new system that Jesus came to install.

While Jesus confronted the existing systems of his day, by speaking to religious leaders and challenging the damaging practices of the institution, he also proactively created a completely new system and structure that would ultimately revolutionize the religious and dominant worldview. This is what would become the church. Although Jesus himself didn't establish the church during his earthly ministry, he laid the foundation for it through the gathering of his missional faith community and the leadership development of the twelve apostles who would launch the early church.

But there was something quite distinct about this new wineskin that Jesus was forming—in some respects, it was the inverse of the religious system that was already in place. Think about some of these points:

- The Twelve wouldn't have been part of the inner circle of the Jewish religious system they were brought up in; they were young adults deemed (or maybe even proven) to not have enough potential for the ultimate positions in the leadership track.
- Although it was recorded that it was Jesus' custom to teach in the synagogue, his formative kingdom teachings (e.g. the Sermon on the Mount) occurred outside the system, on the missional frontier.
- Jesus completely repackaged and renewed the understanding of religious ideas and practices of the existing system—kingdom, Messiah, sabbath, temple, Spirit, etc.—away from worldly expectations and toward heavenly revelation.
- His public "platform" came largely from healing, restoring, and activating the very ones the religious system had marginalized.

- The larger community of disciples he built and organized not only operated outside the existing religious framework but was also made up of individuals and groups who would have been deemed unworthy—women, sinners, the unclean, rebels.
- The practices Jesus adopted for formation reorganized the Jewish system. The most famous and clearest example is the fulfillment of the Sabbath as opposed to the strict observance of technicalities attached to the Sabbath.

These and more bring home the point that, in order to bring about renewal, reformation, and revolution, Jesus created new systems and structures. Jesus birthed a gospel movement with new organizing principles that became the church. Over time, those same systems, structures, and institutions have themselves experienced the inevitable insidious drift away from heaven and toward the world as humanity has operated them. This calls us to question how Jesus invites us to be part of creating new wineskins fit for the kingdom transformation he is doing in our neighborhoods, today.

Jesus' creation of "new wineskins"—new structures—to contain the transformative powers of the gospel is crucial when considering the individual-societal paradox.

Even well-intentioned individuals working within broken systems can only achieve so much. My own experience working in our local school corporation exemplifies this. Initially I was quick to criticize, frustrated by perceived inefficiencies and ineffectiveness. It seemed like, if only there were better leaders in place, things would get better.

However, working within the system revealed a different reality. Two things happened.

First, we started to serve schools. Instead of standing on the outside railing against or observing how easy it would be to make changes, we got inside the schools and joined them on their vision and mission. What we found once inside were people who cared, who were good at their jobs—educators who understood about culture and change. We met principals with bigger visions than we had ever dreamed of having. We saw innovation and love. It was inspiring!

Second, over the course of ten years, we saw the next wave of administrators step into leadership roles. These leaders were people I knew, some even close friends. I knew for a fact that these individuals were high capacity, with grand visions, well versed in the newest literature and best practices. They were certainly more capable than me! In other words, any theory about the wrong people being in the wrong spots to make crucial decisions, well, that just did not float.

The problem wasn't the individuals; it was the system itself. This connects directly to the "Yes, and" dynamic. We can't simply focus on individuals ("Yes") while ignoring the systemic issues ("and"). These systems, as they currently exist, often treat people as faceless members of a crowd, hindering the kind of personalized transformation Jesus modeled. Transformation therefore quires a new-wineskins approach, one that empowers individuals within a new kind of system, enabling them to be agents of change.

The Faceless Crowd

Have you ever stood in a social services line? It's a remarkable experience because, even though you carry many forms of documentation, the process strips away your identity. I have a Social Security card, birth certificate, driver's license, and two pieces of mail with my name and address, all saying I am Austin Maxheimer, and yet I have never felt more like a faceless part of the system than when I stand in those lines. I become merely a number in a program that spits out food stamps.

Besides the cycles of dependency these social services often create, the way they are set up to operate inherently strips the dignity of recipients. This is the limitation of a system that must keep track of hundreds of thousands of people. Not everyone can be ministered to as a neighbor worthy of dignity. There is simply not enough time, staffing, or resources to do so. And people have got to eat!

The intervention we have functionally created becomes the antithesis of Jesus' ministry to the marginalized even as it ostensibly fulfills its purpose. Instead of going to the crowds, where people are, and drawing out individuals, the individual is forced to go to the service provider; their uniqueness is removed, and they become a part of the system—a faceless neighbor. Caring for the whole of the person, restoring their social standing, and activating them into purpose is replaced with meeting one compartmentalized need, perpetuating their social circumstances, and removing their purpose.

We also find that the approach to offering help through these services is depersonalized. This is partly because organizations base their best practices on sociological studies, research, and analysis that inform protocols for social services and nonprofits. Although I believe we can and should study sociological realities that exist at group, community, and societal levels, one of the consequences of this approach—especially when combined with damaging narratives and a deficit-based outlook on proposed interventions—is that programs become divorced from the inclusion of individuals as persons of worth.

For example, a 2010 study by the Organization for Economic Co-Operation and Development showed that appearance—or perception—of peers in a community sets expectations for jobs.[5] Also, what adults do vocationally directly transfers to the next generation. Practically this means that what kids see adults doing is what they envision themselves doing as adults. Surround a kid with a bunch of janitors, and they will aspire to be a janitor; mechanics, and they will aspire to be a mechanic; chemists, and they will aspire to be a chemist, etc.

Again, I'm not saying this isn't extremely important data! It should help set strategies for interventions to break through the lived experiences many marginalized neighbors face. But what it misses is Chade, one of our very real neighbors—a youth who is part of The Promise approach. As a sociological number, Chade is a classic case of someone who will end up on the wrong side of "successful adulthood." She is a young Black woman, growing up in persistent and pervasive poverty,

5   "Education at a Glance: OECD Indicators," *Organization for Economic Co-Operation and Development*, July 9, 2010, last accessed 2018, http://www.oecd.org/education/skills-beyond-school/educationataglance2010oecdindicators.htm.

from a single-parent household, living transiently in multiple disinvested neighborhoods, and a recipient of social services.

As a nameless, faceless demographic, we expect various outcomes for Chade:

- A low-paying job or unemployment
- Receiving social services as an adult
- Living in generational poverty
- A higher chance of teen pregnancy
- Lower educational attainment
- Living in the same neighborhoods she grew up in

These are logical expectations when applied to the faceless crowd. But when we pull this young woman from the crowd, something amazing happens—she becomes Chade, the irascible, confident, talented, leader of her peers. Chade has amazing strengths to build from. Chade is unafraid of adults; she will look you in the eye and let you know what she is thinking. And her thoughts are insightful, intelligent, and full of big ideas. Chade stands forward when others stand back. Although her grades may not reflect it, all of her teachers know her as a quick learner; and one conversation with Chade informs you that she is quick-witted and has a great sense of humor.

The thought that Chade would become part of the next generation of nameless, faceless, non-flourishing numbers on a report, is repulsive and abhorrent. Amazingly, it also feels highly improbable when interacting with her, even if the data overwhelmingly points in that direction. This is the power of the "Yes, and" approach. "Yes," we acknowledge the statistical realities and systemic challenges Chade faces; "and" we refused to let those statistic define her. We recognize her inherent dignity and potential to be an agent of change, both in her own life and in her community.

Jesus' "Yes, and" way corrects the faulty vantage point of the faceless crowd. Jesus certainly ministered to the crowd—think the feeding of the five thousand—but we see time and again, as in his interaction with the woman who was bleeding, that he brought holistic healing to individuals … whom he then sent to be part of bringing societal restoration as activated members of his kingdom.

Therein, we have our approach to neighborhood revitalization. Yes, and. Bringing individual transformation that empowers neighbors to enact societal change.

Neighborhood Revitalization—Old and New

There is a saying along the lines of, "Every system is perfectly designed to produce the results it gets." I think Abraham Lincoln said it first. Or Socrates. Or Steve Jobs.

I have found this idea to be a great explanation for why things in neighborhood revitalization are the way they are. Consider:

- Why is the majority of a city's poverty concentrated in a few urban neighborhoods?
- Why do these neighborhoods experience decades of disinvestment and under-resourcing?
- Why are these neighborhoods full of marginalized neighbors (e.g., poor, racial minorities, immigrants, elderly and aging, those with disabilities)?
- Why are these issues persistent and generational?

We seem to have an emerging answer: Because the systems, institutions, organizations, corporations, and policies, etc., are perfectly designed to create the society we have.

Most neighborhood revitalization initiatives I know of, and definitely most "poverty alleviation" initiatives, only minister at the crowd level. They may know the importance of sharing the story of an individual, but the actual system or program that is operating to effect change isn't set up for real people. Individual success stories remain abstract anomalies rather than the norm.

What's the solution? To pour new wine into new wineskins. To sew a completely new garment. That is what neighborhood revitalization through asset-based community development aims and attempts to do—to design new systems and structures, rooted and enacted by the residents themselves, that build the community from the inside out. Therein residents participate in a new system instead of the old one that has delivered them to their current lived experience.

If all the things we have been doing have taken us to where we are, and we no longer want to be here, then we must insist on paving a new road and creating a new vehicle to take us on the journey. At the very least, we have a hypothesis worth running an experiment.

Now, I am in no way saying we have got it even close to right in our neighborhood initiative; but I will say we are constantly evaluating and experimenting on how to get better at reorienting our approach. Our relentless pursuit of knowing neighbors and building bridges to engagement is the center of our work, and it is the number one metric by which we define success. The tool we utilize is a well-known approach in the business world—customer retention management (CRM)—but the application to neighborhood work is unique, as far as I'm aware.

When we meet neighbors, we let them know there is a group of residents working together for positive change in the neighborhood. If they agree to share their contact information through a connection card, we have moved a member of the "faceless crowd" to what we call a "met neighbor." They are no longer a stranger but a neighbor with a name, place, and uniqueness. We then invite and engage them, until they either decide on their own to opt out or move toward deeper relationship and engagement. We track all of that quantitative and qualitative level of engagement through a simple spreadsheet. When we know a development opportunity comes, we have a bank of real people, with real names and stories, that we can pull from and invite to participate.

In this way, we can allow the neighbors to be the heroes of the story of change, instead of the development itself being the hero. In our neighborhood we do not celebrate that twenty-three trees were planted; we celebrate that Peter led a tree-planting initiative that planted twenty-three trees. That may sound like semantics, but I assure you, the processes in place that create those two different headlines are very different.

If you are operating a ministry to marginalized neighbors, you can use the principle of cerebrating individual agency as the driver of change as your litmus test to see if you are following Jesus in his ministry—are you bringing holistic restoration and activation to a real person with a real name? Do your systems, processes, and measurements support such an endeavor? Are you moving people from a number to a hero of their story of development?

If the answer is no, do not beat yourself up, but make one small change today. You can apply this, regardless of your position on your organizational chart, because all it really takes is seeing a real person among the faceless crowd.

Yet! In the way of Jesus, we cannot forsake the ingrained systems … as much as we (I) may want to. We must be present in the "synagogues and temples," build relationships with the "scribes, Pharisees, Sadducees, priests, and teachers of the Law." Christians need to be the light and yeast in these spaces. Why? Because people are there; and where people are, the body of Christ is called to be living and active.

What does that look like in practice? Here is an example from one of our failures and how we would have adjusted under the new-wine-old-wineskins application.

When we started our neighborhood initiative, there was a strong neighborhood association in place. (Strong in the sense of numbers and presence.) When we kicked off the initiative, the leader of the association asked several new people to get involved, essentially doubling the number of people participating in the leadership and decision-making process. New wine, old wineskins. It was an unmitigated disaster, with one of those new leaders seeking an official vote of "no confidence" in the president within seven months. It was a surreal experience for me as someone new to the work and naively thinking we would all hold hands in harmony as we overturned generational poverty and systemic injustice together.

There were a ton of learned leadership lessons—the importance of team-building and honoring past leadership among them—but maybe the simplest was the application of Jesus' parable for effective change. We could have avoided many of the pitfalls faced by merely starting a second group and giving it a new title. New wine, new wineskins. Let the old guard do their thing, unleash the new energy, and figure out over time how the two groups interact and interface with one another. This echoes Acts 6, where the Twelve addressed how to serve the widows by appointing the Seven. Their solution allowed both groups to function. If we had taken that approach, it could have saved us some heartbreak and lost time.

Many old systems have been corrupted by power. Many old systems are ineffective, inefficient, and full of so much bureaucracy and red tape that you cannot begin to accomplish through them what their purpose intends. And yet, many people depend on these systems. Many people who work in and through them are well-intentioned, high-capacity, and desire to love their fellow humans. I was severely challenged by following Jesus to not forsake these existing systems, but instead start new systems that can travel alongside the old, bringing new life and opportunity, while caring for and being present in the old, in order to love everyone well. Where can you and your organization be wise to start small, fresh, and new initiatives, while loving your community through what already exists? What might it look like to bring the "Yes," of personal transformation that becomes the "and" of societal change?

PART THREE

THE POWER
OF ABCD

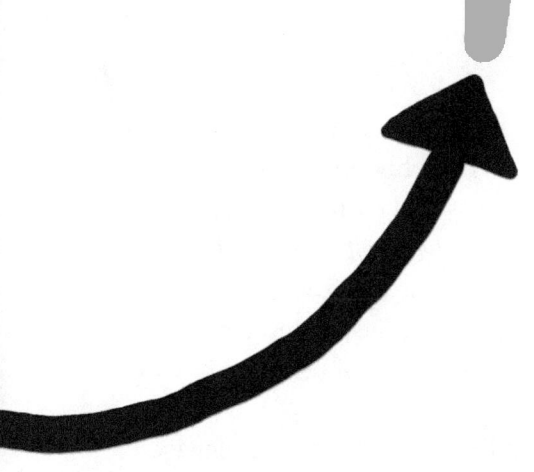

9

LOVE YOUR NEIGHBORHOOD

If you've stuck with me this far, hopefully you've been convinced that neighborhood revitalization is indeed ministry to marginalized neighbors in the way of Jesus and that this is a ministry God's people should participate in.

What I want to do now is break this down in a more practical way. At the organization I work for, we have developed Love Your Neighborhood (LYN)—a framework for community engagement with an accompanying toolkit for practices. I've heard it said there are three aspects to any successful transformative endeavor: inspiration, skill, and tools. Inspiration serves as the catalyst and motivator when energy wanes, skill is the expertise needed to execute the work it takes to actualize the vision, and good tools make the work easier and help you accomplish action in a sustainable way. When these three elements are present, change can occur over time.

In this vein, we developed the Love Your Neighborhood framework for resident-rooted neighborhood revitalization.

Just as a reminder: Neighborhood revitalization is the overarching process of actively improving the quality of life of an under-resourced or disinvested neighborhood by addressing neighbors' lived experiences—e.g., housing, education, infrastructure, safety. Asset-based community development (ABCD) is one approach to neighborhood revitalization. ABCD recognizes that a deficit-based approach has not been successful in eliminating generational poverty, and instead aims to build on the latent and existing asset within a community in order to bring about sustainable change from within. Love Your Neighborhood is the specific approach we take in neighborhood revitalization, built on the foundational concepts of ABCD, with a particular emphasis on resident engagement and incorporating practices from the ministry of Jesus for the restoration and activation of marginalized neighbors. We see neighbors, created in the image of God, as the greatest asset to this work. We want to see them activated to be part of ushering in God's kingdom in their neighborhood.

What you'll find below is an outline for how you can engage in this work. The first three phases are aimed at catalyzing engagement, and the last two phases attempt to move neighbors from engagement to ownership.

Throughout this work, there are three basic players involved:

- Residents—the neighbors who live within the geographical boundaries of the focus area. They are the heart, soul, and purpose of any LYN initiative. It is their vision, voice, engagement, and agency we seek to recognize, resource, and empower. If you are not involving residents at the center of the change process, you may be doing community development, but you are not doing LYN.

- Lead agency partner—any group or organization willing to take on the ten-year commitment. Our recommendation is that this should be a neighborhood-based organization (NBO) already rooted in the community. They are responsible for deploying any personnel and/or operational budget to keep the initiative moving forward ... at the speed of neighbors. Sometimes this role is described as the "backbone," which I like, because the backbone is unseen yet enables the rest of the body to operate.

- Stakeholders—anyone from outside the focus area willing to invest in neighbors' vision for change. Many of the goods, resources, capital, and services that neighbors require to effect change are found in nonprofits, city governments, churches, and individuals that are not explicitly in the geographical focus area. In order to bring that investment into the neighborhood, we build relationships with stakeholders (just like we do with neighbors) and invite them to participate, as long as they honor the resident-centric approach.

As mentioned in previous chapters, commitment is really important—if you're going to empower your neighbors for holistic transformation, you need to walk with them for years, not a few weeks or months. Are you ready to make a ten-year commitment to these neighbors and this neighborhood? There is nothing magical or prescriptive about ten years, but it does carry with it a sense of weight and long-term intention. Neighbors living in disinvested areas are used to being the focus of some outsiders' new initiative or pet project. Such projects and initiatives usually start with a burst of energy, then quickly fade, leaving neighbors behind and the neighborhood in much the same state—only with thicker skin, more apathy, and heightened cynicism for the next over-promised and under-delivered initiative. For anyone starting out on this journey, I would encourage committing first to a period of discernment where you prayerfully consider whether your team/church/ministry is committed to this work for the long term. The Discovery Assessment—a tool we created to see if you are ready to start a Love Your Neighborhood initiative today—is available in appendix one. It explores foundational elements, underlying motivation, current contextual understanding, and existing relationships, and it gauges momentum. The completed assessment, reflection, and evaluation help neighborhood-based organizations identify gaps and plan a path forward to begin implementation of neighborhood revitalization.

Phase 1: Listening and Engagement (1 Year)

The first phase is what we call "listening and engagement." Spending a significant time listening to residents forces you to slow down, meet neighbors, and develop relationships. It also helps you to acquire large amounts of qualitative data rooted in the residents' voices that becomes, alongside relationships with neighbors, the foundation of the neighborhood initiative.

We use two formal listening tools:

- SWOT Analysis—a classic listening tool, simply asks respondents to identify the strengths, weaknesses, opportunities and threats of the neighborhood. We've recently begun using SOAR, which takes a more positive spin (strengths, opportunities, aspirations, and results).
- Influencer Interviews—a set of five questions following an appreciative inquiry approach (asking about good things), designed for anyone who can bring their influence to the change initiative.[1]

You can use whatever listening tools are appropriate for your setting. The important part is to collect as much listening data as you can.

Alongside listening, the major work of this first phase is simply meeting neighbors in every shape, form, and fashion, and through any means possible. Here are some of the ways we go about meeting neighbors:

- Join, attend, and participate in the neighborhood association
- Throw parties in the neighborhood—food, fun, and festivities
- Join the neighborhood school's PTA
- Prayer-walk every street/block in the neighborhood monthly
- Do pop-up experiments
- Serve through local nonprofits that are active in the neighborhood

We like to recommend setting a goal for how many neighbors you will meet in this first phase—for example, 10 percent of the adult population in your geographical focus area. We pulled that number from movement dynamic studies that argue you can begin to influence culture at 10 percent saturation. As an example, our area has around 1,400 residents

---

[1] For a list of "appreciative inquiry" questions, see Catherine Moore, "119+ Appreciative Inquiry Interview Questions and Examples," *Positive Psychology.com*, https://positivepsychology.com/appreciative-inquiry-questions.

over eighteen years of age, so we set a goal to meet 140 neighbors in our first year. We got to 108. The goal pushed us to keep getting out there and held us accountable to doing the connection work.

When we say "met," we mean something different than waving "Hi" and counting in our heads. In order to say we met a neighbor, they have to know something (anything) about the Love Your Neighborhood initiative and agree to exchange contact information. If we are out and about and the conversation is going well, then it could be something as simple as saying, "Hey, we are a group of neighbors coming together to make positive change in the neighborhood. If you want to be connected and stay in the loop, will you fill out a connection card?" If they say yes and fill out that card, that equates to one neighbor met.

In terms of timelines, we have often made this first phase a full year. It's easy to want things to move much more quickly, but taking the time to fully listen to neighbors—and lots of them—is an important foundation to lay before the steps of the next phases.

Of course, there is much more you could and should do in this first phase. There is no end to the possibilities. But if you do nothing else, this is the bare necessity—meet neighbors and listen to them. Collect qualitative data through tools like the SWOT analysis or influencer interviews and begin building relationships through resident engagement.

If you get through that, congratulations! It truly is an accomplishment.

Phase 2: Alignment (6–9 Months)

Now you are ready for the second phase: alignment. I'm going to explain more about the philosophy behind this approach in the next chapter, but here I want to give details of how we practice alignment through our Love Your Neighborhood ministry.

Alignment is done through the publication of the neighborhood's planned change document. This is sometimes called the quality-of-life plan in ABCD. We call ours a "Love Your Neighborhood Vision for

Change." The important part is to collect and publicly share desires, based on what's been learned from listening to residents' voices, for other neighbors to join and contribute to, and for the wider community to be able to invest in.

When we began our lead agency work in the neighborhood, we published a quality-of-life plan because that is what you are "supposed to do" in ABCD. It was a sixty-page document with six priority areas and ninety strategic action goals—a very impressive plan, which I carried around for a couple years in a very impressive binder, showing neighbors who were not very impressed. Its inaccessibility to neighbors and the wider community is why we pivoted to adopt the Love Your Neighborhood framework. This framework is simple—all the content fits in a slim brochure—and is whittled down to three buckets of five actionable projects each.

Through our working experience in four different neighborhood revitalization efforts, we felt confident that we could create three broad categories that all neighbors everywhere care about and that contribute to quality-of-life: 1) livability, 2) youth and lifelong learning, 3) neighboring and community. As an added bonus (thanks to a moment of pure inspiration from my teammate), the categories start with L, Y, and N—just like Love Your Neighborhood. Here's how we described these three areas:

- Livability: This includes everything that makes a neighborhood livable—housing, parks, and green spaces; sidewalks and infrastructure; business and economic development; jobs, etc. This is a big category and is typically the focus of community development efforts. It is indeed very important.
- Youth and lifelong learning: In every neighborhood initiative I have ever been a part of, residents express a desire to see the next generation win. It is one of the things that keeps my hope for humanity alive. Interestingly (at least to me), there is almost an equally prevalent desire to have access to growth opportunities for adults. Therefore, we collapsed these two under the idea of anything that helps people learn and grow.

LOVE YOUR NEIGHBORHOOD

Join our resident-led initiative for positive and sustainable change

LIVABILITY

Enhance the holistic health and well-being of neighborhood residents

- Build a healthy mix of housing options while repairing and rehabbing existing housing stock

- Expand current green space to host recreational sports, exercise groups, family gatherings, and community interaction

- Develop an entrepreneurship ecosystem from within that is inclusive of community residents

- Ensure pedestrian and bicycle-friendly development that blends residential, commercial, cultural, and industrial uses

- Create attractions within the neighborhood that draw people in, become a destination for the larger community, and increase fun and pride for neighbors

- Access to healthy and nutritious food options

YOUTH & LIFELONG LEARNING

Provide access to a rich array of lifelong learning opportunities for all ages

- Create opportunities for children (ages 0–5) to increase success in school and life by obtaining skills and reaching learning benchmarks

- Support the Southside Stars Youth Zone—a resident-led movement providing wrap-around services helping youth in the neighborhood discover their passion and develop a unique pathway to success for each youth

- Empower and resource neighborhood youth during their transitional years from late teens to early adulthood by building mentoring relationships

- Bring existing or create new lifelong learning opportunities—like financial literacy, job fairs, and parenting classes—to neighborhood residents designed uniquely for them

- Connect neighbors to groups, classes, and a social environment that care for all of a person, including social, emotional, trauma, physical, etc.

NEIGHBORING & COMMUNITY

Build a connected community where every person can thrive in dignity

- Create unique neighborhood communication that captures the story of real people and shares the hopes, dreams, and passion of residents within the community

- Install interactive art throughout the neighborhood that contributes to overall beautification and promotes connection between neighbors

- Develop an urban canopy from ground to sky that is pleasing to the eye, provides environmental education, and sparks conversation among neighbors

- Promote natural interactions by improving the built environment, including trail connectivity projects that create walkable corridors and encourage natural interactions

- Design a digital resource that collects neighborhood assets and encourages residents to share their skills, gifts, talents, and resources to help their neighbors

- Neighboring and community: Neighbors seem to always recount the days when everyone on the block knew each other, kids played freely, and they could walk next door to borrow a cup of sugar—even if they never actually experienced it! This stems from humanity's desire to belong and to be a part of a community where they feel like they fit.

You can populate these three categories with five projects in any number of ways: with a representative leadership team from the neighborhood that incorporates the year of listening data; with a facilitated community visioning session; through a series of focus groups; or by using whatever your preferred vehicle is for collecting and capturing residents' voices.

In the end, you should have fifteen or so aspirational goals, projects, and initiatives that neighbors can work on in the next two to three years. The diagram on the previous page shows what came out of our neighborhood.

The aim is that this plan reflects the desires of neighbors, incorporating their goals into actionable steps. It's useful to be able to communicate this to neighbors, but it's also important for the team to be able to use this as a guide to ensure that activities and plans actually line up with what residents want. Also, neighbors are the key to enacting change … and they're not going to be enthusiastic to get involved with implementing actions that aren't reflective of their goals in the first place. Use this plan to ensure that actions are aligned with neighbors' perspectives and engagement.

Phase 3: Action (2 Years)

After you have alignment, it's time for the really fun part: action! This is when transformational change comes to the neighborhood—when you take action on the things neighbors said they wanted to see. It's not rocket-science, and it's fun.

It's also difficult.

I have found that the Action phase is where many neighborhood initiatives begin to die. Just when you would think people would be excited to see their vision come to life, it's at the implementation phase when initiatives often falter. There are many complexities as to why this happens, but here are some of my personal observations about the causes:

- Taking any action requires investment and dedication; it's sometimes more than people are willing to give.
- Creating something from nothing isn't easy! Layer in societal issues like generational poverty and systemic injustices, and you have plenty of barriers.
- Generating genuine community is hard, and accomplishing things by yourself is hard. This is a bad combination.
- Sharing ideas and dreaming about possibilities is fun. Doing the laborious, grinding work of pulling those concepts into reality is not something everyone is willing to invest in.
- Because big dreams are fun, we often miss out on the most successful way to see change occur, and that is through an accumulation of many small actions that produce momentum.

Whatever the reason(s)—or for all the reasons—the actual doing of the thing is where many great ideas for change perish. As lead agency, or backbone support, for the neighborhood initiative, it is incumbent on you to be the steadying force that methodically moves action forward responsibly, meaning you should invest in neighbors not projects. Only move when neighbors are in the center of the work, and discern through relationship when and how to accomplish tasks under the larger action items.

When we think about action, there are four basic concepts we put into practice:

Direct investment to neighbors. Every year, we open up a pool of funds for neighbors to take quick-win action. There is an application process and selection committee so that things are above board, but the basic idea is that any resident can apply for funding ($250–$1,000) to do a project that improves quality of life in the neighborhood. The only "string" attached to the funding is providing a photo of the completed project. As an added bonus, the photos help us tell the story of change over the years.

We are working on more ways for neighbors to receive direct investments. UpTogether has found major returns on investment when giving small amounts of money to neighbors,[2] connecting them to peers also trying to improve their lives, and then believing in them—not managing their spending in any way. This not only helps people escape poverty but also contributes to a social return on that investment.

LYN action teams. This is the vehicle through which we regularly gather neighbors around a table to move projects forward together. The key word in this is "action." It is not another time to sit around and ideate, discuss what-ifs, or get distracted by new initiatives. We do this in teams because we believe that we can do more, and better, together. The last couple of years we have been opening up a relatively small amount of funds for the action teams to either operate or recruit members, but it is not a prerequisite.[3]

Quick-win projects, goals, and initiatives. This is a broad category that includes any action, big or small, that moves resident-voice priorities forward in the neighborhood. This could look like anything from advocating for the local parks department to install bleachers next to the basketball court, to initiating regular "dumpster days" that help with heavy trash pick-up, to saturating the neighborhood with public art. The key here is that something tangible is happening, action is being taken, momentum is building. Neighbors need to see and believe that things will be different this time.

Stakeholder investments in the neighborhood. While we want neighbors to be the heroes of the story of development, the reality

---

[2]   UpTogether is an innovative approach to economic and social mobility that aims to influence policies and change systems through investing in people by recognizing their autonomy in decision-making. You can find multiple years of their impact reports here: https://www. uptogether.org/impact/. See also, Jesus Gerena, *Family Independence Initiative: Trust and Invest in Families,* 2020, 15.

[3]   For the sake of transparency, it's important to say that we have not been able to get action teams operating since the pandemic. We are undergoing a learning season, believing that the core idea behind action teams is still valid but needing to iterate for the future. We are asking this question: "How do people want to come together to make change in their community?"

is that many community partners have access to resources that can help bring transformational change on a shortened timeline. Especially where there is mission alignment, we invite nonprofits, churches, civic organizations, and more to bring their programming, capital, goods, and services to the neighborhood to contribute to the resident-voiced vision for change. The best organizations do this through relational proximity to neighbors; but, in lieu of that, we are more than happy to be the bridge to land these resources responsibly in the neighborhood.

For example, when we kicked off our neighborhood initiative in 2017, safety was a high priority voiced by neighbors. It went in the plan, but not much happened for a while. The issues seemed too complex and out of the control of neighbors. Thankfully, one of our neighborhood leaders had an idea of how to take a relatively small action that could contribute to the overall safety of the neighborhood. She gathered a few neighbors, assigned us streets and alleys, and over the next few weeks we documented every light pole and dark spot in the neighborhood. Compiling all the data, she then took a map of every dark spot or light that wasn't working to our local power company and asked them to replace the lights. Within days, all of the burned-out or defective lights were replaced.

The Importance of Flex

You may be wondering about the timeline for each of these phases. Although it's good to set goals and deadlines to keep momentum, it's often impossible to prescribe how long each phase should take—and that can lead to pushing things forward too quickly.

Forward movement through the phases should be done with an honest assessment of the quality of relationships with neighbors and how they are engaging in the change process. We have coined a phrase, "Move at the speed of the neighborhood." In the first three years of our neighborhood initiative, we experienced a rather ugly blow-up between residents on our leadership team, as well as (hopefully) a once-in-a-generation global pandemic. As hard as it was for me to slow our initiative down, it was the only responsible thing to do in order to keep the change rooted in residents themselves. We had to rebuild the leadership team and reengage neighbors, which pushed back our timelines. That might not be the story of your neighborhood. Maybe you have been rooted in your neighborhood for many years already and have rich relational equity with residents. You might be able to move forward faster. Every neighborhood and neighborhood-based organization is different. What's important is that you're true to your unique situation and flexible to what might be happening in your context.

Phase 4: Ownership (3–4 Years)

One issue with neighborhood revitalization efforts can be that the lead agency builds dependency on itself. Then, if that agency leaves for some reason, the work disappears. That's why, at this stage in our framework, we're aiming for a shift from broad engagement to ownership. We start focusing on individual stories of transformation—because these restored and activated neighbors will restore our neighborhoods. Here are three ways that we cultivate ownership.

Resident stories. There may be no better way to build relational trust with a neighbor than to sit down with them for an hour and ask them to share their story. This serves as a way to build deeper relationship with a neighbor and develop a lead list of potential "owners." Remember, at this point you are years into the LYN initiative, so it is not like you are talking with a stranger. However, now, instead of learning their perspective on the neighborhood (year-one listening), you are getting to know them as an individual. Once the stories are collected and permission granted, begin sharing real stories of transformation that become positive deviations other residents can recognize, learn from, and be inspired and encouraged by. These stories, compiled and shared, are the actualized embodiment of asset-based community. In terms of transitioning the movement to full ownership by neighbors, the stories show that the community is already building itself from the inside out.

Flourishing neighbors. There are many ways you can apply the general principles of helping neighbors create their own customized pathway to flourishing. We utilize a "neighbor navigator" concept, offer The Promise initiative (detailed in chapter five), and do wrap-around care for children and families. UpTogether uses a journaling experience to create peer social capital. We don't want to get to the end of a ten-year investment in a place and its people without seeing neighbors who have moved toward restoration and activation. Having flourishing neighbors leads to greater ownership, as these residents feel empowered to be part of seeing change in their neighborhood. We begin to see the "Yes, and" dynamic at work (see chapter eight).

Transformational projects. We want to focus our lead agency actions on highly visible, tangible projects that bring real change to the physical environment and lived experience of neighbors. We want neighbors to see old dilapidated and abandoned commercial properties transformed into shared-use kitchens run by local residents; empty lots that used to have trash and overgrown weeds transformed into new affordable homes; parks and green spaces that felt run down and unsafe transformed with play equipment that neighbors chose themselves. We want them to proudly say, "Things are different this time, and I helped!" These transformational projects are done in partnership with residents and are aligned to their voiced and documented priorities and goals for their own neighborhood.

Phase 5: Sustainability (2 Years)

In these latter years, we are looking to shift from ownership to sustainability. How can our initiatives empower neighbors to no longer be dependent on a lead agency? It can be a scary thought for the lead agency to "go away," as the very sustainability of the neighborhood revitalization may depend on your existence. I understand and feel this! But I also believe in the axiom that there is always a place in a healthy organization for someone who replaces themselves. I believe this is true of neighborhoods as well.

One of the ways we aim to move toward sustainability is by "hitting the flywheel of neighborhood revitalization."

My coworker reminds me that "hitting the flywheel" is not common parlance. The concept came from Jim Collins in his book *Good to Great*,[4] looking at what separates hyper-successful leaders and businesses. The idea is that anything worth doing well typically takes a massive amount of work. It is a big, heavy thing to move. It simply cannot and will not budge by one giant push. Instead, you move one notch at a time, keep gaining speed by the internal momentum, and eventually you build up to where the flywheel is going on its own with only a small push every now and again due to the established motion.

Getting the gigantic flywheel of neighborhood revitalization going is really the purpose of the Love Your Neighborhood initiative. The overall project is a behemoth. However, it can be turned if it has the proper foundation: execution of listening and engagement, alignment, and action. Momentum is built by achieving enough micro-actions and wins that energize the community and produce stories. These stories then lead to more micro-actions and wins, further energizing the community and generating more stories. Ideally, this cycle continues until the neighborhood revitalization efforts are spinning on their own and are largely, and gloriously, out of your control.

We have boiled down the flywheel effect to four key components, or levers, we want to always be hitting—year in, year out. The actual actions you would take under these headings depend entirely on your context, but these are the bare essentials we have gleaned that need to be always present. We call these our core processes, and they happen

---

4   Jim Collins, *Good to Great: Why Some Companies Make the Leap ... and Others Don't* (New York, NY: HarperBusiness, 2001).

from day one until we hand over the initiative. This is how we build and evaluate sustainability:

- Resident engagement: Are we engaging residents in the change process?
- Quality-of-life accomplishment: Is quality of life improving for neighbors?
- Communication: Is that story of change being communicated to neighbors and the wider community?
- Stakeholder engagement: Are stakeholders investing in the resident-voice vision for change?

Resident Engagement

Resident engagement has to remain the center of the work. Are we meeting new neighbors and helping residents move toward deeper engagement? That is the only question we ultimately care about. To that end, we created a resident engagement database (similar to a customer retention management system) that tracks our relationship to individual neighbors. We came up with our own four categories—Met, Aligned, Connected, Leader—to measure resident engagement. This is the work of year one, continued and expanded. We are constantly meeting neighbors and helping them move forward.

Quality-of-Life Accomplishment

Remember the alignment document? Well, are you actually seeing these resident-voiced projects and initiatives become a reality? This is the more tangible side of the work, and you can track this easily by simply documenting execution and delivery of anything and everything that contributes to a rise in quality of life in the neighborhood—especially when it aligns with the planned-change document. Side note: Often these items are largely out of your control, so we encourage you to track your inputs as a lead agency if you want to make a case for the efficacy of your role. For example, we cannot control whether a local artist creates a mural in the neighborhood, but we can control (to a certain degree) whether we connected a local artist to our arts council. The actual mural is documented in hindsight when it is installed. The connections we make are tracked in real-time and are "proof of a job well done."

Communication

When we talk about communication, we think in terms of two overarching concepts: communication infrastructure and storytelling. The communication infrastructure is how the neighborhood revitalization initiative actively communicates to neighbors—this would include things like SMS, social media, website, mailers, etc. Just as important is the storytelling aspect—what narratives are neighbors and the wider community hearing about your neighborhood? How can you convey the story you want to tell? We produce one or two "neighborhood stories" videos every year,[5] but this goes much deeper. Find ways to encourage advocacy, language, and new reporting of the story of your neighborhood. You have to relentlessly communicate a different perspective in order to shape and change the culture, both internally and externally.

Stakeholder Engagement

Finally, we have stakeholder engagement. We have found that the vast majority of resident-voiced desires and priorities can be met in one form or another through the services, goods, programs, etc., that are provided by various nonprofits, churches, civic agencies, and businesses. The goal is to redirect these resources to the neighborhood and into the flow of neighbors' lives. Similar to our resident engagement, we track the relationships we are developing with these

---

[5] You can see an example of one of our neighborhood stories here: https://vimeo.com/678213492.

organizations in a database, following the same definitions of Met, Aligned, Connect, and Leader. Especially where there is alignment between our resident-voiced mission and the stakeholder's mission, we try to be the bridge to activate a mutually beneficial connection.

We are still living out our commitment to neighborhood revitalization through Love Your Neighborhood—we haven't done ourselves out of a job yet. But my hope is that, as we continue to hit the flywheel and see residents empowered to bring about change in their own neighborhood, we will eventually be surplus to requirement. We see the treasure in the residents who we meet day in and day out, and that gives me great hope that they can bring about the ongoing, sustainable change that's needed to see holistic transformation in our neighborhood.

There is a forgotten area in the center of our city called Jacobsville Park. Natural geographical boundaries block it off to the west, infrastructure developments are to the north and south, and classic sprawl dominates the east—which led to a rather large urban core neighborhood that had experienced decades of disinvestment. However, the community had many existing assets—the largest city park in the area, the third-oldest baseball field in America (used in *A League of Their Own!*), three large employers including a global plastics power, and an historic Main Street with a few locally famous restaurants. The city, to their credit, had plans to bring redevelopment to the area, and they decided to make them coincide with a "formal" resident initiative.

The likely lead organization in that community was the local Habitat for Humanity affiliate. They had led the most recent neighborhood revitalization effort in our city, and their director was a bit of an expert in our area. She also just happened to be part of our local church and motivated by her faith. What's more, she had led our church to kick off a neighborhood revitalization effort across the bridge in her hometown, which is where I happened to cut my teeth in neighborhood work—door knocking, listening to residents, volunteering in working groups—forever revolutionizing how I understood Jesus' ministry to marginalized neighbors.

As the Jacobsville initiative got underway, we wanted to participate as a newly planted church, and so I helped mobilize some of our small groups to be volunteers in the listening kickoff. We became the neighbors that helped gather most of the resident-voiced qualitative data. Unfortunately, my friend and mentor who had started out leading the initiative got pulled off the project and a different neighborhood-based organization was given the lead role. But, the new community mobilizer, who was not a Christian, was very impressed by our church's willingness to be involved and with our ability to mobilize volunteers into the work. We won her over and immediately became a trusted partner in the neighborhood initiative.

On the first mobilization listening day I met Melissa, who lived in the neighborhood. Melissa was in my canvassing group. On sight, Melissa might have been considered "rough": she had many tattoos, used a walker because of a degenerative spinal disorder, and typically had several of her little ones hanging off of her. Melissa was someone you would stereotypically expect to see living in "that neighborhood," and someone I probably would have felt uncomfortable approaching had we not been placed together; it was obvious in one moment that our lives had two very different trajectories. My solidly middle-class upbringing in a relatively healthy and loving family, and my subsequent life experiences, were not the same as those that had shaped and formed Melissa. But thank God we were placed together, because we clicked right away. What's more, any stereotypical facade—going either direction—faded away immediately. Melissa was intelligent, well-spoken, passionate about seeing change in her neighborhood, and she was doing something about it already. On that particular day, we collected six or seven SWOT reports from neighbors, but the lasting discovery for me was in how Melissa reinforced my transformed view of neighbors from being people of need to people of infinite worth. Melissa was a natural leader—an asset to her neighborhood.

About six months into the initiative, the community mobilizer called our church and asked if we would be willing and able to donate $10,000 for new playground equipment for a small pocket park in the neighborhood. It would provide a quick win and a way to build some early momentum. By that time, I had been doing neighborhood work for a whopping eighteen months and had read *Toxic Charity*, so I felt like quite the expert (oh the naiveté!). I responded, "We would love to help out in the park, but we want to engage neighbors in the process and engage our church in the work." She said, "Okay," and we were off!

I made up a quick four-question survey in order to ask neighbors what they wanted to see in the park, gathered up a few small groups as a volunteer base, and then went door-knocking to listen to neighbors in a five-block radius around the park. We had about fifteen people, sent out in twos and threes, and collected forty-eight responses. A pretty good haul of qualitative data—which I did not really know at the time. I just knew that I wanted to do what residents said in order for them to feel valued by looking out their window and seeing the changes to the park that they expressly wanted.

What I had not expected was to learn an invaluable lesson about why you listen. We anticipated hearing that residents wanted things like basketball courts, swing sets, benches, community gardens (people love community gardens!)—and we did hear some of those things here and there; but what came out overwhelmingly was how they wanted the park to *feel*. Forty-six of the forty-eight respondents mentioned safety in one form or another. Neighbors did not feel safe using the park—not because of the equipment, but because of the presence of crime—so to them, it did not really matter what was in it. *Wow!*

So, we began to do our due diligence, and we went to the first place I could think of that might be able to help us create safety—the Evansville Police Department. Armed with our resident-listening data, we met with the neighborhood precinct and asked for their expertise and partnership. In this particular instance, the EPD was great. They agreed to increase patrol around the park and gave us a short list of ways that we could actually contribute to improving safety: add lighting and new signage, do a regular litter pick-up, and put some sort of barrier around the park. Basically, they said the area looked like a vacant lot, and people were treating it that way. It needed to become a park. The final thing they mentioned, fully recognizing it was a "chicken or egg" situation, was that the best way to increase safety is simply to get people to use the park and have friendly neighbors and activities in the park that will displace unfriendly and seedy activity.

We didn't know how to make all that happen, but we wanted to take a small, faithful step forward. First, we created a "border project" for our annual big serve day. We bought two hundred bushes to create a natural hedge around the park. Our church always came out in big numbers on those serve days, but we had several projects going throughout the neighborhood and a lot of bushes to plant, so I was a bit anxious that we would get it done in our three-hour work window. It took forty-five minutes. People were working hard!

On that same day, one of the projects was supporting Melissa's initiative, Throw Your Worries Away. Melissa had started a simple trash pick-up initiative in order to beautify her neighborhood. But more importantly for her, it provided context and opportunity to meet her neighbors, have conversations on front lawns and porches, and build a sense of community in her neighborhood. Since the shrub-planting went so quickly, Melissa got an extra influx of volunteer power. I have a great picture from the day where Melissa is with her family standing in front of a trailer, smiling ear-to-ear, with eighty-plus bags of trash collected. The most they had ever collected before was three! Again, numbers were not the point for Melissa, connections with neighbors were; but she still thought it was amazing that so many people would come out to support her and that they could make such a difference in three hours.

Also, on that day a fourteen-year-old Boy Scout named Dane was part of the hedge-planting team. As he volunteered, he got a vision for his Eagle Scout project—he wanted to bring the biggest, best, most state-of-the-art playground equipment to this small, nearly forgotten pocket park in the middle of a forgotten urban core neighborhood, so neighbors would feel valued and loved. By the end of the day, he had already worked out the plan in his mind and started having conversations. This young man did not lack for self-starting or capacity.

Outside of the big serve day, my small group started hanging out in the park semi-regularly. We would bring a grill and do impromptu cookouts, perform live music, or do a clothing giveaway—really anything that would generate positive energy, bring neighbors out to interact, and give us the opportunity to build relationships with real people. Over time, I was getting to know Melissa more and more. She served as our liaison on the ground, the expert on what was happening in the neighborhood, and she opened doors into the lives of neighbors and their experience. We helped her with another dream of hers— throwing a big blowout block party (called Flower Power) for her neighbors. Eventually, Melissa joined our small group, was baptized,

baptized her daughters, joined and eventually became a leader in our local church, and most importantly (to me), became my close friend and sister in Christ.

In the meantime, Dane was deep into his Eagle Scout project. It is truly impossible to relate all the twists and turns of that story. I freely admit that I even checked out of the process at one point. It was a long, laborious, drawn-out, frustrating process for all involved. But I want to honor Dane and his family by stating that I have never personally experienced more perseverance, ingenuity, relentless problem-solving, optimism, and courage in the face of long odds. It is remarkable that the project got done at all, let alone at the size and scope it did. This teenager and his family willed this project into reality. The end result, after two insanely challenging years, is that Dane had brought over $150,000 of investment into Jacobsville Park and delivered exactly what he set out to provide: the best park equipment in the city. It was the largest Eagle Scout project ever. Moreover, he organized the project in such a way that neighbors could come out and volunteer, engage and participate in the work, and build their own community from the inside out.

Melissa and her girls were ever-present during the buildout, and it is one of my most precious memories seeing her kids be the first to play on that new equipment.

What started as a $10,000 request turned into $200,000 of investment due to the engagement of neighbors and activating faith in the community. Most important of all, real relationships were built. The kingdom of God was revealed, and neighbors received a foretaste of the completed works of Jesus Christ, where we can genuinely experience heaven in the eternal moment of now.

10
LISTEN-ALIGN-
ACT-MEASURE

In the previous chapter we looked at a framework for neighborhood revitalization which details how you can begin to see holistic transformation for neighbors, with neighbors as the central focus of goals, engagement, and empowerment to enact change.

At this point, I want to dig down further into why these practices are vital and a reflection of God's heart for the marginalized, as well as an imitation of Jesus' ways in enacting transformational change.

While some of the practices God called Israel to participate in for holistic restoration to marginalized neighbors are still remarkably relevant and applicable today—such as fair lending and restorative justice—most simply do not have a direct connection to the lived experience of our marginalized neighbors. Gleaning is not an option in most urban core neighborhoods; we do not follow the Hebraic festival calendar; and we don't sacrifice animals at the temple. Marrying next of kin when widowed would be straight-up crazy!

However, even in these outmoded practices, there are kernels of connection to many solid principles. It is worth our time to think about how we might apply those principles to our settings.

This is what Jesus did—how he fulfilled God's ministry to marginalized neighbors—even as he went toward his ultimate mission. In the scenes of Jesus reclining at the table with tax collectors and sinners, we see echoes of Deuteronomy 16:11–14—God's call to include the orphans, widows, and sojourners (OWS) at the festivals. In Jesus standing over the woman accused of adultery, we see a powerful demonstration of his commitment to protecting the vulnerable. In the turning over of the tables at the temple, we see Jesus bringing Scripture to life, as he delivers justice to the corrupt lending systems the Jewish people were explicitly warned against.

Following Jesus into his practices, learning about Israel as God's instrument and vehicle for restoration, and shaping these in your own approach, is a great way to allow Jesus to inform and transform your ministry.

There are four basic practices that are central to asset-based community development that we see clearly in the life of Jesus. For our purposes in neighborhood revitalization, we utilize them as the standard operating procedure for ministry to marginalized neighbors: Listen, align, act, and measure.

Listen

Jesus was famous for asking questions of everyone, but this had special significance for marginalized neighbors. Here are some of the questions he put to them:

- Do you believe that I am able to heal you? (Matt. 9:28)
- What were you discussing along the way? (Mark 9:33)
- Why are you afraid, you of little faith? (Matt. 8:26)
- Why do you ask me what is good? (Matt. 19:17)
- Where is your husband? (John 4:16)
- If I have told you earthly things and you do not believe, how can you believe if I tell you heavenly things? (John 3:12)
- Where are your accusers? (John 8:10)

There are many good reasons to ask questions when interacting with people. It is a great teaching method, as self-realization is more powerful than being told the answers, and this even works for rhetorical questions where the answer is a given. Asking questions gives you a chance to hear the other person's heart, learn what perspectives they hold, and allows you time to process and gauge your own response. We would all do well to ask a few more questions.

However, with marginalized neighbors, *listening* actually becomes ministry. Many marginalized neighbors have had their voices stolen from them. They face discrimination, injustice, bigotry, abuse, etc., on an ongoing basis in their everyday lives. It is a constant weight, which we can never fully understand if we haven't experienced it. We cannot fully understand. But we can listen. We can ask questions and confer dignity and value by that simple act. When we sit down with someone and ask them questions, we activate a forgotten or misplaced person who has been shoved to the margins. We confer the truth that what they have to say really matters.

Listening is integral to the practice of neighborhood revitalization. In our Love Your Neighborhood framework, we suggest a whole year of listening and relationship-building before any public announcement or publication of a plan for change. This is intentional. If you don't have the patience to listen for a year, then you shouldn't get into the neighborhood revitalization game. If you don't have the drive to get out and meet hundreds of neighbors in year one, don't sign on for years two to ten. If you don't believe that residents are the greatest asset in any given community, and therefore you need to hear from them, don't attempt to be part of an asset-based community development.

There are any number of ways to listen—formal and informal. Listening can provide qualitative data that can be analyzed and leveraged as a collective resident-voice for advocacy, and it can serve as a more informal value that permeates everything you do. Here are a few examples from our work:

- Formal listening: In year one of a Love Your Neighborhood initiative, we set a goal to collect a target number of SOAR (strengths, opportunities, aspirations, results) interviews. We collect these throughout the year at meetings, focus groups, door-knocking, and by any other means possible; and then document them for analysis.

- In between formal and informal: You can devise a listening tool at any time you want to discover what you want to learn. This is what we did in the Jacobsville Park story, where we just came up with five questions and then went around talking with neighbors.
- Informal listening: I am always trying to learn and discover more, so at every neighborhood meeting or event I will come prepared with questions—what school did you go to growing up? How did you hear about this event? What would you like to see in the neighborhood? When was the last time you got fresh fruit, and where did you get it from?

Follow in the way of Jesus, and start listening first in your ministry.

Align

Unfortunately, it is the experience of many neighbors that listening is not enough. To illustrate this, I want to briefly tell the story of my friend Lisa:

Lisa is a highly capable, educated, industrious, and relentless person. Her family lives well below the poverty line by lifestyle choice. She quit her job when her triplets were born, and they decided to live off much lower means than the average American family because she wanted to be a homemaker and home-school educator. That choice is how Lisa came to live in our neighborhood—that is where the affordable housing stock was when they were looking to purchase a low-cost home with cash. Lisa is naturally community-minded and grasped the concept and potential of neighborhood revitalization immediately. Because she is a voracious researcher, she learned as much, if not more, about neighborhood work than me in no time flat.

While Lisa chose to live off limited finances, there was abundance in her life in many other areas—certainly in her mindset. She brought this idea of abundance and the principles of ABCD to our initiative as a resident leader. She embodied the we-have-everything-we-need-right-here approach. With the expanded social and financial capital that came through our coordinated work, as well as some early investments from community stakeholders, Lisa catalyzed a housing initiative, started a Youth Zone (loosely based off the Harlem Children's Zone approach), threw block parties, served on the leadership team and influenced decisions positively, and gave her voice as input to the future of our neighborhood. It was inspirational.

Her star was also rising in the wider community of our city. She was invited to give a TEDx talk (she knocked it out of the park) and represented our city at a statewide conference on community development, leading a breakout session on how to engage resident leaders. This led to invitations to boards of nonprofits and seats at tables for city-wide initiatives on poverty alleviation. Lisa felt like this was an opportunity where she could represent the voice of her neighbors, shift the mindsets of decision-makers, and help lead lasting change.

Less than a year later, Lisa was done with all of that larger work, and told me she just wanted to simplify things and get back to working on our neighborhood. Of course, I was ecstatic personally but mournful for the rest of the city. I was also curious as to what had happened. She told me that at those higher levels, she felt like a box that needed to be checked. It was as though they said, "Here is our representative poor person. Let's let her speak, then we can move on with what we already decided to do." They wanted her there so they could show how diverse, equitable, and inclusive they were, without actually giving her any real influence or allowing her to shape decisions. It didn't take her long to comprehend that she was wasting her time. Worse, she was being actively devalued by being "listened" to without bringing any alignment to her voice. Therefore, there was no hope of real action.

While these organizations and initiatives were practicing *listening*, they were not *hearing*.

Alignment, as a practice, serves two main purposes: It 1) shows neighbors that you are hearing what they are saying; and it 2) provides the potential for optimal impact.

1. By organizing formal listening into reports and planned-change documents, you capture and publish to the world the voice of marginalized neighbors. You allow them to inform

and shape what is to be done. This is not directives coming from the outside, initiatives started by detached politicians with agendas, programs started by nonprofits that are built for the organizations that started them, or services offered by social-do-gooders that fit their schedules. It is the voice of the people.

2. Think about a dartboard. You can throw a hundred darts and hit some bullseyes; but, if you create a pipeline that ends at the bullseye and shoot darts through it, you hit 100 bullseyes!

That is the importance of alignment.

Your alignment plan can be written down using something like our Love Your Neighborhood vision for change. It doesn't matter what tool sits in the land between resident voice and community action, but alignment is crucial and often overlooked. Alignment creates the directed purpose at the community level, a shared measurement for success, and a chance for collective action that leads to impact at the community level.

While Jesus certainly never published an alignment document, he was constantly aligning people to the kingdom of God, and his teaching on prayer gives us a glimpse into the ultimate alignment— your kingdom come, your will be done, on earth as it is in heaven (Matt. 6:10). Jesus was playing the game at a different level. The resident voice was his heavenly Father's, and the "alignment document" was Jesus himself, the very Word of God, so all his actions are a foretaste or preview of the kingdom. We continue in that ministry today.

Act

Action at the neighborhood level is a strange beast because, in my experience, it is either the easiest or hardest thing for individuals to do, and therefore it is difficult to execute.

Taking decisive action in anything is a rare gift or skill—natural in some people and needing to be developed through practice in others.

What happens when you get a community of people together to create change is that the "action people" get frustrated by the processes and tend to do their own thing or check-out altogether. What you have left is a bunch of people who either talk a good game but are incapable of action on their own, or people who just want to sit around and complain. This can kill your neighborhood initiative. And it is so frustrating, because you know that everyone wants the same thing—transformational action!

Could you imagine if Jesus had left out action? If he had told the man his sins were forgiven without also telling him to pick up his mat and walk (John 5:8)? If he had told Zaccheaus that salvation had come to his house but then refused to enter it himself and sit at his table (Luke 19:7)? If he had taught the five thousand the words of life but then sent them home with empty bellies (John 6:12)? If he had deemed the lepers clean in spirit but then denied them his physical touch (Mark 1:41)? If he had decried injustice without turning over some tables (Mark 11:15)? If he had called for peace without healing the lopped-off ear of the servant who came to help arrest him (Luke 22:51)? If he had instructed others to forgive sins without going to the cross to reconcile all the marginalized for eternity (John 19:30)?

Words without action don't add up to complete ministry. At least in the way of Jesus.

I want to offer three reasons why I believe action is so vitally important in ministry, specifically to marginalized neighbors:

Marginalized neighbors are used to empty promises. Whether it be from family, government, public services, neighbors, whomever—they have heard over and over again that help is on the way, things are going to be different this time, change is coming, etc., etc. Relief funds during crisis, GED programs, welfare money, the newest federal "zone" designation, and on and on, there is always the next news cycle, political campaign, well-meaning poverty initiative … all of them full of promising language containing all the right things to say. But from a neighbors' perspective, it is a classic case of over-promise, under-deliver. Or no deliver.

Marginalized neighbors need holistic ministry. I know this because we all do! But many of us, living day-to-day above the poverty line do not have as many visible and tangible barriers to loving God with all of our hearts, minds, souls, and strength. While it is relatively easy to take action on bare necessities—food, clothing, and shelter—as important as these are to holistic well-being, they do not create wholeness. That is where things like educational reform, art, leisure activities, access to healthy and nutritious food, music, etc., come into play. In order to bring these into the lives of real people, there must be action! Action moves ideas into reality. Completed action allows a resident to take their neighbor to something, point at a tangible example, and say, "See, things really are different this time."

Ministry to marginalized neighbors is a witness/testimony. Ever wonder why God incessantly reminds Israel to minister to the orphans, widows, and sojourners? Ponder why Jesus spent so much time with those society had deemed the least? I have. Too much maybe. Obviously, there are layered reasons; but I have become convinced that Jesus did this because it is the number one signpost, or heaven-marker, to transcendent reality. Bold statement I know, but think about this: No purely human system would reasonably and logically bring holistic restoration to marginalized people groups. Why would it? Those who hold other worldviews have a very clear internal coherence on what to do with marginalized neighbors:

- Hinduism has the caste system where it is incumbent to the order of things for you to stay on your rung of the ladder.
- Islam easily separates the untouchables as another class to be avoided.
- Communism purposefully sends everyone to the margins in the name of flattening the experience for all.
- Capitalism, in its purest form, places no inherent value on caring for the poor; and since they have nothing to bring to the market, they are pushed to the edges of society.
- While secular humanism typically espouses the Golden Rule (treat others as you would want to be treated), when pressed as to why, the answer gets vague very quickly—there is no real great answer as to why I should love my neighbor instead of leveraging them for personal gain.

I often dream of the church of my city coming together in the name of Jesus to bring wholeness to neighbors and neighborhoods, to bring heaven and earth together, to see restoration and reconciliation occur with no politicking, government assistance, or federal aid. The church of the city, with kingdom resources, in one faith, renewing all the lost and broken places and people of our city. What better witness can there be to the salvific power of God? That would be a testimony that would force the world to look up and wonder what is going on over there! It would move people to see our good works and give glory to God.

Last little side note on action: Action is the most fun! While it may seem like a big step to go from an idea—especially in a community with seemingly little resources and experiencing decades of disinvestment and harmful narratives—toward the tangible delivery of action that accomplishes transformational change, I assure you it is possible. It starts where most things do, with the first faithful step. And along the path toward completion is where all the smiles, laughter, celebrations, and stories occur. Taking action is where you will find the fun!

Measure

I have a love/hate relationship with measurement. The crux of the matter is that I believe we should be faithful and accountable with our kingdom resources as Christians, yet I do not believe our current measurement practices—if they exist at all—have been vetted and filtered through theological reflection and gospel application. In other words, I am in the unenviable position of being an advocate and cynic of measurement.

While you cannot find a clear logic model and measurement system in the life of Jesus presented in the Gospels, I can confidently surmise that Jesus was very concerned with proper stewardship of kingdom resources. This is what the Parable of the Talents (Matt. 25:14–30) is all about, as well as the teaching on the widow's mite (Luke 21:1–4); it is also the focus of large pieces of Jesus' seminal discipleship teaching, the Sermon on the Mount (Matt. 5–7). Jesus' well-documented concern over money was more about idolatry and stewardship of kingdom resources than money itself.

The consistent reference to resources throughout Jesus' ministry is for the purposes of individual and corporate spiritual formation that often takes people away from God instead of toward him. Jesus was shaping a people and community of world changers, and therefore his resourcing the citizens of heaven to be God's missional people for ministries of reconciliation was also a primary concern. There was a practical reason for the constant mentioning of money: When directed to kingdom purposes, money can make the kingdom of God tangible.

There are wide-ranging and divergent opinions on how and what to measure in neighborhood revitalization. A holistic approach to neighborhood revitalization aims for restoration and activation across all aspects of a community, while also addressing generational trends and systemic societal issues, and incorporating traditional community development. When you consider these overlapping realities, the measurement situation can quickly become cloudy.[1] So, I am only going to share what we measure, which is: 1) resident perspective of quality of life; 2) key performance indicators (KPIs) of a healthy neighborhood; and 3) our faithfulness in the work as lead agency. Each of these could be broken down into very lengthy descriptions, but let me summarize.

Resident perspective of quality of life. This is what may be called a "subjective measure," but is central to the efficacy of the work. We want to know if neighbors feel/believe their quality of life is improving. How are residents being affected by the revitalization efforts, and what is their lived experience in the midst of them? We collect this data in survey form. For example, we captured a baseline measurement of residents' perspectives in 2018 and asked the same questions five years later as a follow up in 2023. The questions we ask in the survey are directly tied to the resident-voiced priorities documented in the vision for change plan, as well as their self-reporting in individual flourishing metrics. How are the sidewalks? Do you feel safe? How often do you worry about material needs? Since residents are the center of our work, their perspective is our primary measurement.

---

[1] For a book that is not afraid to dive in to the full complexities, see Bryant L. Myers, *Walking with the Poor*, referenced in chapter two.

Key performance indicators of healthy neighborhoods. As important as resident perspective is, there are more "objective" measures that need to be tracked as well. We want to draw on experts, research, practitioner literature, and best practices to be most effective at loving and serving our neighbors. We can collect and track data over time that point to indicators giving neighbors the best chance to flourish in their neighborhood. Is the housing stock improving? What are the third grade reading levels of neighborhood youth? Has violent crime gone down? These first two measurements ought to work in tandem—if the feeling of safety has lowered, yet violent crime has decreased year over year, we want to explore the reasons why. We also want to correct false narratives, both within and from the wider community, while recognizing and respecting the lived experience of neighbors.

Our faithfulness as lead agency. While we want to see neighbors' quality of life increase and believe that this occurs best when marginalized neighbors themselves are restored and activated into the change process, we cannot force anyone to engage, nor would we want to! What's more, from a faith perspective, we believe that God will bring about kingdom outcomes he desires, and they may not fully align with our limited perspectives and finite timelines. This releasing of the work into the grace gap can be very freeing but also daunting when you have to show funders the efficacy of your work so it can be sustained. So, we track our faithfulness and obedience in the work by creating annual goals, supporting objectives, and action steps around the four Love Your Neighborhood core processes. We do the hard work of getting the water to the feet of Jesus, believing he will turn it into wine!

People of Peace

The key building blocks of listen, align, act, and measure are what make up our work in neighborhood revitalization. But, as mentioned above, we cannot force neighbors to engage with the work—and when your mode of operating is about neighbor-led revitalization, it's not always in our hands to direct what will happen next.

This is where the principle of "people of peace" really helps us out.

In Luke 10, Jesus gives instructions to the seventy-two disciples as they go out to share his good news among the towns and villages. The concept of people or households of peace was the center of the strategy he shared:

> When you enter a house, first say, "Peace to this house." If someone who promotes peace is there, your peace will rest on them; if not, it will return to you. Stay there, eating and drinking whatever they give you, for the worker deserves his wages. Do not move around from house to house.
>
> LUKE 10:5–7 NIV

The idea behind this principle is that, as we go in mission, we should look for "people of peace"—those who welcome us and are open to our message—and when we find them, we should stay with them and allow them to be key operators in the kingdom work we are about. Jesus modeled and practiced this approach throughout his public ministry—he connected with the woman at the well, who was open to his message and became the evangelist to her whole village; and he called out Zacchaeus who immediately opened his home and whose testimony of transformation impacted the community around him. We see this clearly in the first calling of the disciples where Philip chose to follow Jesus and then immediately went and invited Nathaniel to "come and see" (John 1:46). Sometimes it was more of a slow burn of trust building—especially when people had status—as in the cases of Nicodemus (John 3, 7, 19) and Joseph of Arimathea (John 19:38–42).

Jesus' pattern was to prioritize people who would be willing to open up their relational networks, wherever they happened to have influence, so that the gospel could spread more rapidly. This approach was irrespective of formal status or standing, spanning the spectrum of the elite to the disenfranchised to the shamed and outcast to the seemingly inconsequential everyday laborer. The only requirement was reception and opening.

Years ago, I heard someone share the phrase, "Water the green spots." The idea being that instead of pouring water where there is no growth, concentrate your cultivation where green already exists and allow the healthy area to spread. In the arid ground there may or may not be good soil, seeds present, or potential for growth. Watering there, no matter how much and how well, doesn't guarantee a future yield. However, when watering where growth is already proven, chances are good that the healthy growth will spread itself naturally over time into the arid ground. At the very least you will have continued fruit on the proven ground. It's a double win—healthy fruit and expansion of green space.

I have found this to have wide application across many disciplines but none so significant as in relationships. It certainly also applies in discipleship, evangelism, and of course, neighborhood revitalization. You simply cannot have a genuine movement in a resident-led change initiative without being received by neighbors, and without them in turn opening their network. This occurs best when you build genuine trust with a neighbor. Trust is built, at least in part, by investing in them, spending time with them, and resourcing their interests and ideas. It takes time, sometimes years, but when they say, "Hey, you gotta meet …" then you have the potential for multiplication, moving from one investment to the next network branch.

As an outsider—someone not from the neighborhood, race, or socioeconomic background—this opening of networks is the only possibility for relational equity. When LaTreance introduces me to his neighbor, Tashiya introduces me to her brother, and Cord introduces me to other artists he knows, they are taking huge risks because they are vouching for me with their own relational capital. It is a precious resource. In the neighborhood, sometimes this is the best and only capital available to neighbors, and they have spent years, possibly a lifetime, building it up. It is an incredible honor when a person of peace opens up their network to you, putting their chips on the line and placing a bet on you. Be a worthy minister!

In our neighborhood, we have Ms. Edna—the "mom of the block." You know the one. She stands on her front porch during the after-school hours and shepherds kids to their respective homes. She knows everyone by name and is not afraid to call them out, and she has the kids' respect.

There is a backyard where all the retired and unemployed men gather to drink, smoke, play cards, and generally make merry. Any given evening, you can walk by and hear laughter, great discussion, and occasionally see neighbors caring for neighbors in profound ways.

Bryan hangs out at the basketball court several times a week in order to meet young men and have conversations that may turn into a positive, informal, mentoring relationship. A small cadre of neighborhood youth know him and one another.

An intentional urban faith community moved into the neighborhood twelve years ago, and they have been praying for neighbors, rehabbing houses, celebrating feasts, growing produce, and year after year being a positive light in our community.

All of these amazing neighbors, and so many more, have spent years investing in their community, and these investments have returned gains in the form of influence—large and small, individual and community. Each of them, in turn, have opened up their networks to us and the larger neighborhood in order to further the common good and move the vision of the neighborhood forward. And from our perspective, they have fulfilled the ministry of Jesus to marginalized neighbors in tangible ways.

Here are five quick-hit thoughts on combining people of peace and neighborhood revitalization as holistic ministry:

- People of peace are met while *going* (Luke 10:3). People of peace are networked because they are embedded in a community— meaning you have to actually go where they are to meet, interact, and build relationships with them. This is why Jesus *sent* the Seventy-Two. Inviting people to your program, service, or event may or may not uncover a person of peace, but entering into their space, going to their turf, will guarantee you do.

- Come to people of peace as a *learner* (Luke 10:4). Much is made of Jesus' command to take nothing when he sent out the Seventy-Two, but it is clear to me in neighborhood work that every person comes with "the answer" for the poor people. When you literally come with nothing, you position yourself as the learner instead of the expert. Jesus was forcing them to come empty-handed and open-minded.

- Invest in what's important to people of peace (Luke 10:5–6). Jesus tells the Seventy-Two to bless the household that is opened to them, which in their context would have been the epicenter of the person of peace's community influence. Similarly, in our neighborhoods today, influential neighbors will have a "thing" that they call people to and rally around. Bless that thing, whatever it is (assuming it is aligned with the common good). Invest in it, help it succeed, and do so with no expectations that you will get a return on that investment.

- Party with people of peace (Luke 10:7–8). I do not know if there is a social science study on the concept of people of peace and extroversion, but I have a sneaking suspicion that most, if not all, are extroverts. It kind of comes with the territory of being a connector— you probably need to draw energy from being around people. Well, the love language of extroverts, being an extreme one myself, is feasts, laughter, fun! They are social mixers that allow collisions and connections to happen. Go "party" with people of peace, see them in their element, and watch your own network grow.

- Heal when invited (Luke 10:9). As we've thoroughly explored in this book, our initial tendency is to prioritize offering help when engaging with a community. On the positive side, this stems from a genuine desire to serve. On the negative side, it reeks of savior complex. Do the above four activities first, and eventually— whether through earned or transferred trust—the surrounding community will seek you out for healing. Then you heal what is broken.

People of peace are often the gatekeepers to the community, and getting alongside them will allow us to listen, align, act, and measure in a more meaningful way in our neighborhoods. If neighborhood revitalization is all about centering the neighbors, finding people of peace will allow you to find out who those neighbors are, what they really desire, and how you can go about serving them to see transformation realized.

One day we were rolling the tire through the neighborhood ... which of course, is a whole other story. Short version: Dre, one of our neighborhood leaders, started rolling a huge tire around our city to honor his father who had died of cancer. His father had begun rolling the same tire around as a means of staying fit and strong while also taking his mind off his fight with cancer. Dre also wanted to raise awareness of cancer and build community. He called this movement the Keep Rolling Campaign. We hired him to roll the tire through every block of our neighborhood as one more way to meet neighbors.

During one of these rolling sessions, we met LaTreance. He happened to be out and about in the neighborhood when we rolled by and was interested in what was going on. He shared a bit about himself, we shared a bit about the neighborhood revitalization efforts, then he shared a bit about his perspective on the neighborhood. It is the type of conversation that is fairly regular in our line of work, but I never want to take them for granted. This is the center of resident-led change initiatives, and therefore the bullseye for our work.

It was such a good conversation that we exchanged contact information and set a follow-up coffee date to do "formal" listening. In that session we discovered that LaTreance has a passion to mentor youth in the neighborhood—especially those he sees heading down the same path he did, which landed him in federal prison. We let him know that one of the main things his neighbors wanted to see for neighborhood youth was mentoring relationships, and brainstormed some ways to work together. LaTreance had quickly moved from a stranger, to a met neighbor, to an engaged participant in the neighborhood's vision for change. It was a thrilling and encouraging conversation.

As we were saying goodbyes, LaTreance said the three sweetest words we ever hear: "You gotta meet ..."

Those words are key to a neighborhood movement! In most instances the "development" part of community development is relatively easy—relative being the important word because alignment and resource acquisition are often difficult. But it is the "community" part that needs constant attention and investment.

When we meet a neighbor where relationship and trust are immediately established, and they are willing to open up their network of relationships, we feel like we have hit a gold mine. In an asset-based approach, that actually *is* what we hit—the most valuable resource to community development: more neighbors! When we hear, "You gotta meet …" and the neighbor is willing to personally introduce and vouch for us, we know we've found a person of peace.

LaTreance introduced us to Tashiya, his next-door neighbor. Tashiya immediately jumped in, helping with event planning for Dumpster Day and a three-on-three basketball tournament, working on entrepreneurship and economic small business development, and eventually becoming such a trusted volunteer partner that we contracted her to lead initiatives like the Housing Parcel Survey. Tashiya is an absolute unstoppable engine, and I believe her story is just beginning.

Tashiya in turn said, "You gotta meet …" and introduced us to her brother Corderro, who happens to be a remarkably talented artist, with an even bigger vision for his life, work, and business. The first time I met Cord he said he was going to be bigger than Disney. Not with arrogance but with an affable smile and undeniable sense of confidence rooted in reality. He said it in such a way that you definitely wanted him to become bigger than Disney, and thought he just might do it! Cord has gone on to produce art for the neighborhood initiative, including a portrait for a neighborhood hero and a basketball court mural that received city-wide recognition and awards. We have also been able to aid him in the development of his brand and business—an investment with excellent return.

All of these activities—mentoring, event planning, business development, art creation—are community development. They accomplished the specific aspirational goals voiced by residents in our neighborhood:

- Develop an entrepreneurship ecosystem from within that is inclusive of community residents.
- Create attractions within the neighborhood that draw people in, become a destination for the larger community, and increase fun and pride for neighbors.
- Empower and resource neighborhood youth during their transitional years from late teens to early adulthood by building mentoring relationships.
- Install interactive art throughout the neighborhood that contributes to overall beautification and promotes connection between neighbors.

That is asset-based community development at its best. Alive and embodied.

Oh, and by the way, the guy who rolled the tire ... I first saw him about four years before the neighborhood initiative even started. We were at a larger community listening session that I was attending as a lowly interested minister on staff at a church who wanted to discover what God was up to in our city. He was a young, energetic leader with opinions to share. A common friend leaned over as he was sharing his voice and said to me, "You gotta meet Dre ..."

I wonder what image first springs to mind when you think about Jesus. If I'm honest, I don't really think of Jesus as a jovial, life-of-the-party, happy-go-lucky type. I'm more likely to envision him as the mission-driven social activist, or the "Passion-weekend" Jesus—quiet, weighty, serious. To which, I think Jesus himself would ask, "Why so serious?"

The Gospels give us a glimpse of a man who at very least was fun to be around.

People were attracted to Jesus (Luke 12:1). They followed him, drew near to him, sought him out for conversations. This is an understated and underappreciated aspect of Jesus' life, but one we should use as a gauge for our own ministries—are people actively desiring to be around us? Not for what we are offering but for ourselves?

Then there is the iconic image of Jesus "reclining at the table" that permeates all of the Gospel accounts. This setting would have been a major place of social entertainment, full of storytelling, news sharing, and good conversation, probably lasting two to three hours. And yes, there was a lot of wine drinking (Matt. 9:10).

Jesus showed a willingness to be at and contribute to parties. (Turning water into wine in John 2:1–12 as his first miracle is surely significant.) Since Jesus was a faithful observant of the Jewish faith, we can assume and have some evidence for the fact that he would have participated in the festivals, which were day- to week-long parties for the most part!

Further, Jesus regularly, as a rhythm of life, went away for rest, to recharge and spend time with the Father (Matt. 14:13). This may not at first seem like "fun," but good rest is essential to being a whole person, and whole people are a heck of a lot more fun to be around than overworked, overstimulated, over-anxious, drained, and worn-out people.

When I first made these observations, it was a major revelation and critique on my personal approach to disciple-making. Jesus was a fun guy?!

Although understanding Jesus as a mission-driven, movement-starting, social revolutionary was better than begrudgingly believing in something so I wouldn't go to hell, doggedly pursuing that vision had produced urgency, drive, and overwork. Why so serious?! The whole thing came to a head when, out of my relentlessness, I realized I had hurt people in my inner-circle by not caring for them. I was wringing them out in the name of mission and forward movement. It was a major blind spot, and I am grateful for the Lord's correction.

Bringing Rest to Marginalized Neighbors

In the previous chapter I suggested that, when finding people of peace, we should be thinking about whether people are drawn to us for who we are, not just what we do. Do others enjoy your presence, and do you enjoy the presence of others? Are your gatherings, at least occasionally, marked with fun and laughter? Do people in your sphere of influence see you at peace and rest, and are you in turn opening up access for others to experience the same?

While this soaked into my "church work" and disciple-making, I have to admit, it took much longer for the epiphany to shine its light into my work life and neighborhood revitalization efforts.

It was slowly dawning on me that I was creating the same "work-first, nothing-second" mentality in the neighborhood initiative. Besides being unsustainable for me and the neighborhood leadership, I also began to view engagement in the initiative from the marginalized neighbors' perspective—both in a practical sense and in terms of our philosophy and ethos. These are some of the observations I made:

- Many of our neighbors work very hard all day long—either in white- or blue-collar jobs—that exhaust their minds or physical bodies. Piling more work on top of that is not always, if ever, a priority for the vast majority of our neighbors.
- Our neighbors have their own social networks that they manage: friends, family, coworkers, church, and other affinity groups. Relationships are hard! Neighbors may be thinking, *Now you want me to take precious time out of my life and layer in more relationships with strangers, just because I happen to live in the same neighborhood as them?*
- Shifting fully to the neighbors' voice … "You may have all day to sit around learning fancy words like 'asset-based community development' and 'quality of life plans' and 'neighborhood revitalization,' but I just want to see some things change for the better, and I have my own job. You all get paid to do this, so get to it!" or "I see drama-drama-drama all the time, everywhere. If I even get a sniff of this with my leisure and volunteer time, I'm out!"

Those are not only things I have thought; they are near exact quotes I have heard from neighbors. Not exactly the banner endorsements I was looking for to exemplify the leadership of our neighborhood initiative.

What is more, marginalized neighbors constantly have voices crashing into their lives that attack both their being and existence. *You are not good enough. You cannot own this house. You are not qualified to lead this or that activity in the community. This job is definitely not for you. You are an addict/felon/loser. You are not welcome at this table.*

Even if people or organizations are well intentioned, the "help" they offer comes across as marginalized neighbors themselves being the problem that is in need of fixing. *You need* a financial literacy class, *you need* to repair your credit, *you need* to expunge your record, *you need* to sign up for food stamps … you need, you need, you need.

Setting aside the huge problem with power dynamics latent in these relationships, this additional layer of required engagement and relationship-building is simply exhausting for neighbors. What a terrible way to go about life! Surely with all that laying on top of you constantly, it is difficult to have fun.

When we (the neighborhood revitalization team) approach our marginalized neighbors—even with messages centered on their strengths, value, and agency—we still inadvertently place a burden on them by asking for their time and energy. A certain level of seriousness and responsibility is foundational to our approach—"We are *building* a community from the inside out. There is work to do, and you get to do it! Resident-voice and resident-action! We will move at the speed of the neighborhood." But there can be an unstated expectation: "The success of this endeavor rises and falls on you."

The concept of "work hard, play hard" may sound like one of those American axioms that goes against the grain of Christianity, but I have come to believe the exact opposite—that it is in fact vital and aligned with Jesus' way. In the Old Testament, God goes to great lengths to set up a calendar of festivals alongside the Law. In truth, the festivals were part of the Law—there were seven total festivals spanning the course of a year (Lev. 23). That is quite a bit of partying! And yes, they were parties full of food, feasting, music, family and friends, and wine. More than likely, lots of wine.

The main difference between what they experienced in parties and what we typically perceive in partying, is the *telos*—or intended direction and purpose—of the partying. Our party lifestyle is all about self-pleasure. We think of hedonistic pursuits of feeling good through substance abuse, sexual conquest, and overall debauchery. The mantra is more, more, more. The *telos* for Ancient Israelites was communion with God and others. It was an enriching of life instead of a draining and soaking up of resources. "You shall rejoice in your feast, you and your son and your daughter, your male servant and your female servant, the Levite, the sojourner, the fatherless, and the widow who are within your towns" (Deut.16:14 ESV).

This is precisely why God commanded Israel to include orphans, widows, and sojourners in festivals. By virtue of their status, they would have naturally been excluded.

Some of the reasons we might party and celebrate are for:

- Directed purpose—we celebrate what's happening in our neighborhood revitalization, and we intentionally rest because we know that it is beneficial to the work; it is part of sabbath).
- Holistic transformation—fun and feasting is good for our souls; it provides physical, emotional, and spiritual rest for us. This helps those engaging in this work experience holistic transformation more than if we just kept on with the work-work-work approach.
- Community—what better way to encourage deep relationship and bonds of fellowship and friendship than by laughing and eating together. (Jesus' time at the table was a key part of him forming the community which became the early church.)

We need to consider how we are including marginalized neighbors in our communal fun, feasting, and rest practices.

As I write this, I am immediately reminded of my city's First Friday celebration. A few years back, some leaders in our arts district started putting on a First Friday event, familiar to many cities. It includes food, live music, art, drinks, and other entertainment. Its biggest benefit is the throngs of people that come out to participate. It is always a fun night, and there is a definite sense of communing with others. As I knew the organizers, and had always hoped for something like this in our city, I went and participated every month, enjoying the "public space," which I always envisioned was the closest correlation of Jesus going out and about among the crowd.

Coincidentally, the launch of First Fridays was close to the start of my leadership in neighborhood revitalization. Yet, it was not until I moved into the neighborhood a couple years later that I really started to notice how the party lacked inclusivity. I would walk less than a mile from my house down to the heart of the arts district, and the look and feel could not have been more polar opposite. People looked and acted differently; the sights and sounds were different and even the smells! As I walked slowly for ten minutes down the sidewalk, I saw my surroundings literally change beneath my feet. I went from a 60 percent minority neighborhood—with all the classic markers of disinvestment and generational poverty—to white faces, trendy clothes and restaurants, and millions of dollars of infrastructure investment. Again, I was (and still am) a fan of First Fridays and the arts district, but that walk tells quite a tale.

It says to those in our neighborhood: This party is not for you! Sure, they are technically invited. The organizers, who are fairly liberal-minded, would be aghast to think that it is not inclusive. But I have talked with neighbors, and they do not feel that First Fridays are for them. They do not feel welcome. It is similar to the classic nerd caricature at the high school prom—they may be at the dance, but everyone knows the party is really for the prom king and queen and their friends. If the party was actually for them, it would be different, feel different; the messaging, communication, and marketing would be different. Design matters.

What is more, if you expand the definition of parties to include simple entertainment options, then you realize very quickly that there are little to no options within the disinvested community itself. Again, as with all things to do with marginalized neighbors, the reasons behind this are complex, but if we simply focus on functionality, there are no forms of entertainment in my neighborhood. If I want to go to the movies, I have to go to the North-West-East side, because the Southside is the only side of town without a movie theater. There is no art gallery,[1] music venue, coffee shop, roller-rink, bowling alley, or night club. There is not even a sit-down type of restaurant. It is a complete and total black hole of leisure and entertainment venues.

This reality is another in a long list of subliminal messages that constantly convey and reinforce the message to marginalized neighbors: *You are not worthy of these things. They are not for you. You*

---

[1] At the point of writing, a friend has recently taken a significant risk and opened our neighborhood's first art gallery, Twyman Art Gallery. Read about it at Brook Endale, "Evansville artist who didn't feel welcomed in art community created his own space, *Courier and Press*, February 26, 2021, https://www.courierpress.com/story/news/local/2021/02/26/black-art-evansville-artist-billy-twymon-gallery-paintings-indiana/6767258002/.

cannot access these things. If you want to make someone's life seem like nothing but drudgery, pull all of their opportunities and access to fun.

Why so serious?

Partying in the Way of Jesus

So, what are we to do in the name and way of Jesus?

I am not a very fun guy, so my first piece of advice—if you are a hard-charging, mission-driven, goal-achieving, why-so-serious person—is to get a fun person in your life! Get an Enneagram Seven on your group or team. Let the fun people inform and shape pieces and parts of your overall approach.

Beyond this, here are a few more learnings to share from of the life of Jesus:

Join the party already underway. Jesus went to Zacchaeus's house, reclined with the tax collectors and sinners around Matthew's table, observed the celebrations of the community he was a part of, and attended at least one wedding party. Here is the thing: People are going to party. Marginalized neighbors find a way to have fun even in the face of their circumstances, because they are human beings. Of course, this necessitates being on the missional frontier, building relationships with real people, stepping into potentially foreign and uncomfortable settings, and moving toward knowing and integrating into the community. Once you do, go party!

When we began the work in our neighborhood, the neighborhood association had three annual parties already in place—Picnic in the Park, Boo in the Park, and the Christmas party. They weren't great parties. It would have been easy to come in and take over the organization and planning of them, or even easier to let them do their party but start our own new ones. Instead, we made the difficult decision to simply get behind what the resident leaders were doing and offer event-support funding. Seven years later, we now have four annual events officially sponsored by the neighborhood association, and several other events that take place in the neighborhood throughout any given year, attended by hundreds of people and directly in line with resident-voiced priorities. One is the Tepe Park market, where local business owners and creators get to show off their wares and sell them to other neighbors. Our organization hosts zero of these events, as neighbors themselves are the organizers, planners, and hosts. It took some time to build up the muscles, but with a little resourcing and support, these events are made for neighbors, run by neighbors, and they are way better than anything we could have put on.

Shake up the majority's party. As we've already explored, Jesus brought restoration to individuals by both challenging the existing structures that excluded them and by creating new spaces for them to belong. This is at the heart of the table-flipping scene at the temple, his teaching in the Synagogues, and his relentless reimagining of sabbath practices.

We need to consider what the "majority" spaces and parties are where marginalized neighbors are excluded. Marginalized neighbors may not want to access the majority's parties, and that is fine. However, leveraging your position on community-wide events, gatherings, fundraisers, etc., to clear out a space for them, where they otherwise would have the feeling of being uninvited, is following in the way of Jesus.

We partner with an organization that hosts an event called Imagine Evansville (similar to TEDx talks) to purchase seats for anyone who wants to go. We get tickets for the annual Global Leadership Summit for our leadership team. We sponsor residents to go through the local leadership network organization so they can retreat with influential community leaders and people in positions of power. The whole goal of this is to open up access to social capital that our neighbors may not be attuned to. A couple of years ago we got to see Jaidon and Shuron, two young entrepreneurs connected to our neighborhood initiative, working the room at Imagine Evansville, handing out business cards and setting up future business.

Design parties for all. If you are going to plan a party, design it to mirror the citizenship of heaven. When Jesus drew a crowd, the Greek word used to describe it is *oxloi*. This refers to sheer numbers of people, but it also indicates diversity.[2]

While other passages use descriptors like "the Jews" or "the Greeks" or the "religious leaders" or "the disciples"—all of which are tagged onto *oxloi* in other passages—when it is just the crowd standing alone, it is not a homogenous group. This is a crowd of humanity spanning the diversity therein. This echoes the coming diversity of Revelation 7, where every tribe and tongue will worship together. This had already begun in the early church where all were welcomed and where the old hierarchies of holiness were being erased (1 Cor. 12:13).

Twice a year we host a "Love Your Neighbor Day" in the neighborhood. (And by "we," I mean the organization I work for that serves as lead agency in our neighborhood revitalization efforts.) From the outside looking in, it may seem very similar to a classic serve-day experience where the more affluent white suburban churches come and help their poor neighbors that live in the center city—and I'll admit to a fair amount of that tension on these days. However, we do a few things very intentionally to mitigate the tension. We only do projects voiced and prioritized by residents; we invite neighbors to lead projects and serve alongside; and we close the day with food, music, and festivities. At our last Love Your Neighbor Day, there were religious leaders, Jesus-followers, residents, rich and poor, young and old, and diversity in race and ethnicity. This "crowd" were all working and partying shoulder to shoulder.

This is not an exhaustive list, and this isn't just about finding diversity in your neighborhood work—it is just as important, and potentially more uncomfortable and boundary-stretching, to incorporate these principles in your personal life.

How might Jesus' way inform and transform your parties? If neighborhood revitalization is indeed kingdom work, then surely it should be fun, and include a lot of partying. It is not only what marginalized

---

[2] Colin Brown, ed., *The New International Dictionary of New Testament Theology, vol. 2*, s.v. "crowd" (Grand Rapids, MI: Zondervan, 1976), 788–789.

neighbors need but also what God wants for them, what Jesus fulfilled in his ministry, and a pattern for us to follow as the people of God.

Rest as Part of Holistic Ministry

One final thought on fun and partying: Rest is vital if we're going to work hard and play hard. The sabbath rest modeled by God in creation shows the importance of rest. God made one-seventh of his creative work about resting! He then included the command to rest as one of the Ten Commandments—showing its importance in how we should order our lives. And despite the pressing urgency of surrounding circumstances and his cosmic mission, Jesus made it a rhythm of practice to rest. These interludes of rest would often come on the heels of massive public ministry success, where the conventional wisdom would be to leverage the momentum for bigger impact. Instead, Jesus would withdraw from the crowds and place priority on the relationship of prime importance: being with his heavenly Father.

Proper Rest—with a capital R—is essential to being a whole person. You could say that a healthy heart, mind, soul, and strength floats on the buoyancy of good rest. Marginalized neighbors' rest is under constant attack. There is of course a spectrum across which neighbors experience this, but I want to use some real examples from conversations I have had in the last few months:

- Ms. Cassandra has had shots fired three times on her block in the last month, one leaving a bullet hole in her car.
- X-family has had Child Protective Services by their home several times to investigate negligence.
- Tonya heard rustling in her attic that keeps her wide awake at night when she is trying to go to sleep for school. Turns out it was a family of raccoons.
- Walter works fifty-plus hours a week, then volunteers another ten hours at his local church, all while his house is in disrepair. It is difficult to heat and cool the house which makes it hard to rest, as he feels he needs to fix it but is too exhausted to do anything.

- Jay has been searching for a job for three months but deals with mental illness and periodic homelessness. He cannot find anyone to hire him or keep a job; this only exacerbates his mental illness and causes his periodic homelessness.
- Stacy lies awake at night running through the food pantries and agencies she will call tomorrow, and hopefully visit, so she can have food for her children.
- X-neighbor is coming off a three-day meth bender and cannot remember the last time he slept. He certainly won't tonight.
- Lisa, while content in life, has a twinge of jealousy as she sees on social media all the smiling, happy families on summer vacation. She works hard to provide for her kids, but vacations for them are weekend camping trips at the state park, not Disneyland or the beach.

The list of stories could go on and on. Again, this is a sampling from just the last couple of months. The point is that marginalized neighbors are under constant threat in their intellectual, emotional, physical, and spiritual lives. When you are running constantly in the red, it is pretty hard to find a moment of respite, let alone develop any sort of rhythm of rest we need as human beings to be whole.

Rest is not the first thing that springs to mind when you think of helping those in need, but it is acutely felt. Unfortunately, our social services and programmatic interventions are unhelpful in this matter. We heap on more activity, more tasks, more lines and waiting, more certificates, more processes to navigate. And, in the end, they are not really all that helpful to individuals as a blanket response. More burden, fewer results—a recipe for generational poverty.

We need to find solutions that are customized to neighbors' needs, taking into consideration their whole experience. There won't be one solution that helps all of my neighbors. A fitting response could be anything from buying a Temperpedic mattress to financial coaching to helping regulate medications to becoming a foster parent. Finding ways to offer rest to neighbors has to be about people rather than programs.

Ultimately, holistic ministry is about bringing rest. Recall the key encouragement to the woman who was bleeding: "Go, in peace" (Luke 8:38). It is this *shalom* peace—a peace that encompasses all of our heart, mind, soul, and strength—that Jesus came to bring. He pointed to this in his iconic statement, "Come to Me, all who are weary and burdened, and I will give you rest … For My yoke is comfortable, and My burden is light" (Matt. 11:28, 30).

As we participate in the important work of Jesus' kingdom, we must remember how to get this rest ourselves and discover how to include our marginalized neighbors in this rest. Ours should be a work that is restful and restorative, in order that our neighbors can know this comfortable yoke in the transformatory work of the kingdom.

CHURCH ENGAGEMENT IN NEIGHBORHOOD REVITALIZATION

The New Testament epistles read like love letters to me. Each of the authors send encouragement, prayers, teaching and clarification, challenges, and corrections—but underlying all of it is a desire for the church to step into its identity and calling. They care deeply about those they are writing to, the message of the gospel, and how it ought to be lived out in order to see kingdom transformation.

In that vein, this chapter is my attempt to write a love letter of sorts, speaking directly to churches and sharing the working conclusions I have pulled together from practicing neighborhood revitalization as ministry, research in mobilizing Christians into this work, and leading the larger Christian community into missional engagement.[1] You can probably tell that I have a pretty strong belief that Christians should not only be engaging in neighborhood revitalization but also leading efforts in cities all over our nation. In fact, I will go so far as to say that I wish churches and Christians were known for this one thing above all else: Where the church is, there are no marginalized neighbors, only restored communities of belonging.

But currently we don't see this kind of church engagement in ministry to marginalized neighbors.

---

[1] For the purposes of the following discussion, I am talking about "the church" in its local expression, living and active in the world through congregations. When speaking of churches engaging in neighborhood revitalization, I am drawing from the concept of what the universal church (the global body of Christ) should always and necessarily be about but applying these principles to the local church in a given community.

This isn't for lack of resources. Smaller churches (80–120 attendees) have an average annual budget of $220,000; larger churches average $675,000; megachurches … well much more. In my city alone, that equates to approximately $55 million spent annually. Plus, every year in the metropolitan region, you are looking at another $100-plus million given to nonprofits, many of them Christian.

At a national level, US Christians make $5.2 trillion annually in income. A straight-up tithe of that would be $520 billion! Yet only 1.5 million people tithe out of the 247 million US citizens identifying as Christians.[2]

There are fifty-five neighborhoods in my city, and maybe another twenty homeowners' associations in the county—so, seventy-five total neighborhoods. That same area has 250 total churches. Using those figures, each neighborhood could have three to four churches taking responsibility for restoration and belonging. And if we wanted to get even more focused, 80 percent of the poverty in our city resides in just thirteen core neighborhoods.[3] That works out to basically nineteen churches per neighborhood. The local church is the key to tapping latent resources—human and capital—to transform the lived experience of those in poverty in our urban core.

But those kingdom resources would need to be funneled into effective transformational endeavors aligned to the kingdom vision and producing kingdom fruit. Where we spend millions of dollars on feeding ministries and social services—from food pantries to food stamps to backpack programs—we would need to reinvest those resources into the development of people, so that they experience holistic restoration of heart, mind, soul, and strength.

---

[2] These statistics are drawn from the following sources: Carey Nieuwhof, "Church Giving Statistics for 2025: Who's Giving, When, and How Much?" *careynieuwhof.com*, accessed February 20, 2025, https://careynieuwhof.com/church-giving-statistics/; "Impact and Insights," *Wellborn Baptist Foundation*, https://welbornfdn.org/impact-insights/; "Church Giving Stats and Strategies for Adapting to New Trends," *Vanco*, accessed February 20, 2025, https://www.vancopayments.com/egiving/asset-church-giving-statistics-tithing.

[3] See "The State of E Report," *For Evansville*, accessed May 4, 2025, https://www.forevansville.org/stateofe.

We currently spend the lion's share of our church budgets on staff, internal programming, and facilities. Imagine if your average church (with less than two hundred congregants) committed to giving away even 10 percent of their income and invested it directly into the lives of marginalized neighbors for holistic restoration. That would be approximately $20,000 every year for a church to dramatically change the life of a neighbor or two. If you moved up to the city level, it would be $5 million.[4] Think of the impact you could make in the lives of those deemed the "least of these" with a coordinated effort. Wouldn't our communities see our good works and glorify our Father in heaven?

A big part of repositioning our churches to care for marginalized neighbors involves making a change in the way we measure success. When the unspoken (or even spoken) definition is how many people attend a church service, the internal inertia for mobilizing congregants will ultimately be in support of the systems that meet that metric of success. This means that when congregants put their faith in action, it will be expressed primarily through the built-in ministries that make Sunday services happen.

For congregants, ministry has come to be defined by serving with youth in the church building for an hour, leading singing, welcoming people, and other roles to make internal processes work. The greatest purpose of the congregant is to invite someone, or better yet, bring someone on their arm to a Sunday service. In my research, the gravitational pull of these metrics was referenced by ministry leaders. From their perspective, they identified the institutional church, and the perceived expectation of their role as pastors, as a significant barrier to mobilization.

The ministry implication for these observations lies in a redefining of success for local churches. Instead of only counting attendance at

---

4   Admittedly this is more of a mathematical exercise than a practical reality. If you are wondering how I arrived at that number, the equation is: Area Median Income (AMI) for Evansville $50K x 10 percent (Tithe) x 40 households/giving units x 10 percent (Congregation Tithe) = $20K per church. Multiply that by the number of churches in our region (250), and we have arrived at $5 million annually.

church services, a church could also count how many of their disciples are joining with God in his mission of reconciliation. If a church were to express their ministry to marginalized neighbors through a neighborhood revitalization effort, they could measure formation or growth in disciple-making. Each individual congregation would need to define their own metrics and goals for impact, but the aim would be to introduce a sending metric that slowly reorders the natural functions of the local church toward external engagement with the community. (See appendix two, where I give further analysis on organizing principles that can help churches and neighborhood revitalization ministries build momentum as they seek to engage communities.)

The good news is that I believe those sitting in the pews are ready for a change. Through research, we saw a positive correlation between congregants' views of the church and their frequency in putting faith into action. This means that the potential for a social revolution is ready to go if our churches were to leverage their influence for missional engagement in our cities.

Acting Our Way Into a New Way of Thinking

Part of the problem we have in our churches is that we believe we need more head knowledge before we can act differently. However, the research we conducted fits much more firmly within the understanding that the best way to change the way we think is through acting.[5]

We surveyed three groups: congregants, pastors, and practitioners. (See appendix three for more details on the survey.) Of these three groups, there was almost no variance in the responses to belief statements. When asked about some of the most basic foundational

---

[5]   To be clear, this should not be at the expense of "right thinking." Alignment with historical orthodoxy and affirmation of the importance of the fundamental belief statements of the Christian faith for our everyday lives are not to be thrown out in the pursuit of experience. The content is still important. It is just that the content cannot be divorced from experience, and the experience itself should be understood as content, shaping the disciple.

tenets of the Christian faith, nearly all participants showed positive agreement to the concepts presented. This is visually represented by the nearly straight line through the Belief Statements (BS) section.

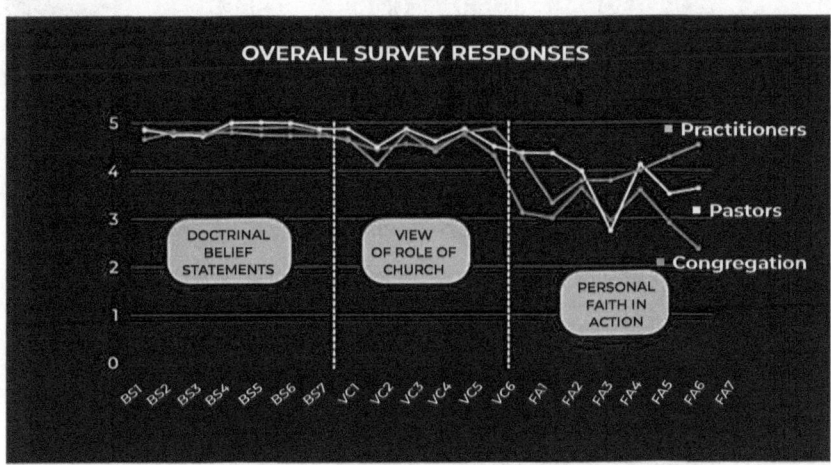

However, once we came to the View of the Role of the Church (VC)—the middle section—the line starts to zig and zag. There is much less agreement about what the church should be doing than what the faith community conceptually believes.

Then, in the Faith in Action (FA) section, there is even greater variance, indicated clearly by the jagged line bouncing all over the place!

What we can take from this is that the Christian community has done a pretty good job of transferring concepts that inform our collective faith. You could say that the vast majority of Christians are "thinking right." But when it comes to expressions of the collective church, and much more so in the personal application of our faith in action, we begin to diverge.

If we look specifically at the responses to questions about faith in action, we can see that congregants and pastors have much lower responses than practitioners.

The three lowest scores for congregants and pastors related to statements 4, 6, and 7: "Have been present at city or community events with the awareness and intentionality of living out my faith and serving as a witness to Jesus Christ"; "Have served or been present with a marginalized population (e.g., homeless, impoverished, felons, etc.) in my community"; "Have spent time in an under-resourced neighborhood in my community with the purpose of living out my faith."[6]

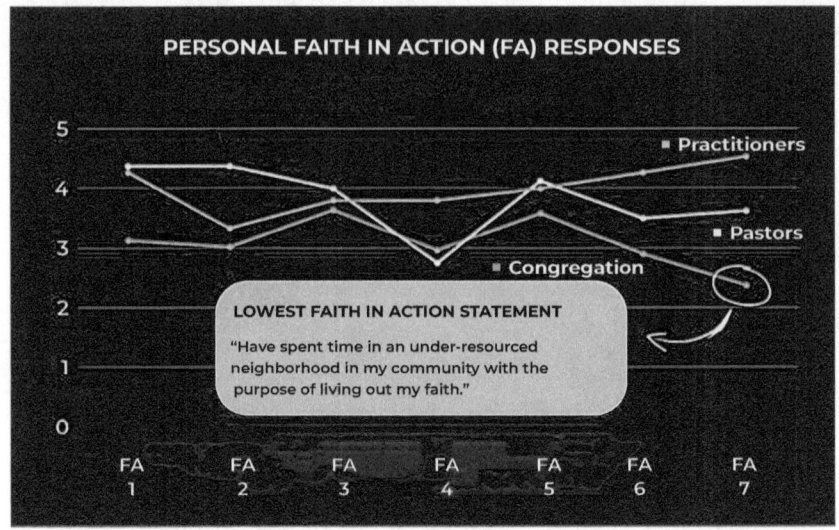

What we can draw from these results is that it's much easier to assent to concepts than to live out faith in action. When it comes to engaging missionally in the community, especially to disinvested neighbors and neighborhoods, congregants and pastors simply are not prioritizing these actions.

Our "thinking" might be right, but our actions don't match up. Perhaps it's time for churches to orient their activities around actions that will align us with the thinking we claim to have.

There is, however, a problem with "right thinking" when it comes to how we view the role of the church. Both congregants and pastors scored lowest on affirmation of the statement, "The church has a specific calling from God to restore the marginalized populations of a

---

6   This finding is supported by a Barna Study commissioned for our city. The report found that 83 percent of the population self-identified as Christians, 54 percent were practicing Christians, and 25 percent were highly engaged in their Christian faith. There is a general disconnect between what Christians say about their faith and what they do in response to their faith. See "Wellborn Baptist Foundation: Target Market Report," accessed May 4, 2025, https://eadn-wc01-11031595.nxedge.io/wp-content/uploads/2022/11/2016_BARNA CommFaithSurvey_WBF.pdf.

community." Conversely, this statement was scored highest by neighborhood revitalization practitioners.

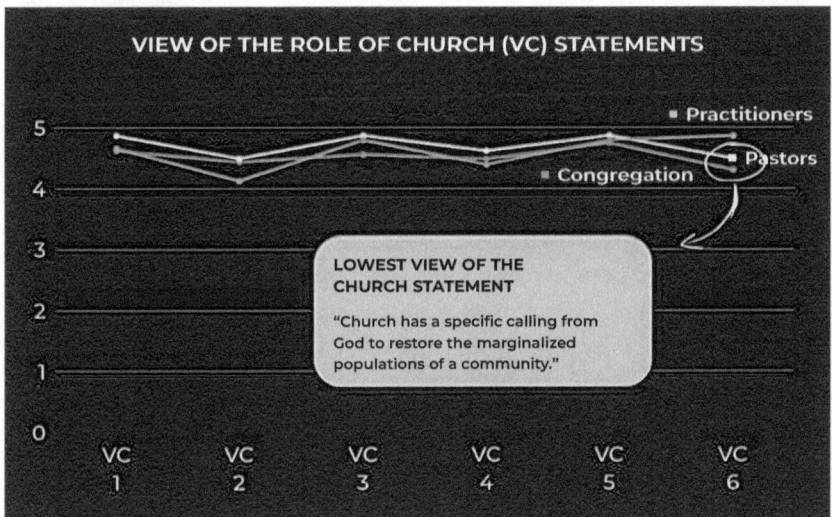

Pastors shouldn't be much of a surprise that congregants report low frequency of faith in action to marginalized neighbors if they are not as certain about the church's role in this ministry. If they're not experiencing the tangible action of their church ministering to marginalized neighbors, they may not be aware that this is part of its mandate.[7]

A further problem in our thinking is that as soon as I start to address the church's role in neighborhood revitalization, there is an immediate danger that I position the church as outside the injunction of ministry to marginalized neighbors. There is a temptation to draw a line between *us*—those delivering the ministry—and *them*—those in need of ministry. This is contrary to the inclusion of marginalized people in the Old Testament (explored in chapter two) and the new kingdom, ushered in by the completed works of Jesus and spoken of in the New Testament (see Eph. 2:11–13, Gal. 3:28). The gospel is not

---

[7] Interestingly, the statement that scored lowest on this section for practitioners was, "The church is the assembled or gathered disciples of Jesus Christ." This could show that practitioners working in neighborhood revitalization experience their roles as lone missionaries, which in turn shapes their view of the church as not supporting their work in the neighborhood.

only the reconciliation of ourselves to God but also the possibility of reconciliation with one another. It is the obliteration of "us and them."

This kingdom reality needs to be kept in mind, even if the language used sometimes leans us away from it. As I lay out church engagement in neighborhood revitalization as holistic ministry to marginalized neighbors, it is from a place of *we*; and where I fail to communicate that properly, it is a failing of mine, not the gospel and way of Jesus.

Again, although this seems to be an issue of correcting "thinking," research (and experience) tells us that proximity to others helps us to break down barriers of "othering."[8] This means that taking action in neighborhood revitalization can help congregants who wouldn't ordinarily come into contact with people from other neighborhoods make relational connections and develop awareness and empathy for the reality of those neighbors' lives. This is much more likely to happen through neighborhood revitalization efforts, where neighbors are centered, rather than through at-arms-length serve ministries.

Needless to say, engaging churches in neighborhood revitalization is important for all. It creates more sustainable, longer-term impact in neighborhoods,[9] and it gives congregants the opportunity to put their faith into action and connect with the work God has called them to.

You may be wondering how you can go about doing this. Well, there are five principles that I believe will mobilize the church into ministry to marginalized neighbors which we can explore now.

---

[8] See Joshua Krook, "How Physical Proximity (and Social Psychology): Can Prevent Racism, Sexism and Discrimination in Our Society," *New Intrigue*, April 29, 2015, https://newintrigue.com/2015/04/29/how-physical-proximity-and-social-psychology-can-prevent-racism-sexism-and-discrimination-in-our-society/.

[9] Early pioneers and practitioners, such as Focused Community Strategies, the Christian Community Development Association, and Shepherd Community Center, evidence that church engagement is needed for neighborhood work to thrive and be sustainable. Shepherd Community Center stated that their church plant allowed them to resource their neighborhood work. (Jay Height, personal interview, February 13, 2018).

Know the Church's Role in Ministry to Marginalized Neighbors

If congregants are lacking clarity on the church's role in ministering to marginalized neighbors, this will need to be addressed first.

Much of the first section of this book gave a detailed analysis of God's heart for the inclusion of marginalized neighbors, and for his people to continually work to ensure that their ability to love him with all of their being isn't restricted.

As those working in neighborhood revitalization, it can be difficult to understand why all Christians aren't convinced of the link between the biblical narrative of caring for the marginalized and living out our faith today.

There are a number of factors I believe may contribute to this:

- Lack of proximity. When we built our cities to separate the haves from the have-nots, we no longer had to come face-to-face with our neighbors. The poor and disenfranchised become a concept instead of a person. This lack of proximity also occurred in our organizational churches as they moved out to the suburbs.
- Government-funded programs as an intervention to poverty. It's no longer the community's responsibility to care for itself but the government's. Churches acquiesced to these interventions, and we vacated our call from God.
- Lack of personal revelation from Jesus. I no longer take for granted that Christians are allowing Jesus' life to inform and transform their own. One of the great revelations I had when our missional small groups initiative stalled was that people won't go on mission with Jesus if they are not spending time sitting at his feet.

These issues are in stark contrast to the neighborhood revitalization practitioners who all mentioned during our survey that their understanding of the mission and call of God to his people is the primary catalyst for their involvement. One practitioner put it beautifully:

"The motivation comes out of our love for God, viewing ourselves as children of God, as missionaries … it's not an extra add on to life, but what we are called to do."

Questions to Consider:

- As a pastor or church leader, how might you create proximity to marginalized neighbors—both for yourself and your congregants?
- How might you see caring for those experiencing poverty as a personal responsibility and mandate, given by God to you as his follower?
- Could you find ways to engage personally, and with your congregation, in the scriptures that highlight God's heart for the marginalized and the ways of Jesus that we are called to imitate? Encourage congregants to ask "What is God saying to me through these passages? And what am I going to do about it?"

Reclaim the Church's Participation in Holistic Ministry

As I have repeatedly highlighted throughout this book, the greatest command we are given is to love God with all of our heart, mind, soul, and strength, and to love our neighbor in the same way (Matt. 22:37–40). Loving people in the whole of their being is the ministry the church should be about. Our ministry to marginalized neighbors should be no different, yet we often build programmatic or service responses that meet only one need or aspect of a person's being.

Even our church activities compartmentalize these aspects instead of integrating them. You get a bit of heart and soul ministry at Sunday services, community and belonging in small group, content for your mind through the mid-week podcast, and physical activation on second Saturday serve days.

Many of our church outreach ministries meet only one need at a time, rather than looking at bringing transformation to the whole of the person.

Conversely, neighborhood practitioners are often motivated to do the work they do because of its holistic nature. They have served in church programs for years, but long for more—wanting to see transformation of people and communities. "We were looking for a new way to serve, something holistic, in a focused way for kingdom impact. We decided to be strategic in the neighborhood."

A starting point for churches is to question whether their local outreach ministries reflect this holistic nature. If you analyze your current ministries and think about what aspect of life they bring transformation to, is it physical, emotional, spiritual, or intellectual? Then consider how you might transfer your focus to become inclusive of the whole person.

A final consideration for churches is whether they actually know what the needs are of marginalized people in their area. Sometimes our ministries are seemingly serving needs but haven't considered what neighbors would want for themselves. Utilizing the listening tools from chapters nine and ten could be a great starting point.

Questions to Consider:

- Are your current outreach ministries holistic in nature?
- What could you do to incorporate other aspects of whole-life transformation into those ministries?
- Do you know the needs and strengths of marginalized neighbors in your neighborhood/town/city?
- What one new ministry could your church start that would bring holistic transformation for these neighbors, even if you're only able to help a few people?

Mobilize Your Congregation to Put their Faith Into Action

One of the most encouraging results from the research was the direct relationship between the view of the role of the church and a person's frequency of putting their faith in action—the higher the view the more it is activated. This means that if churches can rediscover our collective call as the people of God to minister to marginalized neighbors, we will likely find congregants willing to get involved.

Despite all the bad press around churches, everyday followers of Jesus are still looking to their church for ministry direction!

Now for the bad news: Our current primary mode of delivering the content of the Christian faith is ineffective at best, and counter-productive at worst. The number of people identifying as Christians in our community does not correlate with the number of people engaged in missional activities. This likely has to do with lack of opportunity. The overarching approach of most churches I know is that we gather up Christians at our services, give them content and inspiration, and then send them along to live out their faith. This is even true of church ministries like small groups that are supposed to break down these barriers to practicing faith. For example, small groups are often billed as "doing life together"—but do they really? Life does not occur in a living room on Tuesday night for an hour and a half. And the discussion is about the content of faith, not the actual practice of it. I'm not saying Sunday services and small groups are "wrong"; they are just incomplete as vehicles for formation. There has to be a place and space where the content is practiced, and that is the motivation for mobilization.

I find it interesting to reflect on Jesus' interactions with the religious leaders of his day. They certainly knew and assented to proper Jewish doctrine, yet his number one correction for living out their faith was that their actions did not relate to producing kingdom outcomes. So much so that he called them hypocrites.

As we've seen from the research results above, right thinking alone does not lead to right action. We need to create opportunities for our congregants to put their faith into action.

Questions to Consider:

As a leader, how might you create opportunities for both your own and others' faith to be put into action through neighborhood revitalization?

Some potential ideas might be:

- Start a pilot group with congregants who are invited to try out a "faith in action" small group—each week you look at a passage from one of the Gospels and then challenge one another to put what you've learned into action in some way. (A Discovery Bible Study or any obedience-based Bible study tool could be a good starting point.)
- As the church leader, spend time with local practitioners of neighborhood revitalization. Observe their existing involvement, and ask questions about how they see their faith in action through this work. Invite a few key congregants to join you.
- Find out about the work of local neighborhood revitalization organizations and ask how your church can serve them. Rather than setting up your own serve-day events, collaborate with what's already happening to give your congregants the opportunity to put their faith into action—genuinely assisting those already involved in the work (helping not hurting).

See Neighborhood Revitalization as a Formation Opportunity

Many are concerned about the lack of discipleship that happens in churches. As mentioned above, we are seeing a disconnect between belief and action—discipleship cannot just be a case of adhering to a set of faith statements and values, while failing to live life differently. Again, this comes back to the issue of acting our way into a new way of thinking.

When we adopt the perspective that right thinking must precede right acting, we often struggle to create learning opportunities that are action-based. But Jesus modeled a different kind of discipleship—one that involved learning on the job.

Yet, in our church contexts today, it often seems that discipleship and mission have been decoupled from one another.

Attempting to mobilize disciples into neighborhood revitalization over the last eight years has proved difficult in part because it is not seen as discipleship; at best it is seen as an outreach opportunity, and at worst it is seen as an activity for "super-Christians," nonprofits, and city government. But Jesus didn't hold to these false divisions—he discipled those around him in living missionally. The Twelve couldn't have been disciples without participating in Jesus' mission to the world, and those going on mission with Jesus couldn't do so without signing up for his high-bar of discipleship. The two were inextricably linked.

Increased engagement in neighborhood work will occur for local churches if we see it as stepping into the way of Jesus—as an ever-present opportunity for discipleship. This pathway of discipleship must include tangible experiences and not be reduced to content presentation.

In our research, pastors agreed that their role, and by extension the role of the church, was to teach, equip, and empower the congregants. While "sending" was mentioned by several pastors, what was being referenced was the sending of individuals out from the gathered church service into their everyday lives as better equipped disciples and evangelists on behalf of the Christian faith. They did not see their role as leaders of the church to prescribe collective action.

Conversely, neighborhood revitalization practitioners shared with us that they saw their involvement in neighborhood work as a step of faith. Their actions in this work are part of imitating Jesus.

Neighborhood revitalization as a platform for engagement naturally creates tangible opportunities, but it also wouldn't be difficult for a local church body to intentionally build some.

As congregants journey into marginalized communities—seeing the situation for themselves, and meeting neighbors—formation occurs. Coming face-to-face with the challenges that these neighbors experience can open up our hearts to God's heart and lead us to ask him what he would do to bring alleviation and transformation. Existing neighborhood practitioners consistently mentioned the faith formation they experienced as disciples of Jesus involved in this work as the sustaining factor of their ongoing participation in neighborhood engagement.

In this same way, congregants can join with God in his mission of reconciliation and ministry to marginalized neighbors so that they can follow in the way of Jesus and experience the transformative ministry of the people of God.

Furthermore, participants commented on the importance of seeing movement in the revitalization efforts—knowing God is at work sustained their continued commitment to neighborhoods but also was a positive aspect of their discipleship. One practitioner put it this way, "Making progress has sustained me. I've seen God move vividly. Mostly it seems like I'm just following God around. It is easy to see value and investment when tied to these actions. They become fulfilling and empowering."

There was deep belief among practitioners that the God found in the metanarrative of Scripture, who actively participates in restoration, has continuity with the restoration they experience in neighborhood revitalization. This led them to a deeper knowing or experience of God.

I'm not sure we always have the opportunity to experience such a deep and ongoing sense of worship, trust, and intimacy with God when we limit our discipleship to a Sunday service once a week.

When seeking to understand engagement or disengagement in ministry to marginalized populations as a part of an individual's discipleship process and spiritual formation, we need to find ways for congregants to participate and contribute to the mission of God. They are able to bring something—time, skills, gifts—to others as a part of a larger movement of God. The participatory nature of this work helps biblical ideas such as "co-heirs with Christ" and "ministers of reconciliation" to become a real experience.

Questions to Consider:

- How might engagement in neighborhood revitalization address lack of discipleship and formation in your church?
- How could you support congregants to engage in neighborhood revitalization and learn from it as disciples of Jesus?
- Where might there be opportunities to worship God through

neighborhood revitalization, rather than limiting worship and intimacy to Sunday services?

Redefine Success and Measure the Outcomes

As I highlighted at the top of this chapter, if we're to engage our churches with neighborhood revitalization, we're going to need to shift our definition of success.

First, we need to stop seeing attendees at a Sunday service and the amount of money people give as our main metrics of success or failure. How about we begin to measure how well we are participating in God's mission and being formed as disciples instead? Consider how much attention you give to these areas when assessing the health and success of your church.

Second, in terms of participating in God's mission to marginalized people, we need to start measuring the holistic health of our neighbors rather than meals served, people clothed, or children taught to read, etc. In line with an asset-based community development approach, we need to measure success based on the whole-life transformation experienced by neighbors, and based on the areas *they* have communicated they desire to see that transformation in.

Several pioneers are leading the way in these endeavors. The REVEAL Spiritual Life Survey attempts to measure the overall health of the church and includes a measurement of a church's faith in action.[10] LifeWay's Discipleship Pathway Assessment looks at a church and/or individual's current state of discipleship and includes measurements around such items as serving others, sharing Christ, and exercising faith.[11] Many churches are counting how many gospel conversations congregants have

---

[10] See Greg L. Hawkins and Cally Parkinson, *Move: What 1,000 Churches Reveal About Spiritual Growth* (Grand Rapids, MI: Zondervan, 2011).

[11] See the Discipleship Pathway Assessment, Lifeway Christian Resources, accessed May 5, 2025, https://discipleshippathwayassessment.lifeway.com

in their everyday lives. J. D. Greear, in the book *Gaining by Losing*,[12] offers ten "plumb lines" churches can use to gauge whether they are keeping "sending" at the center of their lives and church culture.

These are just a few examples of tools local churches can leverage to convert their congregations toward more missional impact and implement more appropriate metrics. In the area of neighborhood revitalization specifically, the Lupton Center has created a Flourishing Neighborhood Index,[13] which measures the health of a community across economic, social, and structural indicators. This could be used by a local church to pursue impact in the neighborhoods they desire to invest in and to reframe the narrative of engagement for their church.

For churches, perhaps we should consider how we are doing in equipping congregants for the following:

- Love of God, love of neighbors, love of self—loving actions taken in the world
- Gospel conversations—times sharing the good news
- Sent missionaries—how many sent into the world on mission
- Invitations—specifically into a faith community of belonging
- Equipping opportunities—formal and informal, personal and corporate

Taken together, these can create a dashboard that defines success for a local church. If you are equipping the saints for ministry, they will display acts of love, have gospel conversations, be sent into the missional frontier, and invite others into a faith community.

If you are also incorporating neighborhood revitalization into the practices of your church, you can celebrate even more when the above metrics are lived out in the context of your neighborhood focus. Think about incorporating some of these options as well:

---

12 J. D. Greear, *Gaining by Losing: Why the Future Belongs to Churches That Send* (Grand Rapids, MI: Zondervan, 2015).

13 See the Flourishing Neighborhood Index, Lupton Center, accessed May 5, 2025, https://www.luptoncenter.org/flourishing-neighborhood-index/.

- Having a faithful presence—map where you are being the light of Christ in the neighborhood and how long you have consistently shown up there.
- Relational movement—figure out a tracking system for the number of neighbors who have moved from stranger to neighbor to friend. You'll have to define these categories and also be sensitive to the risk of people becoming numbers.
- Quality of life improvement—adopt the neighborhoods' vision-for-change plan as your church's "building campaign." Raise money for them, mobilize volunteers toward them, celebrate and cheer when their goals are accomplished.
- Share stories of transformation—this is a wonderful one because you can actually measure both the transformation and the stories told, all in a way that people can relate to.

Questions to Consider:

- What are your current markers of success?
- How might you shift your understanding of success to orient your church toward ministry to marginalized neighbors?
- How can you share and celebrate to encourage movement and perseverance in this work?

A fundamental reorientation of missional engagement needs to occur within our local churches. I believe as Christians in America we must reflect deeply both on our posture and on our approach to ministering to those pushed to the edges of our society.

Neighborhood revitalization can be a vehicle to move the church into the lives of their marginalized neighbors and to live out the ministry of Jesus that should be a marker of a church and its disciples. It does so in a way that upholds the inherent dignity and infinite worth of neighbors created in the image of God, no longer seeing them as people of need but as people filled with the capacity to be the change they envision for their lives and community.

The final question then becomes: *How?* How do we mobilize and sustain engagement in neighborhood revitalization by local churches? While the solution is complex and multivariant, it is important for churches to create opportunities for congregants to journey into the neighborhood with brothers and sisters in Christ, and to have tangible ministry experiences among their marginalized neighbors. As we follow the way of Jesus, the truth is revealed to us through the experiencing of it, and therefore the abundant life promised by Jesus is found. If the same holds true for disciples and disciple-making today, then church activity should include tangible experience of ministries with our marginalized neighbors and neighborhoods. Consider what next steps you can make in this work. There is so much to be gained for everyone.

CONCLUSION

I have always wanted to be part of a revolution, to be a revolutionary. It is a combination of the idealist in me and never really being settled with the status quo. The desire to participate in revolution goes back as far as my adolescence when Civil Rights and hippie leaders became my heroes—people with great ideals who were willing to act on them, and to do so with others. This is why, for a brief moment in my late teens and early twenties, I identified as a socialist, why I signed up for the Peace Corps at twenty-three, and why I read every book I could on political revolutions. I still love to learn about mini-revolutions in any industry or domain of life.

My faith background is like that of many in the American Bible Belt. I won't go into a full retelling here, but many know the story because you lived it too: grew up in church; learned all the Bible stories; did not actually read the Bible itself; knew all the church rituals; felt like I belonged to a social club; had fun at youth group and church events; and mostly had a fond overall memory of church and Christianity. But Christianity was something best left within the church buildings on Sunday mornings and Wednesday nights. Faith was something that got you out of hell when you died and required you to be as morally good as possible in the meantime.

As I got a little older, I set aside the "faith of my youth" for a while and began looking for something else; but, against all odds and personal desires, I found Jesus. Or he found me. I will leave that distinction to those who care. Needless to say, I found my revolution—something that combined all three of these necessary ingredients at a satisfactorily viable quantity: high ideals I could get behind, a community of others united in ideology, and tangible action I could participate in. A tough formula when you think about it.

In stepped the way of Jesus. Not the flannelgraph, American-PC, conservative-political-party Jesus we often get presented with, but the real Jesus. The revolutionary. The blow-up-your-cultural-norms, say-outrageous-things, live-a-wildly-audacious-life, turn-tables-over, speak-profound-puzzles-of-existence, embrace-both-the-marginalized-and-the-powerful, inspire-two-thousand-years-of-social-revolutionaries-artists-and-thinkers Jesus.

I learned a fuller gospel—that the good news is truly good news ... and infinitely more than a ticket to heaven. Instead, this good news can revolutionize every moment, every relationship, every job, every identity. I remember vividly the precise moment when all the tumblers fell into place after a long, slow-burn of exploring Jesus and the Christian faith anew (an eighteen-month process), and I looked around both excited and confused—*okay, I am in on all this, but where is the revolution? Where is the church changing the world? What are these so-called Christians doing?*

In the day-to-day work of neighborhood revitalization, a tangible presence of the body of Christ engaging in holistic restoration of marginalized neighbors and disinvested neighborhoods is missing. While I believe a revolution can occur when we place genuine value and infinite worth on those society has deemed "the least of these," empowering and resourcing them to be agents of change in the process of transformation, the real revolution I am now pursuing—maybe the only one left to me at mid-life—concerns the way American churches approach what has traditionally been called "outreach ministry." I still dare to dream that we can make even a small dent in the operations of churches in order to help them adopt a completely new way of how and why churches engage their communities. I do this because I have come to believe that it is the way God gave us to witness to his greatness and bring about revolution.

What's central to this is the way of Jesus. This should be an encouragement to church ministries, a reminder that Jesus is not to be assumed in our teaching but should in fact be the culmination—or *telos*—of all our teaching ... and learning ... and practicing of our faith. Having Christianity at the center of American society for so long, we have gradually taken for granted the way of Jesus and Jesus himself as the beginning, middle, and end of our faith. Various strategies for church growth were laid over the life of Jesus because Jesus was assumed in the fabric of our operations. However, with the movement of the church and Christianity from the center of society toward the edges—a mere menu item that can be selected or passed over in the construction of lives and communities—it is time once again to make Jesus explicit. Now is the time to allow Jesus to transform our ministries by reintroducing Jesus into all our content, especially our outreach into the local mission field.

The content requires contextualization as well. It is not necessarily self-evident that large collections of marginalized neighbors living among our cities are concentrated into a few under-resourced neighborhoods. This is a new learning for most congregants, one that must be introduced, taught, and shepherded toward understanding. One of the few unifying beliefs of the Christian faith I have experienced in ten years of ministry in Evansville is the simple command of Jesus to love our neighbors. It is not as intuitive or unifying to love our neighborhoods. Disciples of Jesus understand that they are to love their neighbors where they *are*—where they live, work, play, and worship. But do they understand that they are to love their neighbors where they are *called*—to the least of these, the marginalized living among us? And do they understand that the nature of ministry within that calling is to be holistic and restorative, not merely to meet temporary needs that contribute to the very cycles of dependency we are called to eliminate? Work will need to be done in order to get to know the city and all the complex nuances of disinvestment, generational poverty, and place-based ministry.

I believe that the church is the assembled people of God, the bride of Christ, being built into the very dwelling place of God; the body of Christ, living and active in the world; the light in the darkness, drawing others to the beauty, magnificence, wonder, mystery, and relationship with the foundation of all existence, God himself. I believe that the localized expression of this high ideal is the vehicle of the church, through which God intends to bring about a revolution for world transformation into heaven. The church is who and where the ones called out from the world gather, are shaped, and sent out as his revolutionaries. The quickest and surest way to subvert the status quo is to activate those whom society at large has forgotten, beaten down, and pushed to the margins. The gospel remembers them, raises them up, and empowers them to change the world!

This book has shared my journey in seeking to answer these questions and address these issues, including my research to discover biblical themes and real-life experiences that can help mobilize local churches into holistic ministry to marginalized neighbors. In my own journey, I have experienced many iterations of attempting to join the revolution. Successes and failures, disenchantment, bursts of energy, misplaced priorities, new learnings, old learning refreshed, and much more that could be shared. Through it all, I have continued to desire to be a part of a countercultural revolution that transforms the world. And I still believe that the Christian worldview and gospel message provide the foundation and formula to work.

It is time for us to discover the treasure within our neighborhoods and see neighbors empowered for kingdom transformation—to the glory of God.

ACKNOWLEDGMENTS

I want to give honor and show gratitude to the following people and organizations that made this book possible:

First and foremost, to our Savior and Lord Jesus Christ, who creates, sustains, and fills all things (especially this book), in whom we live, move, and have our being.

Next are the neighbors who show up, against all odds and sensibility, over and over again to come together to build their own communities from the inside out. They do so with no pay and little acclaim in the toughest of environments, and give sacrificially of themselves to love their neighbors. You all are a daily inspiration and joy; may the God of peace make himself known to you.

To my One Life Church family, who got me started in neighborhood work: Thanks for having the foresight to follow Jesus into holistic ministry of marginalized neighbors and for sending, releasing, and resourcing me in the work. While there is danger in singling out individuals, I'd be remiss not to recognize Bret, Natalie, and especially the Bobfather, as friends and mentors.

I definitely need to recognize my Community One team, who trusted me to follow Jesus into the neighborhood and who resource me and the work in crazy and innovative ways. I cannot list every name; still, I have to recognize our founder and my friend, Eric, who boldly created my position and the pioneering work (for our city anyway) of seeing neighborhood revitalization as a platform for kingdom engagement; Courtney, my work confidant and sounding board; Merrick, who helped hack through the jungle of resident engagement with me; and my current Love Your Neighborhood team I get the joy to work with every day—Eric T., Hannah, and Maddie.

Also, to all of the neighborhood-based organizations that trust us enough to coach them through the Love Your Neighborhood approach: You all give me hope that this work can grow, multiply, and transform

214 | NEIGHBORHOODS & JESUS

the world! Special thanks to the practitioners on the ground bringing this work to life.

Thanks to Sarah and Jessica for your friendship; but in this context, thanks especially for helping this social media and tech ignoramus complete a wildly successful crowdfunding campaign that made this book possible. And while I'm at it, thanks to everyone who helped in any way with that!

Thanks to the 100 Movements Publishing crew who picked this book up and made it into something readable—Brenna, Anna, and particularly Helen, who had to put up with editing an absolute mess.

Finally, and to close, to my beloved family who make life a joy: What an amazing tribe we are!

Appendix One
DISCOVERY ASSESSMENT TOOL

Below are questions you should reflect on and take action to answer as you assess the readiness for a potential Love Your Neighborhood initiative.

Foundation

- Is there an organization committed to convening for long-term engagement and participation?
- Has a geographical focus area been defined?
- Has the convening organization defined their desired level of depth and engagement for the neighborhood initiative? This includes but is not limited to:
  - Long-term time frame
  - Amount of dedicated time per week, per month, etc., number of individuals committed to participating (volunteers and/or paid staff)
  - Available budget

Motivation

- Why do you want to do this work?
- Is there a compelling connection (or "why") for the geographic focus for this initiative?
- What is the value exchange? (What's in it for the convening organization and for the neighborhood?)
- What is the ultimate goal? What does success look like?
- If you could only transform one thing in the neighborhood, what would it be? Why?

Understanding

Have you researched and identified neighborhood assets for understanding? These include but are not limited to:

- Who are the anchor organizations in the neighborhood—schools, churches, businesses, nonprofits?
- What school(s) do the neighborhood students go to?
- Are there any restaurants, retail, or attractions in the neighborhood?
- Are there any parks, green spaces, or community gathering spaces?
- Is there an active neighborhood association?
- What is the population?
- How many mailable addresses are in the neighborhood?

Have you researched and identified neighborhood needs/opportunities for understanding? These include but are not limited to:

- Do you have a full demographics report (census) for the neighborhood?
- Do you have any other studies completed by the city for the neighborhood?
- What is the median household income?
- What is the percentage of the population below the poverty level?
- What is the average educational attainment of residents?
- How old are most of the houses?
- What is the distribution between owner-occupied and renter-occupied homes?
- What is the percentage of vacant homes?

Relationships

- Has the convening organization been invited by the neighborhood to lead a neighborhood initiative?

- Does the convening organization have any established relationships with neighborhood residents or stakeholders? Has the convening organization identified any specific neighborhood residents or stakeholders that they must build relationships with to be successful?

Momentum

- Are residents and/or stakeholders currently having conversations about revitalizing the neighborhood?
- Is there a current revitalization effort being led by residents and/or stakeholders?
- Was there a past revitalization effort led by resident and/or stakeholders?
- Are any nonprofits currently investing in or offering services in the neighborhood?
- Is the government (local, state, federal) currently investing in the neighborhood?
- Is there an established communication channel to connect with residents?

Appendix Two
THE ORGANIZING PRINCIPLE

I am fairly obsessed with the organizing principles of social movements. This stems from my wiring of being a Learner and Achiever (StrengthsFinder)—I want to know how things work and can be successfully sustained … then I want to see them work.

For example, the Black Panthers were able to build an alternative educational, financial, social service, and health care system. That level of success did not just magically happen; it took extreme levels of system creation and organization. Any sustained movement must. This fascinates me, and I want to learn from the Black Panther movement and see something similar come into being.

Yet, flying in the face of my need to know "exactly how things work," it is also a well-documented social theory that genuine movements tend to organize themselves in order to create the movement dynamics needed to be birthed and sustained.[1] In fact, over-planning and systematizing trends a movement toward bureaucracy and institution-alism that crushes the movement. The money it takes to keep these bureaucracies and institutions going inflates as investment that used to go into the movement goes into the machine: paid staff replace volun-teers; facilities replace decentralized hubs, removing people from the effective front lines; and red-tape bureaucratic processes replace the free-flowing, fast-action decision-making processes that helped launch the movement in the first place. It is a tale as old as time.

Is there a way to stay in the sweet spot of movement-institution where social change can be sustained but not beached? How would one organize such a change?

Asset-based community development uses the following approx-imate organizing principles:

---

[1] Christian Fuchs, "The Self-Organization of Social Movements," *Systemic Practice and Action Research*, Vol. 19 (1), February 2006.

- Discover individuals' gifts, skills, passions, experience
- Gather larger community around vision for change
- Support "behind the scenes" with a smaller leadership group
- Provide day-to-day backbone support through a lead-agency, typically a neighborhood-based organization
- Start smaller working groups or action teams made up of residents and stakeholders to drive projects and initiatives forward
- Invite community stakeholders (organizations and institutions) to participate and invest
- Periodically regather the larger community at events to sustain excitement and momentum

What struck me at some point in the journey of doing neighborhood work, is that these are almost the exact organizing principles of a typical American Bible-Belt church. Do you see it? The Sunday gathering for the larger community; small groups or Sunday school to move people forward in their faith; staff and elders to plan and steer; and occasional special events to drum up excitement and momentum. My first impression was positive—"That's neat!"—but this quickly gave way to concern: "Uh-oh …"

This diagram attempts to represent these different elements.

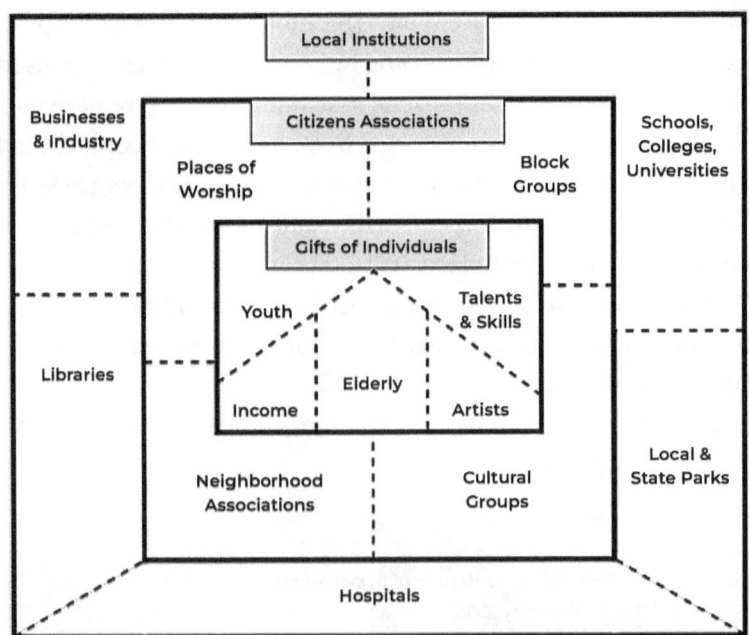

The problem was that personal experience in church leadership and a study of discipleship through the Gospels had convinced me that our churches had actually *inverted* Jesus' organizing principle of Christian community, and I believe that is a major contributing factor to the "discipleship deficit" in our local churches.

What is more, I had participated in two neighborhood initiatives before helping lead another, and both had stalled at the smaller working groups/action team level. As a prescribed, textbook approach, the exact same narrative had played out in both neighborhoods: great engagement by community leaders early in the visioning, steering, and planning phases; some early quick wins and resident engagement flowing from the catalytic start; formation of the "sustainability phase" … where the movement went to die.

Now, I do not think that the working groups/action teams phase of organizing is necessarily the problem, or the only problem, but it is fascinating that both neighborhood initiatives stalled at that point, and the one we are currently leading is also struggling in the same spot. In addition, in my previous role as small-groups pastor, I had experienced a similar organizing difficulty with the church version of "working groups" (small groups). Something seems broken at this critical juncture of organizing, and I needed to know what it was! That need for understanding is what drove me to spend nine months hunkered down at the feet of Jesus, learning about how he organized his movement—and it led me to some working conclusions.

Before sharing those conclusions, I have to make a confession: This is the only idea or concept presented in this book that I have not applied directly in neighborhood revitalization. Everything else you have read has been lived out, experienced; even if it was an utter failure, it has been enacted in real life to some degree. Not so with these thoughts on understanding organizing principles in the way of Jesus. I simply have not yet seen a way forward in our initiatives, and frankly, have not had enough guts to try. But you, dear reader, may be able to figure out a way to apply these ideas in your own neighborhood, especially if you are at the onset and can integrate them seamlessly from the beginning as opposed to course correcting.

As I spent nine months sitting at the feet of Jesus, asking one basic question—why do we have a discipleship deficit?—trying fervently to keep an open mind about how Jesus went about making disciples without importing my own learned biases, one of the biggest learnings was around the idea of organizing principles. The way we organize Christian community today is entirely backward from how Jesus organized his discipleship community. Here's what I mean: Jesus invested the most time, energy, relational equity, etc., with those nearest to him and then brought those into ministry in ever-expanding social-public spaces:

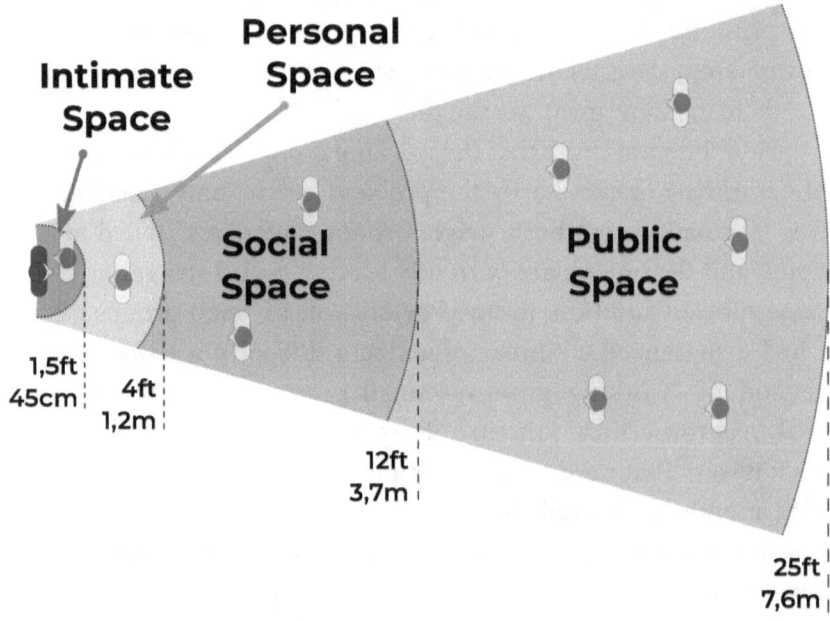

In popular American church culture, we start with the big gathering, drawing a crowd, then move people toward more personal relationships, ultimately getting people into intimate disciple-making relationships. The best churches are intentional about these movements, helping their congregants move into deeper Christian community. However, most churches are simply hopeful that people will progress down the path.

Jesus started with the most intimate discipling relationships, layered them into overlapping and expanding concentric circles of community, ultimately ending up in or among the crowds, with his disciples, doing ministry.

If you know the Gospel accounts well, you will begin to identify this pattern immediately. Seriously, reflect a little right now and see if this bears out in your memory. Jesus had his "inner circle" of three—Peter, James, John—who had more time, access, deeper experiences, and heavier responsibility than any of the other disciples. Then he had the Twelve, which Mark 3 tells us are those whom he called out of the mid-size discipling community—a fluctuating group of approximately 72–120 people. For example, we know in the story of replacing Judas that the requirements were that the person had been a witness from the time of Jesus' baptism to his ascension—basically his entire public ministry (Acts 1:15–26). At least two names were put forward. We also know from John 6:66 that, after a hard teaching, many of Jesus' more distant disciples stopped following him.

So, Jesus, with his closest, most intimate friends and mentees who were part of his personal ministry team, were also part of a larger discipling/missional community that regularly went into the crowds together where people were already present, where they were simply living in the "now" of their everyday lives. In other words, Jesus' methods were the exact opposite of our organizing principles in the American church.

Now, I want to be careful here because I do not think Jesus was writing a missional handbook with a chapter on organizing for kingdom impact to be prescribed across all Christian engagement for all time. Nor was it only one way even in Jesus' life—e.g., sometimes he gathered crowds and went to synagogues. When we become rigid in our applications, we forget the natural "now" of life. It is more often a "Yes, and," all-experiences-go, smash-up of whatever has vibrancy and momentum that is actually effective in reality.

Having said that …

I have been reflecting deeply about how we aim to organize our neighborhood movements, because I believe Jesus is the creator and sustainer of all things, but I am seeing too many parallels to the deficit in churches in our inability to organize for sustainable change. I am wondering if maybe we need a re-org.

Follow me for a minute. A large portion of our energy, planning, and resources goes into gathering a crowd, whether that be at a monthly neighborhood meeting or at various community events that we host. Even though we do not blatantly say it, it feels good when a lot of people show up. It does not feel so great when attendance is low. Sometimes the gatherings are completely about having fun; but oftentimes, once the crowd is gathered, an expert stands in front and delivers a content message, and we invite neighbors to respond: to sign-up for this program, connect to this or that good/service. Then it is our great hope that they will at least come back next Sunday … er, I mean … to next month's meeting or neighborhood event. It would be really great if a neighbor took the bold next step to join a small group … er, I mean … action team. If the cards fall perfectly and we get lucky, we can put them in on the board … er, I mean … in a neighborhood leadership position.

The question becomes, what might different organizing principles look like? How would they work and function? Could they sustain a movement?

Here are Jesus' organizing principles:

Crowds > Come and See
Disciples > Follow Me
Twelve > Disciple Intentionally
Three > Leadership Tree

Now, I am not trying to place modern-day sociology onto ancient paradigms—I just think it is interesting how clearly Jesus' organizing of his faith community aligns with a modern discipline called *proxemics* that looks at the physical space and numbers by which we tend to organize our lives and relationships. Sociologists talk about four different spaces that humans need to operate in for a healthy life: public, social, personal, and intimate. Amazingly (or maybe as we'd expect), Jesus structured his life in just such a manner:

CROWDS → DISCIPLES → TWELVE → THREE
PUBLIC → SOCIAL → PERSONAL → INTIMATE

In other words, Jesus traveled in all of the spaces simultaneously in his ministry so that he could seamlessly transition in and out of discipleship among the various spaces as the situation warranted. This was crucial to Jesus' method of disciple-making because it allowed the main cast of characters to see what was happening and be challenged to make a move. At the exact same time, Jesus was modeling behavior for reproduction. The disciples saw how Jesus interacted with the crowds; they didn't just hear a message about it. Of course, they did hear a message about it as well—the same one as the crowds—but Jesus would then turn to the Twelve and give them a special teaching, telling them why and equipping them to be sent to do the same. It worked the other way too. The crowds saw Jesus living life with the disciples. They observed the relationship, heard the challenges, watched the interactions and bore witness to the relentlessly attractional experience of Jesus Christ. By aligning all of the discipleship spaces into one community, Jesus simplified his life, ministry, and relationships while maximizing his discipleship impact.

Here, I believe, is the connection between how Jesus organized his faith community and neighborhood revitalization because, lest we forget, Jesus also launched the most revolutionary social-impact movement in the history of humanity. Can we try to develop an experiment that adopts and incorporates Jesus' approach? Can we call twelve neighbors, known for doing good works together, into a three-year journey of formation? Can those twelve neighbors participate and move into a larger social-space community that is networked and connected? Can all of those people move together toward a common mission and vision for as long as they self-select to follow the path? Can they live in common union together, being present among the crowds—the residents of a given community? What do those gatherings look like? What does the equipping, empowering, and training entail?

I do not have the answer to these questions, but I think collectively as a wider community we could come up with some interesting cohorts and pilot efforts that try to organize social movements differently and are more aligned with the way of Jesus.

Appendix Three
THE RESEARCH

The ministry problem my research was designed around was to discover what biblical themes and understandings provide the foundation to move disciples of the Christian faith into participation in neighborhood revitalization, and what experiences catalyze and sustain that engagement.

To this end, I built three instruments to support this research and make discoveries:

- A congregational survey with four local churches designed to discover the intersection between belief statements, view of the role of the church, and faith in action.
- Appreciative Inquiry interviews with Christians actively participating in neighborhood revitalization as an expression of their faith. These interviews were conducted with anyone, not just people doing neighborhood work for their job.[1]
- A focus group of ministry leaders who were not personally, nor were their congregations, participating in a neighborhood revitalization initiative.

Methodology

The data for the research was collected through a mixed-methods approach, meaning qualitative and quantitative data—or listening and numbers, as I like to think of them. The listening data came in two forms: 1) One-on-one interviews with Christians who were actively participating in neighborhood revitalization efforts in our community

---

[1]   In case you are unfamiliar with "Appreciative Inquiry," it is based on questions formed to draw out what is good or what already exists in a helpful form, e.g., What is good about your neighborhood? What excites you about your neighborhood? What got you into neighborhood work in the first place?

as an expression of faith, and 2) a focus group of pastors ministering on the same side of town where there was no neighborhood revitalization effort underway. The quantitative data was collected through a twenty–question survey, which sought to discover the correlation and interplay between doctrinal belief statements, view of the role of the church, and personal faith in action.

Congregational Survey

This survey instrument was built in order to discover the relationship between congregants' affirmation of belief statements in their everyday lives, their agreement to statements regarding their view of the church, and the frequency of their faith in action. All three sections used a five-point Likert Scale to indicate the congregants' importance, agreement, and frequency of the indicated statements presented. The practitioners and pastors also completed the survey in order to provide comparative samples.

The survey consisted of twenty questions in three sections:

- Section 1: Doctrinal Belief Statements (BS). Participants were asked how important to their everyday life a set of seven Christian faith statements were.
- Section 2: View of the Role of the Church (VC). Participants were asked to indicate their agreement with six statements regarding the nature and purpose of the church.
- Section 3: Personal Faith in Action (FA). Participants were asked to indicate their frequency involvement in seven activities over the past year.

The codes (such as FA1 or VC4) on the data graphs correspond to the section and the specific question asked in the survey.

Doctrinal Belief Statements (BS):
How important are these faith statements to your everyday life?

1. I believe in the Holy Trinity. I believe in the one true God that eternally exists as three persons—Father, Son, Holy Spirit— and that these three are one God.

[ ] Extremely Important [ ] Very Important [ ] Somewhat Important
[ ] Not too Important [ ] Not at all Important

2. I believe that God created all things through Jesus and all of existence is sustained by the Trinitarian God.

[ ] Extremely Important [ ] Very Important [ ] Somewhat Important
[ ] Not too Important [ ] Not at all Important

3. I believe that God's mission derives from his very nature—the Father sends the Son; the Father and Son send the Spirit; the Father, Son, Spirit send the church into the world.

[ ] Extremely Important [ ] Very Important [ ] Somewhat Important
[ ] Not too Important [ ] Not at all Important

4. I believe the second person of the Trinity (the Son) assumed human form in the person of Jesus Christ, lived life among humanity, and is completely both God and man.

[ ] Extremely Important [ ] Very Important [ ] Somewhat Important
[ ] Not too Important [ ] Not at all Important

5. I believe Jesus Christ was crucified for the rebellion of creation against God, for the purpose of reconciling all things to God.

[ ] Extremely Important [ ] Very Important [ ] Somewhat Important
[ ] Not too Important [ ] Not at all Important

6. I believe Jesus Christ was raised physically from the dead on the third day following his death on the cross, appearing to many followers, and is the foretaste/sign of a future hope brought into the present reality.

[ ] Extremely Important [ ] Very Important [ ] Somewhat Important
[ ] Not too Important [ ] Not at all Important

7. I believe that Jesus Christ ascended to the right hand of the Father and reigns over the kingdom of heaven that is being established by God.

[ ] Extremely Important [ ] Very Important [ ] Somewhat Important [ ] Not too Important [ ] Not at all Important

View of the Role of the Church (VC):

Indicate the degree to which you agree or disagree with the following statements regarding the nature and purpose of the church:

1. Church is a community of people with God, through Jesus Christ, by the Holy Spirit, living life with one another locally, connected to all other Christians through the world and history.

[ ] Strongly Agree [ ] Agree [ ] Neutral [ ] Disagree [ ] Strongly Disagree

2. Church is the assembled or gathered disciples of Jesus Christ.

[ ] Strongly Agree [ ] Agree [ ] Neutral [ ] Disagree [ ] Strongly Disagree

3. The organizational structure of the church should be to build up the body of Christ (internal) and equip the saints for ministry (external).

[ ] Strongly Agree [ ] Agree [ ] Neutral [ ] Disagree [ ] Strongly Disagree

4. The primary practices of church can be described as worship, formation (or discipleship), community, and mission.

[ ] Strongly Agree [ ] Agree [ ] Neutral [ ] Disagree [ ] Strongly Disagree

5. The purpose of church is to carry on the reconciling work of Jesus Christ by proclaiming the gospel and being a light to the world.

[ ] Strongly Agree [ ] Agree [ ] Neutral [ ] Disagree [ ] Strongly Disagree

6. Church has a specific calling from God to restore the marginalized populations of a community.

[ ] Strongly Agree [ ] Agree [ ] Neutral [ ] Disagree [ ] Strongly Disagree

Personal Faith in Action (FA):
Indicate the frequency of your personal involvement in the following activities over the past year:

1. Served at/with/through a local nonprofit or parachurch ministry in my community.

[ ] Often [ ] Regularly [ ] Occasionally [ ] Seldom [ ] Never

2. Served with/through my local church out in the community.

[ ] Often [ ] Regularly [ ] Occasionally [ ] Seldom [ ] Never

3. Built genuine relationships with people not self-identifying as Christians.

[ ] Often [ ] Regularly [ ] Occasionally [ ] Seldom [ ] Never

4. Been present at city or community events with the awareness and intentionality of living out my faith and serving as a witness to Jesus Christ.

[ ] Often [ ] Regularly [ ] Occasionally [ ] Seldom [ ] Never

5. Prayed for the common good of my city and for the kingdom of God to reign in it as in heaven.

[ ] Often [ ] Regularly [ ] Occasionally [ ] Seldom [ ] Never

6. Have served or been present with a marginalized population (e.g., homeless, impoverished, felons, etc.) in my community.

[ ] Often [ ] Regularly [ ] Occasionally [ ] Seldom [ ] Never

7. Have spent time in an under-resourced neighborhood in my community with the purpose of living out my faith.

[ ] Often [ ] Regularly [ ] Occasionally [ ] Seldom [ ] Never

Neighborhood Revitalization Practitioner Interviews:

1. What were your initial inspirations and motivations to get involved in place-based neighborhood revitalization work?
2. Reflecting on your entire experience in neighborhood engagement, remember a time you felt most alive, motivated, excited about your engagement. Describe the circumstances and your involvement.
3. What has sustained your engagement in the neighborhood?
4. What have been the most important experiences, lessons in belief, or steps of faith that have occurred for you in place-based neighborhood revitalization work?
5. Make three wishes for the future of the neighborhood.

Focus Group Questions:

1. If you had to classify an area on the Westside of Evansville as an under-resourced neighborhood, what would it be? What do you believe are the contributing factors?
2. Describe the situation of the neighborhood, both physical environment and the people. Now, what are the perceptions of the surrounding community—think of how people talk about the neighborhood?
3. What do you feel God's heart is for the community? What biblical themes show this?
4. What do you believe is the church's role in neighborhood revitalization?
5. What barriers do you face in leadership and organizationally in mobilizing your congregation into neighborhood engagement?
6. Based on your understanding of the mission of God, make three wishes for the future of the neighborhood.

Survey Responses

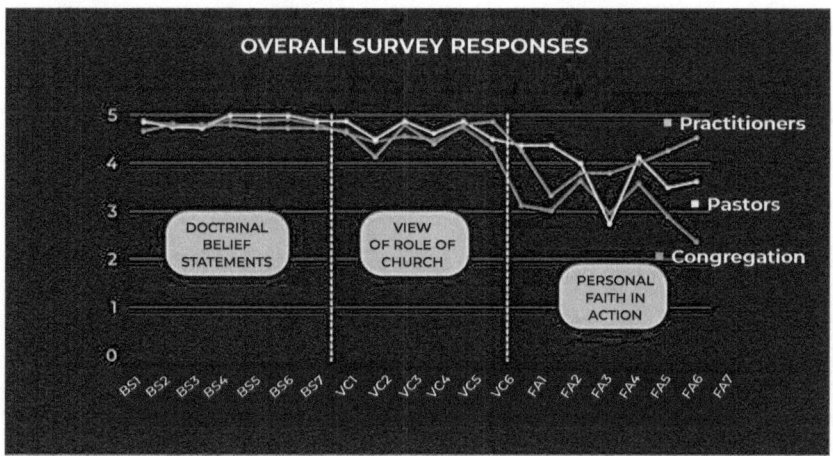

These are the overall responses from the survey of all three groups. At the highest level, there are a few observations:

- There is almost no variance in the responses to the belief statements. When asked about some of the most basic foundational tenets of the Christian faith, nearly all participants showed positive agreement to the concepts presented. This is visually represented by the nearly straight line through the Belief Statements section.
- Once we come to the View of the Role of the Church, the middle section, the line starts to zig and zag. There is much less agreement about what the church should be doing than what the faith community conceptually believes.
- Then in the personal Faith in Action section, there is even greater variance and disparity, indicated clearly by the jagged line bouncing all over the place!

What This Could Mean:

- The Christian community has actually done a pretty good job of transferring concepts that inform our collective faith. You could say that the vast majority of Christians are "thinking right."

- When it comes to expressions of the collective church, and much more so in the personal application of our faith in action, that is where we begin to diverge.

Personal Faith in Action Responses

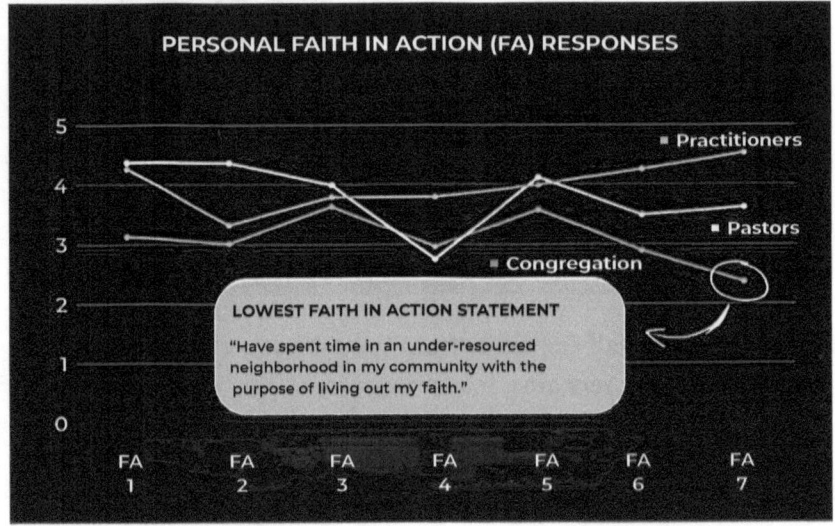

The three lowest scores for congregants and pastors related to statements 4, 6, and 7, which are:

- FA4: Been present at city or community events with the awareness and intentionality of living out my faith and serving as a witness to Jesus Christ.
- FA6: Have served or been present with a marginalized population (e.g., homeless, impoverished, felons, etc.) in my community.
- FA7: Have spent time in an under-resourced neighborhood in my community with the purpose of living out my faith.

What This Could Mean:

- It is much easier to assent to concepts than to live out faith in action.
- When it comes to missionally engaging out in the community, especially to disinvested neighbors and neighborhoods, congregants and pastors simply are not prioritizing those actions.

View of the Role of Church Statements

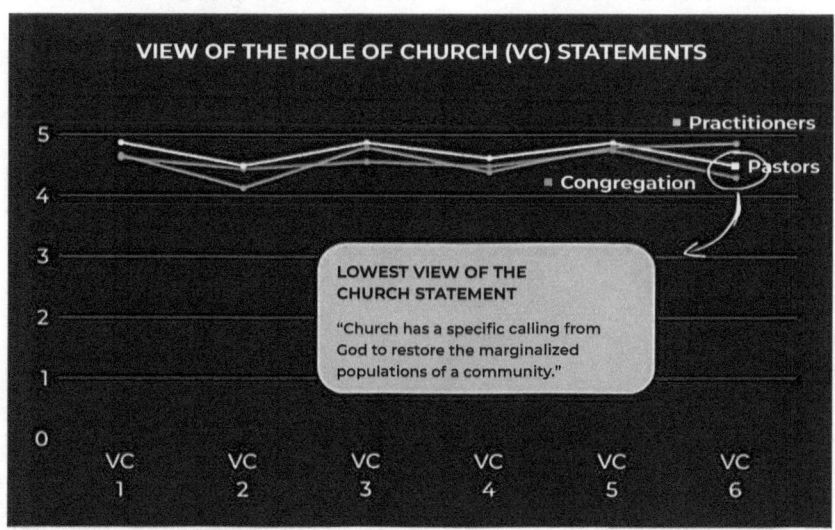

For both congregants and pastors, the lowest score was VC6: "The church has a specific calling from God to restore the marginalized populations of a community." This was the highest score in the view of neighborhood revitalization practitioners.

What This Could Mean:

- It should not be much of a surprise that congregants report low frequency of faith in action to marginalized neighbors if they are not as certain about the church's role in this ministry.
- Interestingly, the lowest score on this section for practitioners was VC2, "Church is the assembled or gathered disciples of Jesus Christ." This could show that their experience as lone missionaries out in the neighborhood shapes their view of the church, or it could come from their experience of church as not supporting their work in the neighborhood.

Correlations

Below is an analysis of the correlations between the responses of congregants and practitioners. I wanted to show the correlation between what people believed about their faith with how their faith was activated. At the highest level of understanding, if the bar goes up, there is a positive correlation; and if it goes down, there is a negative correlation. While I am well aware that correlation is not causation, what emerged is fascinating.

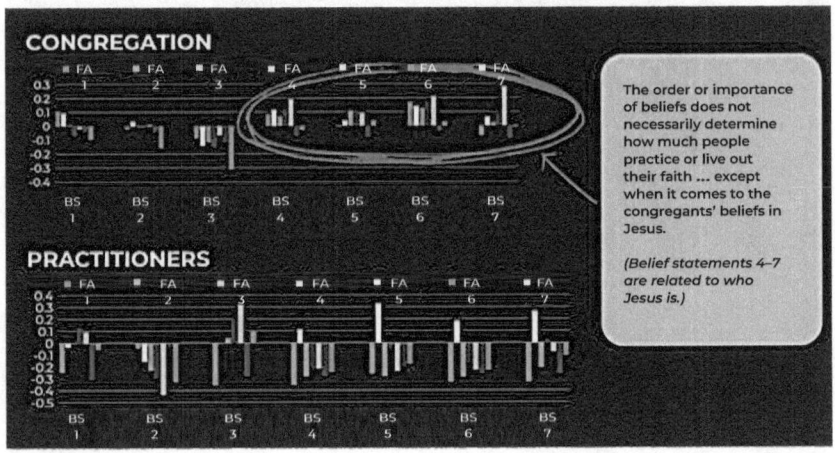

What This Could Mean:

- For congregants there was a strong positive correlation between belief statements 4–7 and the frequency of their faith in action. Questions 4–7 had to do with the person and nature of Jesus. It seems the firmer their belief in Jesus, the more they live out their faith.

- However, for congregants there is also a negative correlation nearly across the board in FA6–7. These were the questions dealing directly with ministry to marginalized neighbors and being present in under-resourced neighborhoods with the intention of living out their faith. In keeping with what we have presented above, this may show that—especially in the context of engaging in neighborhood revitalization—right thinking does not necessarily lead to right action.

- These conclusions are further supported by the strong negative correlation between belief statements and faith in action for neighborhood revitalization practitioners.

- In other words, the more confident the respondents were in their belief statements, the less action they took in ministry to marginalized neighbors and neighborhoods. Or stated another way, the more the respondents participated in ministry to marginalized neighbors and neighborhoods, the less confident they were in their statements of belief.

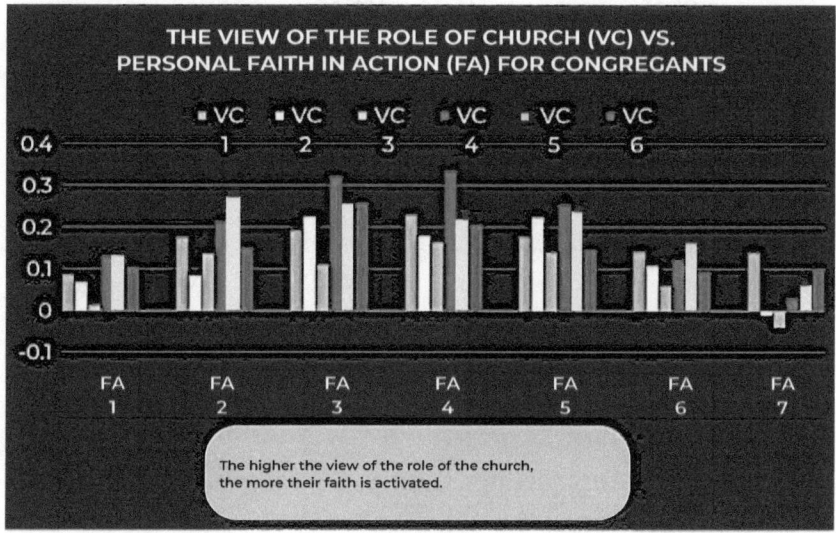

What this shows is the correlation between a congregants' view of the role of the church and their frequency of faith in action. It is nearly all positive. The higher the respondent's view of the role of the church, the more they put their faith into action. This does indeed include the two actions that dealt directly with marginalized neighbors and neighborhoods.

What This Could Mean:

- Congregants generally have a very positive view of the role of the church in the world—and the stronger their views, the more their faith is activated. This provides an opportunity to reimagine what the church is doing in the world.
- This should be encouraging, but we also must be aware of why the church is not transforming marginalized neighbors and neighborhoods—because they do not have as much certainty that they

should! This is a clear opportunity for discipleship and recapturing God's calling to restore and activate marginalized neighbors.

What the Data Says: Interviews and Focus Group

The qualitative data was produced from hours of listening to practitioners and pastors through the one-on-one interviews and focus groups. Here are the most noteworthy takeaways from this part of the research.

Three key areas were noteworthy from this part of the research.

Key biblical themes catalyze engagement in neighborhood revitalization. Five biblical themes or understandings catalyze engagement in neighborhood revitalization as an expression of the Christian faith:

- Calling: both personal (I am called) and corporate (we the people of God are called).
- Evangelism-Discipleship: sharing of faith and growing in faith were interchangeable.
- Mission of God: especially as expressed through creation and reconciliation of all things.
- Hope: tied directly to the resurrection of Jesus Christ.
- Incarnation: stepping into the life of Jesus, as Jesus stepped into the world and our lived experience.

Key initial experiences move Jesus' followers toward participation. Three clear themes emerged:

- Invitation: someone, or some organization, extended a personal invitation to come and check out the neighborhood work.
- Step of faith: at a point in their personal faith journey and growth, they felt like it was a movement into deeper faith.
- Participation in holistic ministry: there was clear discontent with one-off ministry opportunities or "toxic charity" that did not minister to the whole of a person.

Key elements help sustain the work. Last, but certainly not least, was discovering what sustained followers of Jesus in the work itself. Timelines on neighborhood revitalization are long, success is not guaranteed, and trust is difficult to develop. All of that leads to attrition in engagement, so I wanted to discover the most helpful experiences that sustained disciples in ministry to marginalized neighbors through neighborhood work. Three clear categories emerged:

- Seeing progress: This is a very broad category—anything from seeing a house rehabbed, to a youth program started, to a neighbor being baptized. The important connection was that they saw clear and tangible progress or outcomes from their work.
- Getting to know neighbors: pretty simple, the more neighbors they met, and the deeper the relationships, the more sustained they were in the work.
- Serving in community: this was in reference to serving with others, especially but not exclusive to, brothers and sisters in Christ.

ABOUT THE AUTHOR

AUSTIN MAXHEIMER has been a practitioner of neighborhood revitalization for over fifteen years. He began participating in neighborhood work through his local church as they began an engagement initiative alongside marginalized neighbors within a disinvested neighborhood. It was through this work that his understanding of Christian outreach and mission was transformed into more holistic expressions. He spent several years mobilizing missional communities and local churches into missional engagement before shifting into full-time vocational ministry and leading neighborhood revitalization initiatives. Austin remains a practitioner and coach of other neighborhood-based organizations.

DONOR LIST

Nick and Rebekah Basham

Steve and Sue Below

Katye Bennett

Jonathan and Alex Boettcher

Bre and Andrew

Matt and Amanda Breivogel

Chris Buckman

The Corbett Family

Pat and Martha Creech

Eric and Lynda Cummings

Ryan and Chelsea England

Jeremy and Tara Evans

Heath and Rachel Farmer

Brian and Chris Fleming

Amy and Andy Hanson

Jim and Carol Havens

Tim and Cathy Hesse

Sarah Inman

Kelly and Kelley

Martin and Kera Koen

Jake and Kristen Kuhn

Darin and Courtney Lander

Danny and Amy Maxheimer

Zach Maxheimer

John and Andi Miles

Brian and Kim Reinitz

Crystal and Andrew Roberson

Bob and Kathy Seymore

Josh and Kelsey Stanley

Cara Steinkul

Alex and Jill Strohm

Jeff and Lisa Taylor

Judy Vos

Mark and Betsy Wade

Mark and Cindy Weaver

Hannah Wehr

Sean and Jessica Welcher

Debbie Wiseman

Kelly Zindel

If this content and our learning journey so far resonated with you, we would love for you to continue the conversation at www.community1.org/lyn.